SQL Server Backup and Restore

By Shawn McGehee

First published by Simple Talk Publishing April 2012

Technical Review by Eric Wisdahl
Cover Image by Andy Martin
Edited by Tony Davis
Typeset & Designed by Peter Woodhouse & Gower Associates

Table of Contents

Chapter 6: Log Restores

Chapter 8: Database Backup and Restore with SQL Backup 243

Chapter 9: File and Filegroup Backup and Restore 301

Chapter 10: Partial Backup and Restore _____355

About the author

Shawn McGehee

Shawn is a DBA living in Orlando, FL. He has been working in IT since graduating high school in 1997, in positions ranging from web developer, to help desk operative, to his current position as a Senior DBA. He is heavily involved in the SQL Server community, speaking at and organizing local users' groups in Florida since 2008, and is currently President of the OPASS group in Lake Mary, FL. Shawn is also a contributing author on the Apress book, *Pro SQL Server Reporting Services 2012*.

Acknowledgements

I would like to thank everyone who helped and supported me through the writing of this book. I would especially like to thank my editor, Tony Davis, for sticking with me during what was a long and occasionally daunting process, and helping me make my first single-author book a reality. I also need to give a special thank you to all of my close friends and family for always being there for me during all of life's adventures, good and bad.

– Shawn McGehee

About the technical reviewer

Eric Wisdahl

Eric is a development DBA working in the e-commerce industry. He spends what little free time he has reading, playing games, or spending time with his wife and dogs. In a past life he has worked as an ETL/BI Specialist in the insurance industry, a pizza boy, patent examiner, Pro-IV code monkey and .NET punching bag.

Introduction

My first encounter with SQL Server, at least from an administrative perspective, came while I was still at college, working in a small web development shop. We ran a single SQL Server 6.5 instance, on Windows NT, and it hosted every database for every client that the company serviced. There was no dedicated administration team; just a few developers and the owner.

One day, I was watching and learning from a fellow developer while he made code changes to one of our backend administrative functions. Suddenly, the boss stormed into the room and demanded everyone's immediate attention. Whatever vital news he had to impart is lost in the sands of time, but what I do remember is that when the boss departed, my friend returned his attention to the modified query and hit **Execute**, an action that was followed almost immediately by a string of expletives so loud they could surely have been heard several blocks away. Before being distracted by the boss, he'd written the DELETE portion of a SQL statement, but not the necessary WHERE clause and, upon hitting **Execute**, he had wiped out all the data in a table.

Fortunately, at least, he was working on a test setup, with test data. An hour later we'd replaced all the lost test data, no real harm was done and we were able to laugh about it. As the laughter subsided, I asked him how we would have gotten that data back if it had been a live production database for one of the clients or, come to think of it, what we would do if the whole server went down, with all our client databases on board. He had no real answer, beyond "Luckily it's never happened." There was no disaster recovery plan; probably because there were no database backups that could be restored! It occurred to me that if disaster ever did strike, we would be in a heap of trouble, to the point where I wondered if the company as a whole could even *survive* such an event. It was a sobering thought.

That evening I did some online research on database backups, and the very next day performed a full database backup of every database on our server. A few days later, I had jobs scheduled to back up the databases on a regular basis, to one of the local hard drives on that machine, which I then manually copied to another location. I told the boss what I'd done, and so began my stint as the company's "accidental DBA."

Over the coming weeks and months, I researched various database restore strategies, and documented a basic "crash recovery" plan for our databases. Even though I moved on before we needed to use even one of those backup files, I felt a lot better knowing that, with the plan that I'd put in place, I left the company in a situation where they could recover from a server-related disaster, and continue to thrive as a business. This, in essence, is the critical importance of database backup and restore: it can mean the difference between life or death for a business, and for the career of a DBA.

The critical importance of database backup and restore

The duties and responsibilities of a Database Administrator (DBA) make a long and dynamically changing list, ranging from offering query tuning advice, to cutting stored procedures, all the way through to system process design and implementation for high availability. A DBA's tasks, from day to day, are rarely constant; with one exception: the need to ensure each and every day that any database in their charge can be restored and recovered, in the event of error or disaster. This means that if a database, for whatever reason, gets corrupted, dropped, or otherwise becomes unusable, then it is the DBA's responsibility to restore that database to the state it was in before the problem occurred, or as close as is possible.

Of course, this doesn't mean that a DBA is required to restore a database each and every day, just that, if disaster does strike, the DBA must be prepared to deal with it, regardless of when or why it occurs. If a DBA isn't prepared, and significant data is lost or databases become unavailable to end-users for long periods of time, then that DBA probably won't be in their job for too long. This is why a good, and tested, SQL Server backup and restore plan must be at the top of every administrative DBA's list of tasks.

Such a plan needs to be developed for each and every user database in your care, as well as supporting system databases, and it should be tailored to the specific requirements of each database, based on the type of data being stored (financial, departmental, personal, and so on), the maximum acceptable risk of potential data loss (day? hour? minute?), and the maximum acceptable down-time in the event of a disaster.

Each of these factors will help decide the types of backup required, how often they need to be taken, how many days' worth of backup files need to be stored locally, and so on. All of this should be clearly documented so that all parties, both the DBAs and application/database owners, understand the level of service that is expected for each database, and what's required in the plan to achieve it.

At one end of the scale, for a non-frontline, infrequently-modified database, the backup and recovery scheme may be simplicity itself, involving a nightly full database backup, containing a complete copy of all data files, which can be restored if and when necessary. At the opposite end of the scale, a financial database with more or less zero tolerance to data loss will require a complex scheme consisting of regular (daily) full database backups, probably interspersed with differential database backups, capturing all changes since the last full database backup, as well as very regular transaction log backups, capturing the contents added in the database log file, since the last log backup. For very large databases (VLDBs), where it may not be possible to back up the entire database in one go, the backup and restore scheme may become more complex still, involving backup of individual data files, for filegroups, as well as transaction logs. All of these backups will need to be carefully planned and scheduled, the files stored securely, and then restored in the correct sequence, to allow the database to be restored to the exact state in which it existed at any point in time in its history, such as the point just before a disaster occurred.

It sounds like a daunting task, and if you are not well prepared and well practiced, it will be. However, with the tools, scripts, and techniques provided in this book, and with the requisite planning and practice, you *will* be prepared to respond quickly and efficiently to a disaster, whether it's caused by disk failure, malicious damage, database corruption or the accidental deletion of data. This book will walk you step by step through the process of capturing all types of backup, from basic full database backups, to transaction log backups, to file and even partial backups. It will demonstrate how to perform all of the most common types of restore operation, from single backup file restores, to complex point-in-time restores, to recovering a database by restoring just a subset of the files that make up the database.

As well as allowing you to recover a database smoothly and efficiently in the face of one of the various the "doomsday scenarios," your well-rounded backup and recovery plan, developed with the help of this book, will also save you time and trouble in a lot of other situations including, but not limited to those below.

- **Refreshing development environments** – periodically, developers will request that their development environments be refreshed with current production data and objects.

- **Recovering from partial data loss** – occasionally, a database has data "mysteriously disappear from it."

- **Migrating databases to different servers** – you will eventually need to move databases permanently to other servers, for a variety of reasons. The techniques in this book can be used for this purpose, and we go over some ways that different backup types can cut down on the down-time which this process may cause.

- **Offloading reporting needs** – reporting on data is becoming more and more of a high priority in most IT shops. With techniques like log shipping, you can create cheap and quick reporting solutions that can provide only slightly older reporting data than High Availability solutions.

I learned a lot of what I know about backup and restore the hard way, digging through innumerable articles on Books Online, and various community sites. I hope my book will serve as a place for the newly-minted and accidental DBA to get a jump on backups and restores. It can be a daunting task to start planning a Backup and Restore SLA from scratch, even in a moderately-sized environment, and I hope this book helps you get a good start.

How the book is structured

In this book, you'll discover how to perform each of these backup and restore operations using SQL Server Management Studio (SSMS), basic T-SQL scripts and Red Gate's SQL Backup tool. Capturing backups using SSMS or simple scripts is perfectly fine for one-off backup operations, but any backups that form part of the recovery strategy for any given database *must* be automated and you'll also want to build in some checks that, for example, alert the responsible DBA immediately if a problem arises. The tool of choice in this book for backup automation is Red Gate SQL Backup. Building your own automated solution will take a lot of work, but we do offer some advice on possible options, such as PowerShell scripting, T-SQL scripts and SQL Server Agent jobs. Broadly, the book breaks down into four sections.

Prerequisites – everything you need to know and consider *before* you start performing backup and restore.

- **Chapter 1** describes the data and log files that comprise a database, and all the basic types of backup that are possible for these file, and explains the available database recovery models and what they mean.

- **Chapter 2** takes a detailed look at all of the major aspects of planning a backup and recovery strategy, from choosing and configuring hardware, gathering and documenting the requirements for each database, selecting the appropriate backup tool, scheduling considerations, running backup verification checks, and more.

Basic backup and restore – how to capture and restore all of the basic backup types, using SSMS and T-SQL.

- **Chapters 3 and 4** cover how to take standard and compressed **full database backups**, and restore them.

- **Chapters 5 and 6** cover how to take **transaction log backups**, and then use them in conjunction with a full database backup to restore a database to a particular point in time. They also cover common transaction log problems and how to resolve them.

- **Chapter 7** covers standard and compressed **differential database backup and restore**.

Basic backup and restore with SQL Backup – how to capture and restore all basic backup types using Red Gate SQL Backup.

- **Chapter 8** – third-party tools such as Red Gate SQL backup aren't free, but they do offer numerous advantages in terms of the ease with which all the basic backups can be captured, automated, and then restored. Many organizations, including my own, rely on such tools for their overall backup and restore strategy.

Advanced backup and restore – how to capture and restore file and filegroup backups, and partial database backups.

- **Chapter 9** – arguably the most advanced chapter in the book, explaining the filegroup architectures that enable file-based backup and restore, and the complex process of capturing the necessary file backups and transaction log backups, and using them in various restore operations.

- **Chapter 10** – a brief chapter on partial database backups, suitable for large databases with a sizeable portion of read-only data.

- Finally, **Appendix A** provides a quick reference on how to download, install, and configure the SQL Backup tool from Red Gate Software, so that you can work through any examples in the book that use this tool.

Who this book is for

This book is targeted toward the novice Database Administrator with less than a year of experience, and toward what I call "accidental" or "inheritance" DBAs, who are those who have inherited the duties of a DBA, by luck or chance, without any training or prior experience.

If you have some experience, feel free to skip through some of the more basic topics and head to the more advanced sections. If you are one of our newly-minted DBA brothers and sisters, or someone who's had these duties thrust upon you unexpectedly, reading these prerequisite and basic sections will be a very worthwhile task.

Software Requirements and Code Examples

Throughout this book are scripts demonstrating various ways to take and restore backups, using either native T-SQL or SQL Backup scripts. All the code you need to try out the examples in this book can be obtained from the following URL:

WWW.SIMPLE-TALK.COM/RedGateBooks/ShawnMcGehee/SQLServerBackupAndRestore_Code.zip.

Examples in this book were tested on SQL Server 2008 and SQL Server 2008 R2 Standard Edition, with the exception of the online piecemeal restore in Chapter 9, which requires Enterprise Edition. Red Gate SQL Backup v.6.4.056 was used in all SQL Backup examples, in Chapters 8 and 9 of this book.

Chapter 1: Basics of Backup and Restore

Before we dive into the mechanisms for taking and restoring backups, we need to start with a good basic understanding of the files that make up a SQL Server database, what they contain, how and when they can be backed up, and the implications this has with regard to potential data loss in the event of a disaster in which a database is damaged, or specific data accidentally lost, and needs to be restored.

Specifically, in this chapter, we will cover:

- **components of a SQL Server database** – primary and secondary files and filegroups, plus log files

- **how SQL Server uses the transaction log** – and its significance in regard to restore capabilities

- **possible types of SQL Server backup** – full and differential database backups, transaction log backups and file backups

- **SQL Server database recovery models** – the available recovery models and what they mean in terms of backups

- **restoring databases** – the various available types of database restore, plus special restores, such as system database restores.

Components of a SQL Server Database

Ultimately, a relational database is simply a set of files that store data. When we make backups of these files, we capture the objects and data within those files and store them in a **backup file**. So, put simply, a database backup is just a copy of the database as it existed at the time the backup was taken.

Before we dive into the backup files themselves, however, we need to briefly review the files that comprise a SQL Server database. At its simplest, a database is composed of two files, both created automatically upon execution of a `CREATE DATABASE` command: a **data file** and a **log file**. However, in larger, more complex databases, the data files may be broken down into multiple **filegroups**, each one containing multiple files.

Let's discuss each of these components in a little more detail; we won't be delving too deep right now, but we need at least to cover what each file contains and what roles it plays in a day-to-day database backup and recovery strategy.

Data files

Data files in a SQL Server database refer to the individual data containers that are used to store the system and user-defined data and objects. In other words, they contain the data, tables, views, stored procedures, triggers and everything else that is accessed by you, and your end-users and applications. These files also include most of the system information about your database, including permission information, although not including anything that is stored in the `master` system database.

Each database must have one, and only one, **primary data file**, typically denoted by the .MDF extension, which will be stored in the `PRIMARY` filegroup. It may also have some **secondary data files**, typically denoted by the .NDF extension. Note that use of the `.MDF` and `.NDF` extensions are convention rather than necessity; if you enjoy confusing your fellow DBAs, you can apply any extensions you wish to these files.

The primary data file will contain:

- all system objects and data

- by default, all user-defined objects and data (assuming that only the MDF file exists in the PRIMARY filegroup)

- the location of any secondary data files.

Many of the databases we'll create in this book will contain just a primary data file, in the PRIMARY filegroup, although in later chapters we'll also create some secondary data files to store user-defined objects and data.

Writes to data files occur in a random fashion, as data changes affect random pages stored in the database. As such, there is a potential performance advantage to be had from being able to write simultaneously to multiple data files. Any secondary data files are typically denoted with the NDF extension, and can be created in the PRIMARY filegroup or in separate user-defined filegroups (discussed in more detail in the next section). When multiple data files exist within a single filegroup, SQL Server writes to these files using a proportional fill algorithm, where the amount of data written to a file is proportionate to the amount of free space in that file, compared to other files in the filegroup.

Collectively, the data files for a given database are the cornerstone of your backup and recovery plan. If you have not backed up your live data files, and the database becomes corrupted or inaccessible in the event of a disaster, you will almost certainly have lost some or all of your data.

As a final point, it's important to remember that data files will need to grow, as more data is added to the database. The manner in which this growth is managed is often a point of contention among DBAs. You can either manage the growth of the files manually, adding space as the data grows, or allow SQL Server to auto-grow the files, by a certain value or percentage each time the data file needs more space. Personally, I advocate leaving auto-growth enabled, but on the understanding that files are sized initially to cope with current data and predicted data growth (over a year, say) without undergoing an excessive number of auto-growth events. We'll cover this topic more thoroughly in the *Database creation* section of Chapter 3, but for the rest of the discussion here, we are going to assume that the data and log files are using auto-growth.

Filegroups

A filegroup is simply a logical collection of one or more data files. Every filegroup can contain one or more data files. When data is inserted into an object that is stored in a given filegroup, SQL Server will distribute that data evenly across all data files in that filegroup.

For example, let's consider the **PRIMARY** filegroup, which in many respects is a "special case." The **PRIMARY** filegroup will *always* be created when you create a new database, and it must *always* hold your primary data file, which will *always* contain the pages allocated for your system objects, plus "pointers" to any secondary data files. By default, the **PRIMARY** filegroup is the **DEFAULT** filegroup for the database and so will also store all user objects and data, distributed evenly between the data files in that filegroup. However, it is possible to store some or all of the user objects and data in a separate filegroup.

For example, one commonly cited best practice with regard to filegroup architecture is to store system data separately from user data. In order to follow this practice, we might create a database with both a **PRIMARY** and a secondary, or user-defined, filegroup, holding one or more secondary data files. All system objects would automatically be stored in the **PRIMARY** data file. We would then **ALTER** the database to set the secondary filegroup as the **DEFAULT** filegroup for that database. Thereafter, any user objects will, by default, be stored in that secondary filegroup, separately from the system objects.

There may also be occasions when we want to store just certain, specific user objects separately, outside the **PRIMARY** filegroup. To store an object in a secondary, rather than the **PRIMARY**, filegroup, we simply specify this during object creation, via the **ON** clause, as in the example below.

```
CREATE TABLE TableName
    (
        ColumnDefinitionList
    )
ON  [SecondaryFilegroupName]
GO
```

Any data files in the secondary filegroup can, and typically will, be stored on separate physical storage from those in the PRIMARY filegroup. When a BACKUP DATABASE command is issued it will, by default, back up all objects and data in all data files in all filegroups. However, it's possible to specify that only certain filegroups, or specific files within a filegroup are backed up, using file or filegroup backups (covered in more detail later in this chapter, and in full detail in Chapter 9, *File and Filegroup Backup and Restore*). It's also possible to perform a partial backup (Chapter 10, *Partial Backup and Restore*), excluding any read-only filegroups. Given these facts, there's a potential for both performance and administrative benefits, from separating your data across filegroups.

For example, if we have certain tables that are exclusively read-only then we can, by storing this data in a separate filegroup, exclude this data from the normal backup schedule. After all, performing repeated backups of data that is never going to change is simply a waste of disk space.

If we have tables that store data that is very different in nature from the rest of the tables, or that is subject to very different access patterns (e.g. heavily modified), then there can be performance advantages to storing that data on separate physical disks, configured optimally for storing and accessing that particular data. Nevertheless, it's my experience that, in general, RAID (Redundant Array of Inexpensive Disks) technology and SAN (Storage Area Network) devices (covered in Chapter 2) automatically do a much better job of optimizing disk access performance than the DBA can achieve by manual placement of data files.

Also, while carefully designed filegroup architecture can add considerable flexibility to your backup and recovery scheme, it will also add administrative burden. There are certainly valid reasons for using secondary files and filegroups, such as separating system and user data, and there are certainly cases where they might be a necessity, for example, for databases that are simply too large to back up in a single operation. However, they are not required on every database you manage. Unless you have experience with them, or know definitively that you will gain significant performance with their use, then sticking to a single data file database will work for you most of the time (with the data being automatically striped across physical storage, via RAID).

Finally, before we move on, it's important to note that SQL Server transaction log files are never members of a filegroup. Log files are always managed separately from the SQL Server data files.

Transaction log

A transaction log file contains a historical account of all the actions that have been performed on your database. All databases have a transaction log file, which is created automatically, along with the data files, on creation of the database and is conventionally denoted with the LDF extension. It is possible to have multiple log files per database but only one is required. Unlike data files, where writes occur in a random fashion, SQL Server always writes to the transaction log file sequentially, never in parallel. This means that it will only ever write to one log file at a time, and having more than one file will not boost write-throughput or speed. In fact, having more multiple files could result in performance degradation, if each file is not correctly sized or differs in size and growth settings from the others.

Some inexperienced DBAs don't fully appreciate the importance of the transaction log file, both to their backup and recovery plan and to the general day-to-day operation of SQL Server, so it's worth taking a little time out to understand how SQL Server uses the transaction log (and it's a topic we'll revisit in more detail in Chapter 5, *Log Backups*).

Whenever a modification is made to a database object (via Data Definition Language, DDL), or the data it contains (Data Manipulation Language, DML), the details of the change are recorded as a **log record** in the transaction log. Each log record contains details of a specific action within the database (for example, starting a transaction, or inserting a row, or modifying a row, and so on). Every log record will record the identity of the transaction that performed the change, which pages were changed, and the data changes that were made. Certain log records will record additional information. For example, the log record recording the start of a new transaction (the LOP_BEGIN_XACT log record) will contain the time the transaction started, and the LOP_COMMIT_XACT (or LOP_ABORT_XACT) log records will record the time the transaction was committed (or aborted).

From the point of view of SQL Server and the DBA looking after it, the transaction log performs the following critical functions:

- ensures transactional durability and consistency

- enables, via log backups, point-in-time restore of databases.

Transactional durability and consistency

Via a Write Ahead Logging (WAL) mechanism that ensures that change descriptions are written to the transaction log before the actual data changes are written to the data files, SQL Server guarantees that all valid, committed data will be written to the data files and that the effects of any partial, uncommitted transactions, in the data file, can be "undone," via transaction rollback.

As noted previously, the database's log file provides a record of all transactions performed against that database. When a data modification is made, the relevant data pages are read from the data cache, first being retrieved from disk if they are not already in the cache. Data is modified in the data cache, and the log records describing the effects of the transaction are created in the log cache. Any page in the cache that has been modified since being read from disk is called a "dirty" page. When a periodic CHECKPOINT operation occurs, all dirty pages, regardless of whether they relate to committed or uncommitted transactions, are flushed to disk. The WAL protocol dictates that, before a data page is modified in non-volatile storage (i.e. on disk), the description of the change must first be "hardened" to stable storage. SQL Server or, more specifically, the buffer manager, makes sure that the change descriptions (log records) are written to the physical transaction log file *before* the data pages are written to the physical data files.

The Lazy Writer

Another process that scans the data cache, the Lazy Writer, may also write dirty data pages to disk, outside of a checkpoint, if forced to do so by memory pressures.

By always writing changes to the log file first, SQL Server can guarantee that the effects of all committed transactions will ultimately be reflected in the data files, and that any data modifications on disk that originate from incomplete transactions, i.e. those for which neither a COMMIT nor a ROLLBACK have been issued are ultimately *not* reflected in the data files.

This process of reconciling the contents of the data and log files occurs during the **database recovery process** (sometimes called Crash Recovery), which is initiated automatically whenever SQL Server restarts, or as part of the RESTORE command. Say, for example, a database crashes after a certain transaction (T1) is "hardened" to the transaction log file, but before the actual data is written from memory to disk. When the database restarts, a **recovery** process is initiated, which reconciles the data file and log file. All of the operations that comprise transaction T1, recorded in the log file, will be "rolled forward" (redone) so that they are reflected in the data files.

During this same recovery process, any data modifications on disk that originate from incomplete transactions, i.e. those for which neither a COMMIT nor a ROLLBACK have been issued, are "rolled back" (undone), by reading the relevant operations from the log file, and performing the reverse physical operation on the data. More generally, this rollback process occurs if a ROLLBACK command is issued for an explicit transaction, or if an error occurs and XACT_ABORT is turned on, or if the database detects that communication has been broken between the database and the client that instigated the transactions. In such circumstances, the log records pertaining to an interrupted trans-action, or one for which the ROLLBACK command is explicitly issued, are read and the changes rolled back.

In these ways, SQL Server ensures that, either all the actions associated with a transaction succeed as a unit, or that they all fail, and so guarantees data consistency and integrity during normal day-to-day operation.

Log backups and point-in-time restore

As we've discussed, each log record contains the details of a specific change that has been made to the database, allowing that change to be performed again as a part of REDO, or undone as a part of UNDO, during crash recovery. Once captured in a log backup file, the log records can be subsequently applied to a full database backup in order to perform a database restore, and so re-create the database as it existed at a previous point in time, for example right before a failure. As such, regular backups of your log files are an essential component of your database backup and restore strategy for any database that requires point-in-time restore.

The other very important reason to back up the log is to control its size. Since your log file has a record of all of the changes that have been made against it, it will obviously take up space. The more transactions that have been run against your database, the larger this log file will grow. If growth is left uncontrolled, the log file may even expand to the point where it fills your hard drive and you receive the dreaded "9002 (transaction log full)" error, and the database will become read-only, which we definitely do not want to happen. We'll discuss this in more detail in Chapter 5.

SQL Server Backup Categories and Types

The data files, filegroups, and log files that make up a SQL Server database can, and generally should, be backed up as part of your database backup and recovery strategy. This includes both user and system databases. There are three broad categories of backup that a DBA can perform: database backups, file backups and transaction log backups, and within these categories several different types of backup are available.

- **Database backups** – copy into a backup file the data and objects in the primary data file and any secondary data files.
  - *Full database backup* – backs up all the data and objects in the data file(s) for a given database.
  - *Differential database backup* – backs up any data and objects in data file(s) for a given database that have changed since the last full backup.
- **Transaction log backups** – copy into a backup file all the log records inserted into the transaction log LDF file since the last transaction log backup.
- **File backups** – copy into a backup file the data and objects in a data file or filegroup.
  - *Full file backup* – backs up all the data and objects in the specified data files or filegroup.
  - *Differential file backup* – backs up the data and objects in the specified data files or filegroup that have changed since the last full file backup.
  - *Partial backup* – backs up the complete writable portion of the database, excluding any read-only files/filegroups (unless specifically included).
  - *Differential partial backup* – backs up the data and objects that have changed since the last partial backup.

In my experience as a DBA, it is rare for a database to be subject to file backups, and some DBAs never work with a database that requires them, so the majority of this book

(Chapters 3 to 8) will focus on database backups (full and differential) and transaction log backups. However, we do cover file backups in Chapters 9 and 10.

Note that the exact types of backup that can be performed, and to some extent the restore options that are available, depend on the **recovery model** in which the database is operating (SIMPLE, FULL or BULK_LOGGED). We'll be discussing this topic in more detail shortly, in the *Recovery Models* section, but for the time being perhaps the most notable point to remember is that it is not possible to perform transaction log backups for a database operating in SIMPLE recovery model, and so log backups play no part of a database RESTORE operation for these databases. Now we'll take a look at each of these types of backup in a little more detail.

SQL Server database backups

The database backup, which is a backup of your primary data file plus any secondary database files, is the cornerstone of any enterprise's backup and recovery plan.

Any database that is not using file backups will require a strategy for performing database backups. Consider, for example, the situation in which a SQL Server database crashes, perhaps due to a hardware failure, and the live data file is no longer accessible. If no backups (copies) of this file exist elsewhere, then you will suffer 100% data loss; the "meltdown" scenario that all DBAs must avoid at all costs.

Let's examine the two types of database backup, full and differential. Each of them contains the same basic type of information: the system and user data and objects stored in the database. However, viewed independently, the former contains a more complete picture of the data than the latter.

Full database backups

You can think of the full database backup file as a complete and total archive of your database as it existed when you began the backup. Note though that, despite what the term "full" might suggest, a full backup does not fully back up *all* database files, only the data files; the transaction log must be backed up separately.

A full database backup will contain every detail of your database: tables, stored procedures, functions, views, permission information, indexes and, of course, the data stored within those tables. It will also contain just enough information from the transaction log to guarantee that the database can be restored to a consistent state (for example, it needs to back up enough of the log to be able to roll back any transactions that started before the backup and had not committed by backup completion), and to get the database back online in the case of failure during a restore operation.

Generally speaking, we can consider that restoring a full database backup will return the database to the state it was in at the time the backup process started. However, it is possible that the effects of a transaction that was in progress when the backup started will *still* be included in the backup. Before SQL Server begins the actual data backup portion of the backup operation, it reads the Log Sequence Number (LSN; see Chapter 5), then reads all the allocated data extents, then reads the LSN again; as long as the transaction commits before the second LSN read, the change will be reflected in the full backup.

Full database backups will most likely be your most commonly used backup type, but may not be the only type of backup you need, depending on your data recovery requirements. For example, let's say that you rely exclusively on full backups, performing one every day at midnight, and the server experiences a fatal crash at 11 p.m. one night. In this case, you would only be able to restore the full database backup taken at midnight the previous day, and so you would have lost 23 hours' worth of data.

If that size of potential loss is unacceptable, then you'll need to either take more frequent full backups (often not logistically viable, especially for large databases) or take transaction log backups and, optionally, some differential database backups, in order to minimize the risk of data loss. A full database backup serves as the **base** for any subsequent differential database backup.

Copy-only full backups

There is a special type of full backup, known as a copy-only full backup, which exists independently of the sequence of backup files required to restore a database, and cannot act as the base for differential database backups. This topic is discussed in more detail in Chapter 3, Full Database Backups.

Differential database backups

The differential backup is very similar to the full backup, in that it contains a record of the objects and data contained within the data file or files, but the differential backup file will contain only the data that has been changed since the last full backup was taken.

This means that a full database backup must be taken before a differential database backup can be performed, otherwise the system will not have a way of knowing what data has been modified. This full backup is known as the **base** of the differential.

If you're interested to know how SQL Server knows which data has changed, it works like this: for all of the data extents in the database the server will keep a bitmap page that contains a bit for each separate extent (an extent is simply a collection of consecutive pages stored in your database file; eight of them, to be exact). If the bit is set to 1, it means that the data in one or more of the pages in the extent has been modified since the base backup, and those eight pages will be included in the differential backup. If the bit for a given extent is still 0, the system knows that it doesn't need to include that set of data in the differential backup file.

Some DBAs avoid taking differential backups where possible, due to the perceived administrative complexity they add to the backup and restore strategy; they prefer instead to rely solely on a mix of full and regular transaction log backups. Personally, however, I find them to be an invaluable component of the backup strategy for many of my databases. Furthermore, for VLDBs, with a very large full backup footprint, differential backups may become a necessity. Even so, it is still important, when using differential backups, to update the base backup file at regular intervals. Otherwise, if the database is large and the data changes frequently, our differential backup files will end up growing to a point in size where they don't give us much value. We will discuss differential backups further in Chapter 7, where we will dive much deeper into best practices for their use as part of a backup and recovery strategy.

SQL Server transaction log backups

As a DBA, you will in many cases need to take regular backups of the transaction log file for a given database, in addition to performing database backups. This is important both for enabling point-in-time restore of your database, and for controlling the size of the log file.

A full understanding of log backups, how they are affected by the database recovery model, and how and when space inside the log is reused, requires some knowledge of the architecture of the transaction log. We won't get to this till Chapter 5, so we'll keep things as simple as possible here, and get into the details later.

Essentially, as discussed earlier, a transaction log file stores a series of log records that provide a historical record of the modifications issued against that database. As long as the database is operating in the **FULL** or **BULK LOGGED** recovery model then these log records will remain in the live log file, and never be overwritten, until a log backup operation is performed.

Therefore, the full transaction "history" can be captured into a backup file by **backing up the transaction log**. These log backups can then be used as part of a database RESTORE operation, in order to roll the database forward to a point in time at, or very close to, when some "disaster" occurred.

The log chain

For example, consider our previous scenario, where we were simply taking a full database backup once every 24 hours, and so were exposed to up to 24 hours of data loss. It is possible to perform differential backups in between the full backups, to reduce the risk of data loss. However both full and differential backups are I/O intensive processes and are likely to affect the performance of the database, so they should not be run during times when users are accessing the database.

If a database holds business-critical data and you would prefer your exposure to data loss to be measured in minutes rather than hours, then you can use a scheme whereby you take a full database backup, followed by a series of frequent transaction log backups, followed by another full backup, and so on. As part of a database restore operation, we can then restore the most recent full backup (plus differentials, if taken), followed by the **chain** of available log file backups, up to one covering the point in time to which we wish to restore the database.

In order to restore a database to a point in time, either to the end of a particular log backup or to a point in time within a particular log backup, there must exist a full, unbroken chain of log records, from the first log backup taken after a full (or differential backup), right up to the point to which you wish to recover. This is known as the **log chain**. If the log chain is broken (for example, by switching a database to SIMPLE recovery model, then it will only be possible to recover the database to some point in time before the event occurred that broke the chain. The chain can be restarted by returning the database to FULL (or BULK LOGGED) recovery model and taking a full backup (or differential backup, if a full backup was previously taken for that database). See Chapter 5, *Log Backups*, for further details.

Tail log backups

In the event of a failure affecting a database operating in FULL or BULK_LOGGED recovery model, the first action after the failure should be to perform what is known as a **tail log backup** of the live transaction log, which captures the remaining contents of this file. In fact, a subsequent RESTORE operation may otherwise fail, unless the command includes WITH REPLACE, indicating that the existing database should be overwritten, or WITH STOPAT, indicating that there is a specific point at which we wish to stop the restore operation.

If a database is corrupted in some way, but is still online and we wish to restore over that database, then performing a tail log backup with BACKUP LOG...WITH NORECOVERY, will capture the remaining contents of the live log file and put the database into a restoring state, so that no further transactions against that database will succeed, and we can begin the restore operation.

This sort of tail log backup, as well as normal log backups, require the database to be online (I believe, so that information regarding the log backup can be stamped into the database header). If the database is offline, and an attempt to bring it back online fails, perhaps because a data file is unavailable, then a tail log backup WITH NORECOVERY, as well as any normal log backups, will fail. However, it may still be possible to perform a tail log backup, but using the NO_TRUNCATE option instead, BACKUP LOG...WITH NO_TRUNCATE. This operation backs up the log file without truncating it and doesn't require the database to be online.

Of course, any sort of tail log backup will only be possible if the log file is still accessible and undamaged but, assuming this is the case, it should be possible to restore right up to the time of the last transaction committed and written to the log file, before the failure occurred.

Finally, there is a special case where a tail log backup may not succeed, and that is if there are any minimally logged transactions, recorded while a database was operating in BULK_LOGGED recovery model, in the live transaction log, and a data file is unavailable as a result of the disaster. A tail log backup using NO_TRUNCATE may "succeed" (although with reported errors) in these circumstances but a subsequent attempt to restore that tail log backup will fail. This is discussed in more detail in the *Minimally logged operations* section of Chapter 6.

Log space reuse (a.k.a. log truncation)

When using any recovery model other than SIMPLE, it is *vital* to take regular log backups, not only for recovery purposes, but also to **control the growth** of the log file. The reason for this relates to how and when space in the log is made available for reuse; a process known as **log truncation**.

We'll go into deeper detail in Chapter 5 but, briefly, any segment of the log that contains only log records that are no longer required is deemed "inactive," and any inactive segment can be truncated, i.e. the log records in that segment can be overwritten by log records detailing new transactions. These "segments" of the log file are known as virtual log files (VLFs).

If a VLF contains even just a single log record that relates to an open (uncommitted) transaction, or that is still *required* by some other database process (such as replication), or contains log records that are more recent than the log record relating to the oldest open or still required transaction, it is deemed "active." Any active VLF can *never* be truncated.

Any inactive VLF can be truncated, although the point at which this truncation can occur depends on the recovery model of the database. In the SIMPLE recovery model, truncation can take place immediately upon occurrence of a CHECKPOINT operation. Pages in the data cache are flushed to disk, having first "hardened" the changes to the log file. The space in any VLFs that becomes inactive as a result, is made available for reuse. Therefore, the space in inactive portions of the log is continually overwritten with new log records, upon CHECKPOINT; in other words, a complete "log record history" is not maintained.

In the FULL (or BULK LOGGED) recovery model, once a full backup of the database has been taken, the inactive portion of the log is no longer marked as reusable on CHECKPOINT, so records in the inactive VLFs are retained alongside those in the active VLFs. Thus we maintain a complete, unbroken series of log records, which can be captured in log backups, for use in point-in-time restore operations. Each time a BACKUP LOG operation occurs, it marks any VLFs that are no longer necessary as inactive and hence reusable.

This explains why it's vital to back up the log of any database running in the FULL (or BULK LOGGED) recovery model; it's the only operation that makes space in the log available for reuse. In the absence of log backups, the log file will simply continue to grow (and grow) in size, unchecked.

File backups

In addition to the database backups discussed previously, it's also possible to take file backups. Whereas database backups back up all data files for a given database, with file backups we can back up just a single, specific data file, or a specific group of data files (for example, all the data files in a particular filegroup).

For a VLDB that has been "broken down" into multiple filegroups, file backups (see Chapter 9) can decrease the time and disk space needed for the backup strategy and also, in certain circumstances, make disaster recovery much quicker. For example, let's assume that a database's architecture consists of three filegroups: a primary filegroup holding only system data, a secondary filegroup holding recent business data and a third filegroup holding archive data, which has been specifically designated as a READONLY filegroup.

If we were to perform database backups, then each full backup file would contain a lot of data that we know will never be updated, which would simply be wasting disk space. Instead, we can take frequent, scheduled file backups of just the system and business data.

Furthermore, if a database suffers corruption that is limited to a single filegroup, we may be able to restore just the filegroup that was damaged, rather than the entire database.

For instance, let's say we placed our read-only filegroup on a separate drive and that drive died. Not only would we save time by only having to restore the read-only filegroup, but also the database could remain online and just that read-only data would be unavailable until after the restore. This latter advantage only holds true for user-defined filegroups; if the primary filegroup goes down, the whole ship goes down as well. Likewise, if the disk holding the file storing recent business data goes down then, again, we may be able to restore just that filegroup; in this case, we would also have to restore any transaction log files taken after the file backup to ensure that the database as a whole could be restored to a consistent state.

Finally, if a catastrophe occurs that takes the database completely offline, and we're using SQL Server Enterprise Edition, then we may be able to perform an online restore, restoring the primary data file and bringing the database back online before we've restored the other data files. We'll cover all this in a lot more detail, with examples, in Chapter 9.

The downside of file backups is the significant complexity and administrative burden that they can add to the backup strategy. Firstly, it means that a "full backup" will consist of capturing several backup files, rather than just a single one. Secondly, in addition, we will have to take transaction log backups to cover the time between file backups of different file groups. We'll discuss this in fuller detail in Chapter 9 but, briefly, the reason for this is that while the data is stored in separate physical files it will still be relationally connected; changes made to data stored in one file will affect related data in other files, and since the individual file backups are taken at different times, SQL Server needs any subsequent log backup files to ensure that it can restore a self-consistent version of the database.

Keeping track of all of the different backup jobs and files can become a daunting task. This is the primary reason why, despite the potential benefits, most people prefer to deal with the longer backup times and larger file sizes that accompany full database backups.

Full and differential file backups

As noted earlier, a full file backup differs from the full database backup in that it doesn't back up the entire database, but just the contents of one or more files or filegroups. Likewise, differential file backups capture all of the data changes made to the relevant files or filegroups, since the last full file backup was taken.

In VLDBs, even single files or filegroups can grow large, necessitating the use of differential file backups. The same caveat exists as for differential database backups: the longer the interval between refreshing the base file backup, the larger the differential backups will get. Refresh the base full file backup at least once per week, if taking differential file backups.

Partial and differential partial backups

Partial backups, and differential partial backups, are a relative innovation, introduced in SQL Server 2005. They were specifically designed for use with databases that are comprised of at least one read-only filegroup and their primary use case was for databases operating within the SIMPLE recovery model (although they are valid for any of the available recovery models).

By default, a partial backup will create a full backup of the primary filegroup plus any additional read/write filegroups. It will not back up any read-only filegroups, unless explicitly included in the partial backup.

A typical use case for partial backups would be for a very large database (VLDB) that contains a significant portion of read-only data. In most cases, these read-only file groups contain files of archived data, which are still needed by the front end application for reference purposes. However, if this data is never going to be modified again, we don't want to waste time, CPU, and disk space backing it up every time we run a full database backup.

So, a partial full backup is akin to a full database backup, but omits all **READONLY** filegroups. Likewise, a partial differential backup is akin to a differential database backup, in that it only backs up data that has been modified since the base partial backup and, again, does not explicitly back up the **READONLY** filegroups within the database. Differential partial backups use the last partial backup as the base for any restore operations, so be sure to keep the base partial on hand.

It is recommended to take frequent base partial backups to keep the differential partial backup file size small and manageable. Again, a good rule of thumb is to take a new base partial backup at least once per week, although possibly more frequently than that if the read/write filegroups are frequently modified.

Finally, note that we can only perform partial backups via T-SQL. Neither SQL Server Management Studio nor the Maintenance Plan Wizard supports either type of partial backup.

Recovery Models

A recovery model is a database configuration option, chosen when creating a new database, which determines whether or not you need to (or even can) back up the transaction log, how transaction activity is logged, and whether or not you can perform more granular restore types that are available, such as file and page restores. All SQL Server database backup and restore operations occur within the context of one of three available **recovery models** for that database.

- **SIMPLE recovery model** – certain operations can be minimally logged. Log backups are not supported. Point-in-time restore and page restore are not supported. File restore support is limited to secondary data files that are designated as **READONLY**.

- **FULL recovery model** – all operations are fully logged. Log backups are supported. All restore operations are supported, including point-in-time restore, page restore and file restore.

- **BULK_LOGGED recovery model** – similar to FULL except that certain bulk operations can be minimally logged. Support for restore operations is as for FULL, except that it's not possible to restore to a specific point in time within a log backup that contains log records relating to minimally logged operations.

Each model has its own set of requirements and caveats, so we need to choose the appropriate one for our needs, as it will dramatically affect the log file growth and level of recoverability. In general operation, a database will be using either the SIMPLE or FULL recovery model.

Can we restore just a single table?

Since we mentioned the granularity of page and file restores, the next logical question is whether we can restore individual tables. This is not possible with native SQL Server tools; you would have to restore an entire database in order to extract the required table or other object. However, certain third-party tools, including Red Gate's SQL Compare, do support object-level restores of many different object types, from native backups or from Red Gate SQL Backup files.

By default, any new database will inherit the recovery model of the model system database. In the majority of SQL Server editions, the model database will operate with the FULL recovery model, and so all new databases will also adopt use of this recovery model. This may be appropriate for the database in question, for example if it must support point-in-time restore. However, if this sort of support is not required, then it may be more appropriate to switch the database to SIMPLE recovery model after creation. This will remove the need to perform log maintenance in order to control the size of the log. Let's take a look at each of the three recovery models in a little more detail.

Simple

Of the three recovery models for a SQL Server database, SIMPLE recovery model databases are the easiest to manage. In the SIMPLE recovery model, we can take full database backups, differential backups and file backups. The one backup we cannot take, however, is the transaction log backup.

As discussed earlier, in the *Log space reuse* section, whenever a CHECKPOINT operation occurs, the space in any inactive portions of the log file belonging to any database operating SIMPLE recovery model, becomes available for reuse. This space can be overwritten by new log records. The log file does not and cannot maintain a complete, unbroken series of log records since the last full (or differential) backup, which would be a requirement for any log backup to be used in a point-in-time restore operation, so a log backup would be essentially worthless and is a disallowed operation.

Truncation and the size of the transaction log

There is a misconception that truncating the log file means that log records are deleted and the file reduces in size. It does not; truncation of a log file is merely the act of making space available for reuse.

This process of making log space available for reuse is known as **truncation**, and databases using the SIMPLE recovery model are referred to as being in **auto-truncate** mode.

In many respects, use of the SIMPLE recovery model greatly simplifies log file management. The log file is truncated automatically, so we don't have to worry about log file growth unless caused, for example, by some large and/or long-running batch operation. If a huge number of operations are run as a single batch, then the log file can grow in size rapidly, even for databases running in SIMPLE recovery (it's better to run a series of smaller batches).

We also avoid the administrative burden of scheduling and testing the log backups, and the storage overhead required for all of the log backup files, as well as the CPU and disk I/O burden placed on the server while performing the log backups.

The most obvious and significant limitation of working in SIMPLE model, however, is that we lose the ability to perform point-in-time restores. As discussed earlier, if the exposure to potential data loss in a given database needs to be measured in minutes rather than hours, then transaction log backups are essential and the SIMPLE model should be avoided for that database.

However, not every database in your environment needs this level of recoverability, and in such cases the SIMPLE model can be a perfectly sensible choice. For example, a Quality Assurance (QA) server is generally subject to a very strict change policy and if any changes are lost for some reason, they can easily be recovered by redeploying the relevant data and objects from a development server to the QA machine. As such, most QA servers can afford to operate in SIMPLE model. Likewise, if a database that gets queried for information millions of time per day, but only receives new information, in a batch, once per night, then it probably makes sense to simply run in SIMPLE model and take a full backup immediately after each batch update.

Ultimately, the choice of recovery model is a business decision, based on tolerable levels of data loss, and one that needs to be made on a database-by-database basis. If the business requires full point-in-time recovery for a given database, SIMPLE model is not appropriate. However, neither is it appropriate to use FULL model for every database, and so take transaction log backups, "just in case," as it represents a considerable resource and administrative burden. If, for example, a database is read-heavy and a potential 12-hours' loss of data is considered bearable, then it may make sense to run in SIMPLE model and use midday differential backups to supplement nightly full backups.

Full

In FULL recovery model, all operations are fully logged in the transaction log file. This means all INSERT, UPDATE and DELETE operations, as well as the full details for all rows inserted during a bulk data load or index creation operations. Furthermore, unlike in SIMPLE model, the transaction log file is *not* auto-truncated during CHECKPOINT operations and so an unbroken series of log records can be captured in log backup files.

As such, FULL recovery model supports restoring a database to any point in time within an available log backup and, assuming a tail log backup can be made, right up to the time of the last committed transaction before the failure occurred. If someone accidentally deletes some data at 2:30 p.m., and we have a full backup, plus valid log backups spanning the entire time from the full backup completion until 3:00 p.m., then we can restore the database to the point in time directly before that data was removed. We will be looking at performing point-in-time restores in Chapter 6, *Log Restores*, where we will focus on transaction log restoration.

The other important point to reiterate here is that inactive VLFs are not truncated during a CHECKPOINT. The only action that can cause the log file to be truncated is to perform a backup of that log file; it is only once a log backup is completed that the inactive log records captured in that backup become eligible for truncation. This means that log backups play a vital dual role: firstly in allowing point-in-time recovery, and secondly in controlling the size of the transaction log file.

In the FULL model, the log file will hold a full and complete record of the transactions performed against the database since the last time the transaction log was backed up. The more transactions your database is logging, the faster it will fill up. If your log file is not set to auto-grow (see Chapter 3 for further details), then this database will cease to function correctly at the point when no further space is available in the log. If auto-grow is enabled, the log file will grow and grow until either you take a transaction log backup or the disk runs out of space; I would recommend the first of these two options.

In short, when operating in FULL recovery model, you must be taking transaction log backups to manage the growth of data in the transaction log; a full database backup does not cause the log file to be truncated. Once you take a transaction log backup, space in inactive VLFs will be made available for new transactions (except in rare cases where you specify a copy-only log backup, or use the NO_TRUNCATE option, which will not truncate the log).

Bulk Logged

The third, and least frequently used, recovery model is BULK_LOGGED. It operates in a very similar manner to FULL model, except in the extent to which bulk operations are logged, and the implications this can have for point-in-time restores. All standard operations (INSERT, UPDATE, DELETE, and so on) are fully logged, just as they would be in the FULL recovery model, but many bulk operations, such as the following, will be *minimally* logged:

- bulk imports using the BCP utility

- BULK INSERT

- INSERT … SELECT * FROM OPENROWSET(bulk…)

- SELECT INTO

- inserting or appending data using WRITETEXT or UPDATETEXT

- index rebuilds (ALTER INDEX REBUILD).

In FULL recovery model, every change is fully logged. For example, if we were to use the BULK INSERT command to load several million records into a database operating in FULL recovery model, each of the INSERTs would be individually and fully logged. This puts a tremendous overhead onto the log file, using CPU and disk I/O to write each of the transaction records into the log file, and would also cause the log file to grow at a tremendous rate, slowing down the bulk load operation and possibly causing disk usage issues that could halt your entire operation.

In BULK_LOGGED model, SQL Server uses a bitmap image to capture only the extents that have been modified by the minimally logged operations. This keeps the space required to record these operations in the log to a minimum, while still (unlike in SIMPLE model) allowing backup of the log file, and use of those logs to restore the database in case of failure. Note, however, that the size of the log backup files will not be reduced, since SQL Server must copy into the log backup file all the actual extents (i.e. the data) that were modified by the bulk operation, as well as the transaction log records.

Tail log backups and minimally logged operations

If the data files are unavailable as a result of a database failure, and the tail of the log contains minimally logged operations recorded while the database was operating in BULK_LOGGED recovery model, then it will not be possible to do a tail log backup, as this would require access to the changed data extents in the data file.

The main drawback of switching to BULK_LOGGED model to perform bulk operations, and so ease the burden on the transaction log, is that it can affect your ability to perform point-in-time restores. The series of log records is always maintained but, if a log file contains details of minimally logged operations, it is not possible to restore to a specific point in time represented within that log file. It is only possible to restore the database to the point in time represented by the final transaction in that log file, or to a specific point in time in a previous, or subsequent, log file that does not contain any minimally logged transactions. We'll discuss this in a little more detail in Chapter 6, *Log Restores*.

There is a time and place for use of the BULK_LOGGED recovery model. It is not recommended that this model be used for the day-to-day operation of any of your databases. What is recommended is that you switch from FULL recovery model to BULK_LOGGED recovery model only when you are using bulk operations. After you have completed these operations, you can switch back to FULL recovery. You should make the switch in a way that minimizes your exposure to data loss; this means taking an extra log backup immediately before you switch to BULK_LOGGED, and then another one immediately after you switch the database back to FULL recovery.

Restoring Databases

Of course, the ultimate goal of our entire SQL Server backup strategy is to prepare ourselves for the, hopefully rare, cases where we need to respond quickly to an emergency situation, for example restoring a database over one that has been damaged, or creating a second copy of a database (see HTTP://MSDN.MICROSOFT.COM/EN-US/LIBRARY/MS190436. ASPX) in order to retrieve some data that was accidentally lost from that database. In non-emergency scenarios, we may simply want to restore a copy of a database to a development or test server.

For a user database operating in FULL recovery model, we have the widest range of restore options available to us. As noted throughout the chapter, we can take transaction log backups and use them, in conjunction with full and differential backups, to restore a database to a specific point within a log file. In fact, the RESTORE LOG command supports several different ways to do this. We can:

- **recover to a specific point in time** – we can stop the recovery at a specific point in time within a log backup file, recovering the database to the point it was in when the last transaction committed, before the specified STOPAT time

- **recover to a marked transaction** – if a log backup file contains a marked transaction (defined using BEGIN TRAN TransactionName WITH MARK 'Description...') then we can recover the database to the point that this transaction starts (STOPBE- FOREMARK) or completes (STOPATMARK)

- **recover to a Log Sequence Number** – stop the recovery at a specific log record, identified by its LSN (see Chapter 6, *Log Restores*).

We'll cover several examples of the first option (which is by far the most common) in this book. In addition, we can perform more "granular" restores. For example, in certain cases, we can recover a database by restoring only a single data file (plus transaction logs), rather than the whole database. We'll cover these options in Chapters 9 and 10.

For databases in BULK_LOGGED model, we have similar restore options, except that none of the point-in-time restore options listed previously can be applied to a log file that contains minimally logged transactions.

For SIMPLE recovery model databases, our restore options are more limited. In the main, we'll be performing straightforward restores of the full and differential database backup files. In many cases, certainly for a development database, for example, and possibly for other "non-frontline" systems, this will be perfectly adequate, and will greatly simplify, and reduce the time required for, the backup and restore strategies for these databases.

Finally, there are a couple of important "special restore" scenarios that we may run into from time to time. Firstly, we may need to restore one of the system databases. Secondly, if only a single data page is damaged, it may be possible to perform a page restore, rather than restoring the whole database.

Restoring system databases

The majority of the discussion of backing up and restoring databases takes place in the context of protecting an organization's business data. However, on any SQL Server instance there will also be a set of system databases, which SQL Server maintains and that are critical to its operation, and which also need to be backed up on a regular schedule.

The full list of these databases can be found in Books Online (HTTP://MSDN.MICROSOFT. COM/EN-US/LIBRARY/MS190190.ASPX), but there are three in particular that must be included in your backup and recovery strategy.

The **master** database holds information on all of your other databases, logins and much more. If you lose your master database you are in a bad spot unless you are taking backups and so can restore it. A full backup of this database, which operates in SIMPLE recovery model, should be part of your normal backup procedures for each SQL Server instance, along with all the user databases on that instance. You should also back up master after a significant RDBMS update (such as a major Service Pack). If you find yourself in a situation where your master database has to be rebuilt, as in the case where you do not have a backup, you would also be rebuilding the msdb and model databases, unless you had good backups of msdb and model, in which case you could simply restore them.

The **msdb** database contains SQL Agent jobs, schedules and operators as well as historical data regarding the backup and restore operations for databases on that instance. A full backup of this database should be taken whenever the database is updated. That way, if a SQL Server Agent Job is deleted by accident, and no other changes have been made, you can simply restore the msdb database and regain that job information.

Finally, the model database is a "template" database for an instance; all user databases created on that instance will inherit configuration settings, such as recovery model, initial file sizes, file growth settings, collation settings and so on, from those stipulated for the model database. By default, this database operates in the FULL recovery model. It should rarely be modified, but will need a full backup whenever it is updated. Personally, I like to back it up on a similar rotation to the other system databases, so that it doesn't get overlooked. We'll walk through examples of how to restore the master and the msdb databases in Chapter 4, *Restoring From Full Backup*.

Restoring single pages from backup

There is another restore type that can be performed on SQL Server databases that can save you a huge amount of time and effort. When you see corruption in a database, it doesn't have to be corruption of the entire database file. You might find that only certain segments of data are missing or unusable. In this situation, you can restore single or multiple pages from a database backup. With this method, you only have to take your database down for a short period of time to restore the missing data, which is extremely helpful when dealing with VLDBs. We won't cover an example in this book, but further details can be found at HTTP://MSDN.MICROSOFT.COM/EN-US/LIBRARY/MS175168.ASPX.

Summary

In this chapter, we've covered a lot of necessary ground, discussing the files that comprise a SQL Server database, the critical role played by each, why it's *essential* that they are backed up, the types of backup that can be performed on each, and how this is impacted by the recovery model chosen for the database.

We're now ready to start planning, verifying and documenting our whole backup strategy, answering questions such as:

- Where will the backups be stored?

- What tools will be used to take the backups?

- How do I plan and implement an appropriate backup strategy for each database?

- How do I verify that the backups are "good?"

- What documentation do I need?

To find out the answers to these questions, and more, move on to Chapter 2.

Chapter 2: Planning, Storage and Documentation

Having covered all of the basic backup types, what they mean, and why they are necessary, we're now ready to start planning our overall backup and restore strategy for each of the databases that are in our care.

We'll start our discussion at the hardware level, with consideration of the appropriate storage for backup files, as well as the live data and log files, and then move on to discuss the tools available to capture and schedule the backup operations.

Then, in the heart of the chapter, we'll describe the process of planning a backup and restore strategy, and developing a Service Level Agreement that sets out this strategy. The SLA is a vital document for setting appropriate expectations with regard to possible data loss and database down-time, as well as the time and cost of implementing the backup strategy, for both the DBA, and the application owners.

Finally, we'll consider how best to gather vital details regarding the file architecture and backup details for each database into one place and document.

Backup Storage

Hopefully, the previous chapter impressed on you the need to take database backups for *all* user and system databases, and transaction log backups for any user databases that are not operating in SIMPLE recovery mode. One of our basic goals, as a DBA, is to create an environment where these backups are stored safely and securely, and where the required backup operations are going to run as smoothly and quickly as possible.

The single biggest factor in ensuring that this can be achieved (alongside such issues as careful backup scheduling, which we'll discuss later in the chapter) is your backup storage architecture. In the examples in this book, we back up our databases to the same disk drive that stores the live data and log files; of course, this is purely a convenience, designed to make the examples easy to practice on your laptop. In reality, we'd *never* back up to the same local disk; after all if you simply store them on the same drive as the live files, and that drive becomes corrupt, then not only have you lost the live files, but the backup files too!

There are three basic options, which we'll discuss in turn: **local disk storage, network storage**, and **tape storage**. Each of these media types has its pros and cons so, ultimately, it is a matter of preference which you use and how. In many cases, a mixture of all three may be the best solution for your environment. For example, you might adopt the scheme below.

1. **Back up the data and log files to local disk storage** – either Direct Attached Storage (DAS) or a Storage Area Network (SAN). In either case, the disks should be in a RAID configuration. This will be quicker for the backup to complete, but you want to make sure your backups are being moved immediately to a separate location, so that a server crash won't affect your ability to restore those files.

2. **Copy the backup files to a redundant network storage location** – again, this space should be driven by some sort of robust storage solution such as SAN, or a RAID of local physical drives. This will take a bit longer than the local drive because of network overhead, but you are certain that the backups are in a separate/secure location in case of emergency.

3. **Copy the files from the final location to a tape backup library** for storage in an offsite facility. I recommend keeping the files on disk for at least three days for daily backups and a full seven days for weekly (or until the next weekly backup has been taken). If you need files older than that, you can retrieve them from the tape library.

The reason I offer the option to write the backups to local storage initially, instead of straight to network storage, is that it avoids the bottleneck of pushing data through the network. Generally speaking, it's possible to get faster write speeds, and so faster backups, to a local drive than to a drive mapped from another network device, or through a drive space shared out through a distributed file system (DFS). However, with storage networks becoming ever faster, it is becoming increasingly viable to skip Step 1, and back up the data and log files directly to network storage.

Whether you write first to locally attached storage, or straight to a network share, you'll want that disk storage to be **as fast and efficient as possible**, and this means that we want to write, not to a single disk, but to a RAID unit, provided either as DAS, or by a SAN. We also want, wherever possible, to **use dedicated backup** storage. For example, if a particular drive on a file server, attached from the SAN, is designated as the destination for our SQL Server backup files, we don't want any other process storing their data in that location, competing with our backups for space and disk I/O.

Local disk (DAS or SAN)

Next on our list of backup media is the local disk drive. The main benefit of backing up to disk, rather than tape is simply that the former will be much faster (depending on the type and speed of the drive). Of course, any consideration of local disk storage for backup files is just as relevant to the storage of the online data and log files, since it's likely that the initial backup storage will just be a separate area in the same overall SQL Server storage architecture.

Generally speaking, SQL Server storage tends to consist of multiple disk drives, each set of disks forming, with a controller, a **Redundant Array of Inexpensive Disks** (RAID) device, configured appropriately according the files that are being stored.

These RAID-configured disks are made available to SQL Server either as part of **Directly Attached Storage**, where the disks (which could be SATA, SCSI or SAS) are built into the server or housed in external expansion bays that are attached to the server using a RAID controller, or as **Storage Area Network** – in layman's terms, a SAN is a big box of hard drives, available via a dedicated, high performance network, with a controller that instructs individual "volumes of data" known as Logical Unit Numbers (LUNs) to interact with certain computers. These LUNs appear as local drives to the operating system and SQL Server. Generally, the files for many databases will be stored on a single SAN.

RAID configuration

The RAID technology allows a collection of disks to perform as one. For our data and log files RAID, depending on the exact RAID configuration, can offer some or all of the advantages below.

- **Redundancy** – if one of the drives happens to go bad, we know that, depending on the RAID configuration, either the data on that drive will have been mirrored to a second drive, or it will be able to be reconstructed, and so will still be accessible, while the damaged drive is replaced.

- **Improved read and write I/O performance** – reading from and writing to multiple disk spindles in a RAID array can dramatically increase I/O performance, compared to reading and writing from a single (larger) disk.

- **Higher storage capacity** – by combining multiple smaller disks in a RAID array, we overcome the single-disk capacity limitations (while also improving I/O performance).

For our data files we would, broadly speaking, want a configuration optimized for maximum read performance and, for our log file, maximum write performance. For backup files, the simplest backup storage, if you're using DAS, may just be a separate, single physical drive.

However, of course, if that drive were to become corrupted, we would lose the backup files on that drive, and there isn't much to be done, beyond sending the drive to a recovery company, which can be both time consuming and expensive, with no guarantee of success. Therefore, for backup files it's just as important to take advantage of the redundancy advantages offered by RAID storage.

Let's take just a brief look at the more popular of the available RAID configurations, as each one provides different levels of protection and performance.

RAID 0 (striping)

This level of RAID is the simplest and provides only performance benefits. A RAID 0 configuration uses multiple disk drives and stripes the data across these disks. Striping is simply a method of distributing data across multiple disks, whereby each block of data is written to the next disk in the stripe set. This also means that I/O requests to read and write data will be distributed across multiple disks, so improving performance.

There is, however, a major drawback in a RAID 0 configuration. There is no fault tolerance in a RAID 0 setup. If one of the disks in the array is lost, for some reason, the entire array will break and the data will become unusable.

RAID 1 (mirroring)

In a RAID 1 configuration we use multiple disks and write the same data to each disk in the array. This is called mirroring. This configuration offers read performance benefits (since the data could be read from multiple disks) but no write benefits, since the write speed is still limited to the speed of a single disk.

However, since each disk in the array has a mirror image (containing the exact same data) RAID 1 does provide redundancy and fault tolerance. One drive in the mirror set can be lost without losing data, or that data becoming inaccessible. As long as one of the disks in the mirror stays online, a RAID 1 system will remain in working order but will take a hit in read performance while one of the disks is offline.

RAID 5 (striping with parity)

RAID 5 disk configurations use block striping to write data across multiple disks, and so offer increased read and write performance, but also store **parity data** on every disk in the array, which can be used to rebuild data from any failed drive. Let's say, for example, we had a simple RAID 5 setup of three disks and were writing data to it. The first data block would be written to Disk 1, the second to Disk 2, and the parity data on Disk 3. The next data blocks would be written to Disks 1 and 3, with parity data stored on Disk 2. The next data blocks would be written to Disks 2 and 3, with the parity being stored on Disk 1. The cycle would then start over again.

This allows us to lose any one of those disks and still be able to recover the data, since the parity data can be used in conjunction with the still active disk to calculate what was stored on the failed drive. In most cases, we would also have a hot spare disk that would immediately take the place of any failed disk, calculate lost data from the other drives using the parity data and recalculate the parity data that was lost with the failure.

This parity does come at a small cost, in that the parity has to be calculated for each write to disk. This can give a small hit on the write performance, when compared to a similar RAID 10 array, but offers excellent read performance since data can be read from all drives simultaneously.

RAID 10 (striped pairs of mirrors)

RAID 10 is a hybrid RAID solution. Simple RAID does not have designations that go above 9, so RAID 10 is actually RAID 1+0. In this configuration, each disk in the array has at least one mirror, for redundancy, and the data is striped across all disks in the array. RAID 10 does not require parity data to be stored; recoverability is achieved from the mirroring of data, not from the calculations made from the striped data.

RAID 10 gives us the performance benefits of data striping, allowing us to read and write data faster than single drive applications. RAID 10 also gives us the added security that losing a single drive will not bring our entire disk array down. In fact, with RAID 10, as long as at least one of the mirrored drives from any set is still online, it's possible that more than one disk can be lost while the array remains online with all data accessible. However, loss of both drives from any one mirrored set will result in a hard failure.

With RAID 10 we get excellent write performance, since we have redundancy with the need to deal with parity data. However, read performance will generally be lower that a RAID 5 configuration with the same number of disks, since data can be read simultaneously from only half the disks in the array.

Choosing the right storage configuration

All SQL Server file storage, including storage for database backup files, should be RAID-configured, both for redundancy and performance. For the backup files, what we're mainly after is the "safety net" of storage redundancy, and so the simplest RAID configuration for backup file storage would be RAID 1. However, in my experience, it's quite common that backup files simply get stored on the slower disks of a SAN, in whatever configuration is offered (RAID 5, in my case).

Various configurations of RAID-level drive failure protection are available from either DAS or SAN storage. So, in cases where a choice exists, which one should we choose?

SAN vs. DAS

With the increasing capacity and decreasing cost of hard drives, along with the advent of Solid State Drives, it's now possible to build simple but pretty powerful DAS systems. Nevertheless, there is an obvious physical limit to how far we can expand a server by attaching more hard drives. For VLDBs, this can be a problem and SAN-attached storage is still very popular in today's IT infrastructure landscape, even in smaller businesses.

For the added cost and complexity of SAN storage, you have access to storage space far in excess of what a traditional DAS system could offer. This space is easily expandable (up to the SAN limit) simply by adding more disk array enclosures (DAEs), and doesn't take up any room in the physical server. Multiple database servers can share a single SAN, and most SANs offer many additional features (multiple RAID configurations, dynamic snapshots, and so on).

SAN storage is typically provided over a fiber optic network that is separated from your other network traffic in order to minimize any network performance or latency issues; you don't have to worry about any other type of network activity interfering with your disks.

RAID 5 vs. RAID 10

There is some debate over which of these two High Availability RAID configurations is best for use when storing a relational database. The main point of contention concerns the write penalty of recalculating the parity data after a write in a RAID 5 disk array.

This was a much larger deal for RAID disks a few years ago than it is in most of today's implementations. The parity recalculation is no longer an inline operation and is done by the controller. This means that, instead of the parity recalculation happening before you can continue with I/O operations, the controller takes care of this work separately and no longer holds up the I/O queue. You do still see some overhead when performing certain types of write, but for the most part this drawback has been obfuscated by improved hardware design.

Nevertheless, my general advice, where a choice has to be made, is to go for a RAID 10 configuration for a database that is expected to be subject to "heavy writes" and RAID 5 for read-heavy databases. However, in a lot of cases, the performance gain you will see from choosing one of these RAID configurations over the other will be relatively small.

My experience suggests that advances in controller architecture along with increases in disk speed and cache storage have "leveled the playing field." In other words, don't worry overly if your read-heavy database is on RAID 10, or a reasonably write-heavy database is on RAID 5; chances are it will still perform reliably, and well.

Network device

The last option for storing our backup files is the network device. Having each server backing up to a separate folder on a network drive is a great way to organize all of the backups in one convenient location, which also happens to be easily accessible when dumping those files to tape media for offsite storage.

We don't really care what form this network storage takes, as long as it is as stable and fault tolerant as possible, which basically means RAID storage. We can achieve this via specialized Network Attached Storage (NAS), or simply a file server, backed by physical disks or SAN-attached space.

However, as discussed earlier, backing up directly to a network storage device, across a highly utilized network, can lead to latency and network outage problems. That's why I generally still recommend to backup to direct storage (DAS or SAN) and then copy the completed backup files to the network storage device. A good solution is to use a scheduled job, schedulable utility or, in some cases, a third-party backup tool to back up the databases to a local drive and then copy the results to a network share. This way, we only have to worry about latency issues when copying the backup file, but at least at this stage we don't put any additional load on the SQL Server service; if a file copy fails, we just restart it. Plus, with utilities such as **robocopy**, we have the additional safety net of the knowing the copy will automatically restart if any outage occurs.

Tape

Firstly, I will state that tape backups should be part of any SQL Server backup and recovery plan and, secondly, that I have never in my career backed up a database or log file *directly* to tape. The scheme to go for is to back up to disk, and then archive to tape.

There are several reasons to avoid backing up directly to tape, the primary one being that writing to tape is *slow*, with the added complication that the tape is likely to be attached via some sort of relatively high-latency network device. This is a big issue when dealing with backup processes, especially for large databases. If we have a network issue after our backup is 90% completed, we have wasted a lot of time and resources that are going to have to be used again. Writing to a modern, single, physical disk, or to a RAID device, will be *much* faster than writing to tape.

Some years ago, tape storage might still have had a cost advantage over disk but, since disk space has become relatively cheap, the cost of LTO-4 tape media storage is about the same as comparable disk storage.

Finally, when backing up directly to tape, we'll need to support a very large tape library in order to handle the daily, weekly and monthly backups. Someone is going to have to swap out, label and manage those tapes and that is a duty that most DBAs either do not have time for, or are just not experienced enough to do. Losing, damaging, or overwriting a tape by mistake could cost you your job.

Hopefully, I've convinced you not to take SQL Server backups directly to tape, and instead to use some sort of physical disk for initial storage. However, and despite their other shortcomings, tape backups certainly do have a role to play in most SQL Server recovery plans. The major benefit to tape media is *portability*. Tapes are small, take up relatively little space and so are ideal for offsite storage. Tape backup is the last and best line of defense for you and your data. There will come a time when a restore operation relies on a backup file that is many months old, and you will be glad you have a copy stored on tape somewhere.

With tape backups stored offsite, we also have the security of knowing that we can recover that data even in the event of a total loss of your onsite server infrastructure. In locations where the threat of natural disasters is very real and very dangerous, offsite storage is essential (I have direct experience of this, living in Florida). Without it, one hurricane, flood, or tornado can wipe out all the hard work everyone put into backing up your database files. Storing backup file archive on tape, in a secure and structurally reinforced location, can mean the difference between being back online in a matter of hours and not getting back online at all.

Most DBA teams let their server administration teams handle the task of copying backups to tape; I know mine does. The server admins will probably already be copying other important system backups to tape, so there is no reason they cannot also point a backup-to-tape process at the disk location of your database and log backup files.

Finally, there is the prosaic matter of who handles all the arrangements for the physical offsite storage of the tapes. Some smaller companies can handle this in-house, but I recommend that you let a third-party company that specializes in data archiving handle the long-term secure storage for you.

Backup Tools

Having discussed the storage options for our data, log, and backup files, the next step is to configure and schedule the SQL Server backup jobs. There are several tools available to do this, and we'll consider the following:

- **maintenance plans** – the simplest, but also the most limited solution, offering ease of use but limited options, and lacking flexibility
- **custom backup scripts** – offers full control over how your backup jobs execute, but requires considerable time to build, implement, and maintain

- **third-party backup tools** – many third-party vendors offer powerful, highly configurable backup tools that offer backup compression and encryption, as well as well-designed interfaces for ease of scheduling and monitoring.

All environments are different and the choice you make must be dictated by your specific needs. The goal is to get your databases backed up, so whichever one you decide on and use consistently is going to be the right choice.

Maintenance plan backups

The Maintenance Plan Wizard and Designer is a built-in SQL Server tool that allows DBAs to automate the task of capturing full and differential database backups, and log backups. It can also be used to define and schedule other essential database maintenance tasks, such as index reorganization, consistency checks, statistics updates, and so on.

I list this tool first, not because it is the best way to automate these tasks, but because it is a simple-to-use, built-in option, and because scheduling backup and other maintenance tasks this way sure is better than not scheduling them at all!

In fact, however, from a SQL Server backup perspective, maintenance plans are the weakest choice of the three we'll discuss, for the following reasons:

- **backup options are limited** – file or partial backups are not supported

- **configurability is limited** – we are offered a strict set of options in configuring the backup task and we cannot make any other modifications to the process, although it's possible (via the designer) to include some pre- and post-backup logic

- **some important tasks are not supported** – such as proper backup verification (see later in the chapter).

Under the covers, maintenance plans are simply SSIS packages that define a number of maintenance tasks, and are scheduled for execution via SQL Server Agent jobs. The Maintenance Plan Wizard and Designer makes it easy to build these packages, while removing a lot of the power and flexibility available when writing such packages directly in SSIS.

For maintenance tasks of any reasonable complexity, it is better to use Business Intelligence Design Studio to design the maintenance packages that suit your specific environment and schedule them through SQL Server Agent. It may not be a traditional maintenance plan in the same sense as one that the wizard would have built, but it is a maintenance package none the less.

Custom backup scripts

Another option is to write a custom maintenance script, and run it in a scheduled job via SQL Server Agent or some other scheduling tool. Traditionally, DBAs have chosen T-SQL scripts or stored procedures for this task, but PowerShell scripting is gaining in popularity due to its versatility (any .NET library can be used inside of a PowerShell script).

Custom scripting is popular because it offers the ultimate flexibility. Scripts can evolve to add more and more features and functionality. In this book, we'll create custom scripts that, as well as backing up our databases, will verify database status and alert users on failure and success. However, this really only scratches the surface of the tasks we can perform in our customized backup scripts.

The downside of all this is that "ultimate flexibility" tends to go hand in hand with increasing complexity and diminishing consistency, and this problem gets exponentially worse as the number of servers to be maintained grows. As the complexity of a script increases, so it becomes more likely that you'll encounter bugs, especially the kind that might not manifest themselves immediately as hard errors.

If a script runs on three servers, this is no big deal; just update the code on each server and carry on. What if it must run on 40 servers? Now, every minor improvement to the backup script, or bug fix, will entail a major effort to ensure that this is reflected consistently on all servers.

In such cases, we need a way to centralize and distribute the code so that we have consistency throughout the enterprise, and a quick and repeatable way to make updates to each machine, as needed.

Many DBA teams maintain on each server a "DBA database" that holds the stored procedures for all sorts of maintenance tasks, such as backups, index maintenance and more. For example, my team maintains a "master" maintenance script, which will create this database on a server, or update the objects within the database if the version on the server is older than what exists in our code repository. Whenever the script is modified, we have a custom .NET tool that will run the script on every machine, and automatically upgrade all of the maintenance code.

Third-party tools

The final option available to the DBA is to create and schedule the backup jobs using a third-party tool. Several major vendors supply backup tools but the one used in my team, and in this book, is Red Gate SQL Backup (www.red-gate.com/products/dba/sql-backup/). Details of how to install this tool can be found in Appendix A, and backup examples can be found in Chapter 8.

With SQL Backup, we can create a backup job just as easily as we could with the maintenance plan wizard, and with a lot more flexibility. We can create SQL Server Agent jobs that take full, differential, transaction log or file and filegroup backups from a GUI wizard. We can set up a custom schedule for the backups. We can configure numerous options for the backup files, including location, retention, dynamic naming convention, compression, encryption, network resilience, and more.

Be aware, though, that a tool that offers flexibility and ease of use can lead down the road of complex backup jobs. Modifying individual steps within such jobs requires T-SQL proficiency or, alternatively, you'll need to simply drop the job and build it again from scratch (of course, a similar argument applies to custom scripts and maintenance plan jobs).

Backup and Restore Planning

The most important point to remember is that, as DBAs, we do not devise plans to *back up* databases successfully; we devise plans to *restore* databases successfully. In other words, if a database owner expects that, in the event of an outage, his database and data will be back online within two hours, with a maximum of one hour's data loss, then we must devise a plan to support these requirements, assuming we believe them to be reasonable. Of course, a major component of this plan will be the details of the types of backup that will be taken, and when, but never forget that the ultimate goal is not just to take backups, but to support specific restore requirements.

This backup and restore plan will be agreed and documented in a contract with the database users, called a **Service Level Agreement**, or SLA, which will establish a certain level of commitment regarding the availability and recoverability of their database and data.

Planning an SLA is a delicate process, and as DBAs we have to consider not only our own experiences maintaining various databases and servers, but also the points of view of the application owners, managers, and end-users. This can be a tricky task, since most owners and users typically feel that their platform is the most important in any enterprise and that it should get the most attention to detail, and highest level of service. We have to be careful not to put too much emphasis on any one system, but also to not let anything fall through the cracks.

So how do we get started, when devising an appropriate backup and restore plan for a new database? As DBAs, we'd ideally be intimately familiar with the inner and outer workings of every database that is in our care. However, this is not always feasible. Some DBAs administer too many servers to know exactly what is on each one, or even what sort of data they contain. In such cases, a quick 15-minute discussion with the application owner can provide a great deal of insight into the sort of database that we are dealing with.

Over the coming sections, we'll take a look at factors that affect each side of the backup-restore coin, and the sorts of questions we need to ask of our database owners and users.

Backup requirements

The overriding criterion in determining the types of backup we need to take, and how frequently, is the maximum toleration to possible data loss, for a particular database. However, there are a few other factors to consider as well.

On what level of server does this database reside?

For example, is it a development box, a production server or a QA machine? We may be able to handle losing a week's worth of development changes, but losing a week's work of production data changes could cost someone their job, especially if the database supports a business-critical, front-line application

Do we need to back up this database at all?

Not all data loss is career-ending and, as a DBA, you will run into plenty of situations where a database doesn't need to be backed up at all. For example, you may have a development system that gets refreshed with production data on a set schedule. If you and your development team are comfortable not taking backups of data that is refreshed every few days anyway, then go for it. Unless there is a good reason to do so (perhaps the data is heavily modified after each refresh) then you don't need to waste resources on taking backups of databases that are just copies of data from another server, which does have backups being taken.

How much data loss is acceptable?

Assuming this is a system that has limits on its toleration of data loss, then this question will determine the need to take supplemental backups (transaction log, differential) in addition to full database (or file) backups, and the frequency at which they need to be taken. Now, the application owner needs to be reasonable here. If they state that they cannot tolerate any down-time, and cannot lose any data at all, then this implies the need for a very high availability solution for that database, and a very rigorous backup regime, both of which are going to cost a lot of design, implementation and administrative effort, as well as a lot of money. If they offer more reasonable numbers, such as one hour's potential data loss, then this is something that can be supported as part of a normal backup regime, taking hourly transaction log backups.

Do we need to take these hourly log backups all day, every day, though? Perhaps, yes, but it really depends on the answer to next question.

At what times of the day is this database heavily used?

What we're trying to find out here is when, and how often, backups need to be taken. Full backups of large databases should be carried out at times when the database is least used, and supplemental backups need to be fitted in around our full backup schedule. We'll need to start our log backup schedules well in advance of the normal database use schedules, in order to capture the details of all data changes, and end them after the traffic subsides. Alternatively, we may need to run these log file backups all day, which is not a bad idea, since then we will never have large gaps in time between the transaction log backup files.

What are the basic characteristics of the database?

Here, we're interested in other details that may impact backup logistics. We'll want to find out, for example:

- **How much data is stored** – the size of the database will impact backup times, backup scheduling (to avoid normal database operations being unduly affected by backups), amount of storage space required, and so on.

- **How quickly data is likely to grow** – this may impact backup frequency and scheduling, since we'll want to control log file size, as well as support data loss requirements. We will also want to plan for the future data growth to make sure our SQL Server backup space doesn't get eaten up.

- **The nature of the workload**. Is it OLTP, with a high number of both reads and writes? Or mainly read-only? Or mixed and, if so, are certain tables exclusively read-only?

Planning for backup and restore starts, ideally, right at the very beginning of a database's life, when we are planning to create it, and define the data and log file properties and architecture for the new database. Answers to questions such as these will not only help define our backup requirements, but also the appropriate file architecture (number of filegroups and data files) for the database, initial file sizes and growth characteristics, as well as the required hardware capacity and configuration (e.g. RAID level).

Data and log file sizing and growth

We'll discuss this in more detail in Chapter 3, but it's worth noting that the initial size, and subsequent auto-growth characteristics, of the data and log files will be inherited from the properties of the model *database for that instance, and there is a strong chance that these will not be appropriate for your database.*

Restore requirements

As well as ensuring we have the appropriate backups, we need a plan in place that will allow us to perform "crash recovery." In other words, we need to be sure that we can restore our backups in such a way that we meet the data loss requirements, and complete the operation within an acceptable period of down-time.

An acceptable recovery time will vary from database to database depending on a number of factors, including:

- **the size of the database** – much as we would like to, we cannot magically restore a full backup of a 500 GB database, and have it back online with all data recovered in 15 minutes

- **where the backup files are stored** – if they are on site, we only need to account for the time needed for the restore and recovery process; if the files are in offsite storage, we'll need to plan extra time to retrieve them first

- **the complexity of the restore process** – if we just need to restore a full database backup, this is fairly straightforward process; but if we need to perform a complex point-in-time restore involving full, differential, and log files, this is more complex and may require more time – or at least we'll need to practice this type of restore more often, to ensure that all members of our team can complete it successfully and within the required time.

With regard to backup file locations, an important, related question to ask your database owners is something along the lines of: *How quickly, in general, will problems be reported?*

That may sound like a strange question, but its intent is to find out how long it's necessary to retain database backup files on network storage before deleting them to make room for more backup files (after, of course, transferring these files to tape for offsite storage).

The location of the backup file will often affect how quickly a problem is solved. For example, let's say the company policy is to keep backup files on site for three days, then archive them to tape, in offsite storage. If a data loss occurs and the error is caught quickly, the necessary files will be at hand. If, however, it's only spotted five days later, the process of getting files back from the offsite tape backups will push the recovery time out, and this extra time should be clearly accounted for in the SLA. This will save the headache of having to politely explain to an angry manager why a database or missing data is not yet back online.

An SLA template

Having asked all of these question, and more, it's time to draft the SLA for that database. This document is a formal agreement regarding the backup regime that is appropriate for that database, and also offers a form of insurance to both the owners and the DBA. You do not, as a DBA, want to be in a position of having a database owner demanding to know why you can't perform a log restore to get a database back how it was an hour before it went down, when you know that they told you that only weekly full backups were required for that database, but you have no documented proof.

Figure 2-1 offers a SLA template, which will hopefully provide a good starting point for your Backup SLA contract. It might not have everything you need for your environment, but you can download the template from the supplemental material and modify it, or just create your own from scratch.

Server Name: MYCOMPANYDB1
Server Category: Production / Development / QA / Staging

Application Name: Sales-A-Tron
Application Owner: Sal Esman

Database Name :   salesDB
Data Loss: 2 Hours
Recovery Time: 4 Hours

Full Backups: Daily / Weekly / Monthly
Diff Backups: Daily / Weekly
Log Backups: Daily @ _____ Hour Intervals
File Backups: Daily / Weekly / Monthly
File Differentials: Daily / Weekly

Database Name :   salesArchives
Data Loss: 4 Hours
Recovery Time: 6 Hours

Full Backups: Daily / Weekly / Monthly
Diff Backups: Daily / Weekly
Log Backups: Daily @ _____ Hour Intervals
File Backups: Daily / Weekly / Monthly
File Differentials: Daily / Weekly

Database Name :   resourceDB
Data Loss: 2 Hours
Recovery Time: 3 Hours

Full Backups: Daily / Weekly / Monthly
Diff Backups: Daily / Weekly
Log Backups: Daily @ _____ Hour Intervals
File Backups: Daily / Weekly / Monthly
File Differentials: Daily / Weekly

Database Administrator:
Application Owner:
Date of Agreement:

Figure 2-1:   An example backup and restore SLA.

Example restore requirements and backup schemes

Based on all the information gathered for the SLA, we can start planning the detailed backup strategy and restore for each database. By way of demonstrating the process, let's walk through a few common scenarios and the recommended backup strategy. Of course, examples are only intended as a jumping-off point for your own SQL Server backup and restore plans. Each server in your infrastructure is different and may require completely different backup schedules and structures.

Scenario 1: Development server, VLDB, simple file architecture

Here, we have a development machine containing one VLDB. This database is not structurally complex, containing only one data file and one log file. The developers are happy to accept data loss of up to a day. All activity on this database takes place during the day, with a very few transactions happening after business hours.

In this case, it might be appropriate to operate the user database in **SIMPLE** recovery model, and implement a backup scheme such as the one below.

1. Perform full nightly database backups for the system databases.

2. Perform a full weekly database backup for the VLDB, for example on Sunday night.

3. Perform a differential database backup for the VLDB on the nights where you do not take the full database backups. In this example, we would perform these backups on Monday through Saturday night.

Scenario 2: Production server, 3 databases, simple file architecture, 2 hours' data loss

In the second scenario, we have a production server containing three actively-used databases. The application owner informs us that no more than two hours of data loss can be tolerated, in the event of corruption or any other disaster. None of the databases are complex structurally, each containing just one data file and one log file.

With each database operating in FULL recovery model, an appropriate backup scheme might be as below.

1. Perform full nightly database backups for every database (plus the system databases).

2. Perform log backups on the user databases every 2 hours, on a schedule starting after the full backups are complete and ending before the full backup jobs starts.

Scenario 3: Production server, 3 databases, complex file architecture, 1 hour's data loss

In this final scenario, we have a production database system that contains three databases with complex data structures. Each database comprises multiple data files split into two filegroups, one read-only and one writable. The read-only file group is updated once per week with newly archived records. The writable file groups have an acceptable data loss of 1 hour. Most database activity on this server will take place during the day.

With the database operating in FULL recovery model, the backup scheme below might work well.

1. Perform nightly full database backups for all system databases.

2. Perform a weekly full file backup of the read-only filegroups on each user database, after the archived data has been loaded.

3. Perform nightly full file backups of the writable file groups on each user database.

4. Perform hourly log backups for each user database; the log backup schedule should start after the nightly full file backups are complete, and finish one hour before the full file backup processes start again.

Backup scheduling

It can be a tricky process to organize the backup schedule such that all the backups that are required to support the Backup and Restore SLA fit into the available maintenance windows, don't overlap, and don't cause undue stress on the server.

Full database and file backups, especially of large databases, can be CPU- and Disk I/O-intensive processes, and so have the propensity to cause disruption, if they are run at times when the database is operating under its normal business workload. Ideally, we need to schedule these backups to run at times when the database is not being accessed, or at least is operating under greatly reduced load, since we don't want our backups to suffer because they are fighting with other database processes or other loads on the system (and vice versa). This is especially true when using compressed backups, since a lot of the load that would be done on disk is moved to the CPU in the compression phase.

Midnight is usually a popular time to run large backup jobs, and if your shop consists of just a few machines, by all means schedule all your full nightly backups to run at this time. However, if you administer 20, 30, or more servers, then you may want to consider staggering your backups throughout the night, to avoid any possible disk or network contention issues. This is especially true when backing up directly to a network storage device. These devices are very robust and can perform a lot of operations per second, but there is a limit to how much traffic any device can handle. By staggering the backup jobs, you can help alleviate any network congestion.

The scheduling of differential backups will vary widely, depending on their role in the backup strategy. For a VLDB, we may be taking differential backups every night, except for on the night of the weekly full backup. At other times, we may run differential backups at random times during the day, for example as a way to safeguard data before performing a large modification or update.

Transaction log backups are, in general, much less CPU- and I/O-intensive operations and can be safely run during the day, alongside the normal database workload. In fact, there isn't much point having a transactional backup of your database if no one is actually performing any transactions! The scheduling of log backups may be entirely dictated by the agreed SLA; if no more than five minutes of data can be lost, then take log backups every five minutes! If there is some flexibility, then try to schedule consecutive backups close enough so that the log file does not grow too much between backups, but far enough apart that it does not put undue stress on the server and hardware.

As a general rule, don't take log backup much more frequently than is necessary to satisfy the SLA. Remember, the more log backups you take, the more chance there is that one will fail and possibly break your log chain. However, what happens when you have two databases on a server that both require log backups to be taken, but at different intervals? For example, Database A requires a 30-minute schedule, and Database B, a 60-minute schedule. You have two choices:

1. create two separate log backup jobs, one for **DB_A** running every 30 minutes and one for **DB_B**, every 60 minutes; this means multiple SQL Agent / scheduled jobs and each job brings with it a little more maintenance and management workload

2. take log backups of both databases using a single job that runs every 30 minutes; you'll have fewer jobs to schedule and run, but more log backup files to manage, heightening the risk of a file being lost or corrupted.

My advice in this case would be to create one log backup job, taking log backups every 30 minutes; it satisfies the SLA for both databases and is simpler to manage. The slight downside is that the time between log backups for databases other than the first one in the list might be slightly longer than 30 minutes, since the log backup for a given database in the queue can't start till the previous one finishes. However, since the backups are frequent and so the backup times short, any discrepancy is likely to be very small.

Backup Verification and Test Restores

Whether there are 10 databases in our environment or 1,000, as DBAs, we must ensure that all backups are valid and usable. Without good backups, we will be in a very bad spot when the time comes to bring some data back from the dead. Backup verification is easy to integrate into normal backup routines, so let's discuss a few tips on how to achieve this.

The first, and most effective, way to make sure that the backups are ready for use is simply to perform some test restores. This may seem obvious, but there are too many DBAs who simply assume that their backups are good and let them sit on the shelf. We don't need to restore every backup in the system to check its health, but doing random spot checks now and again is an easy way to gain peace of mind regarding future restores.

Each week, choose a random database, and restore its last full backup. If that database is subject to differential and log backups as well, choose a point-in-time test restore that uses a full, differential and a few log backup files.

Since it's probably unrealistic to perform regular test restores on every single database, there are a few other practices that a DBA can adopt to maximize the likelihood that backup files are free of any corruption and can be smoothly restored.

Back up WITH CHECKSUM

We can use the **WITH CHECKSUM** option, as part of a backup operation, to instruct SQL Server to test each page with its corresponding checksum to makes sure that no corruption has happened in the I/O subsystem.

```
BACKUP DATABASE <DatabaseName>
TO  DISK =  '<Backup_location>'
 WITH CHECKSUM
GO
```

Listing 2-1: Backup WITH CHECKSUM syntax.

If it finds a page that fails this test, the backup will fail. If the backup succeeds then the backup is valid...or maybe not.

In fact, this type of validation has gotten many DBAs into trouble. It does not guarantee that a database backup is corruption free. The **CHECKSUM** only verifies that we are not backing up a database that was already corrupt in some way; if the corruption occurs in memory or somehow else during the backup operation, then it will not be detected.

As a final note, my experience and that of many others, suggests that, depending on the size of the database that is being used, enabling checksums (and other checks such as torn page detection) will bring with it a small CPU overhead and may slow down your backups (often minimally). However, use of the **WITH CHECKSUM** option during backups is a valuable safeguard and, if you can spare the few extra CPU cycles and the extra time the backups will take, go ahead. These checks are especially valuable when used in conjunction with restore verification.

Verifying restores

Since we cannot rely entirely on page checksums during backups, we should also be performing some restore verifications to make sure our backups are valid and restorable. As noted earlier, the surest way to do this is by performing test restores. However, a good additional safety net is to use the RESTORE VERIFYONLY command.

This command will verify that the structure of a backup file is complete and readable. It attempts to mimic an actual restore operation as closely as possible without actually restoring the data. As such, this operation only verifies the backup header; it does not verify that the data contained in the file is valid and not corrupt.

However, for databases where we've performed BACKUP...WITH CHECKSUM, we can then re-verify these checksums as part of the restore verification process.

```
RESTORE VERIFYONLY
FROM DISK= '<Backup_location>'
WITH CHECKSUM
```

Listing 2-2: RESTORE VERIFYONLY WITH CHECKSUM syntax.

This will recalculate the checksum on the data pages contained in the backup file and compare it against the checksum values generated during the backup. If they match, it's a good indication that the data wasn't corrupted during the backup process.

DBCC CHECKDB

One of the best ways to ensure that databases remain free of corruption, so that this corruption does not creep into backup files, making mincemeat of our backup and restore planning, is to run DBCC CHECKDB on a regular basis, to check the logical and physical integrity of all the objects in the specified database, and so catch corruption as early as possible.

We will not discuss this topic in detail in this book, but check out the information in Books Online (HTTP://MSDN.MICROSOFT.COM/EN-US/LIBRARY/MS176064.ASPX) and if you are not already performing these checks regularly, you should research and start a DBCC CHECKDB regimen immediately.

Documenting Critical Backup Information

Properly documenting your backup and restore plan goes beyond the SLA which we have previously discussed. There is a lot more information that you must know, and document, for each of the databases in your care, and the backup scheme to which they are subject.

The following checklist summarizes just some of the items that should be documented. For further coverage, Brad McGehee is currently writing a series of articles on documenting SQL Server databases, covering the information listed below, and much more. See, for example, WWW.SIMPLE-TALK.COM/SQL/DATABASE-ADMINISTRATION/DATABASE-PROPERTIES-HEALTH-CHECK/.

Database File Information

- Physical File Name:

- MDF Location:

- NDF Location(s) (add more rows as needed):

- Filegroup(s) (add more rows as needed):

- Includes Partitioned Tables/Indexes:

- Database Size:

- Has Database File Layout Been Optimized:

Log File Information

- Physical File Name:

- LDF Location:

- Log Size:

- Number of Virtual Log Files:

Backup Information

- Types of Backups Performed (Full, Differential, Log):

- Last Full Database Backup:

- Last Differential Database Backup:

- Last Transaction Log Backup:

- How Often are Transaction Logs Backed Up:

- Average Database Full Backup Time:

- Database Full Backup Size:

- Average Transaction Log Backup Size:

- Number of Full Database Backup Copies Retained:

- Backups Encrypted:

- Backups Compressed:

- Backup To Location:

- Offsite Backup Location:

- Backup Software/Agent Used:

This information can be harvested in a number of different ways, but ideally will be scripted and automated. Listing 2-3 shows two scripts that will capture just some of this information; please feel free to adapt and amend as is suitable for your environment.

```
SELECT   d.name ,
         MAX(d.recovery_model) ,
         is_Password_Protected , --Backups Encrypted:
       --Last Full Database Backup:
         MAX(CASE WHEN type = 'D' THEN backup_start_date
                  ELSE NULL
              END) AS [Last Full Database Backup] ,
       --Last Transaction Log Backup:
         MAX(CASE WHEN type = 'L' THEN backup_start_date
                  ELSE NULL
              END) AS [Last Transaction Log Backup] ,
       --Last Differential Log Backup:
         MAX(CASE WHEN type = 'I' THEN backup_start_date
                  ELSE NULL
              END) AS [Last Differential Backup] ,
       --How Often are Transaction Logs Backed Up:
         DATEDIFF(Day, MIN(CASE WHEN type = 'L' THEN backup_start_date
                            ELSE 0
                       END),
               MAX(CASE WHEN type = 'L' THEN backup_start_date
                    ELSE 0
               END)) / NULLIF(SUM(CASE WHEN type = 'I' THEN 1
                                   ELSE 0
                              END), 0) [Logs BackUp count] ,
       --Average backup times:
         SUM(CASE WHEN type = 'D'
              THEN DATEDIFF(second, backup_start_date,
                                Backup_finish_date)
              ELSE 0
          END) / NULLIF(SUM(CASE WHEN type = 'D' THEN 1
                           ELSE 0
                      END), 0) AS [Average Database
                                 Full Backup Time] ,
         SUM(CASE WHEN type = 'I'
              THEN DATEDIFF(second, backup_start_date,
                                Backup_finish_date)
              ELSE 0
          END) / NULLIF(SUM(CASE WHEN type = 'I' THEN 1
```

```
                              ELSE 0
                         END), 0) AS [Average Differential
                                          Backup Time] ,
        SUM(CASE WHEN type = 'L'
                THEN DATEDIFF(second, backup_start_date,
                                    Backup_finish_date)
                ELSE 0
           END) / NULLIF(SUM(CASE WHEN type = 'L' THEN 1
                              ELSE 0
                         END), 0) AS [Average Log Backup Time] ,
        SUM(CASE WHEN type = 'F'
                THEN DATEDIFF(second, backup_start_date,
                                    Backup_finish_date)
                ELSE 0
           END) / NULLIF(SUM(CASE WHEN type = 'F' THEN 1
                              ELSE 0
                         END), 0) AS [Average file/Filegroup
                                              Backup Time] ,
        SUM(CASE WHEN type = 'G'
                THEN DATEDIFF(second, backup_start_date,
                                    Backup_finish_date)
                ELSE 0
           END) / NULLIF(SUM(CASE WHEN type = 'G' THEN 1
                              ELSE 0
                         END), 0) AS [Average Differential
                                          file Backup Time] ,
        SUM(CASE WHEN type = 'P'
                THEN DATEDIFF(second, backup_start_date,
                                    Backup_finish_date)
                ELSE 0
           END) / NULLIF(SUM(CASE WHEN type = 'P' THEN 1
                              ELSE 0
                         END), 0) AS [Average partial Backup Time] ,
        SUM(CASE WHEN type = 'Q'
                THEN DATEDIFF(second, backup_start_date,
                                    Backup_finish_date)
                ELSE 0
           END) / NULLIF(SUM(CASE WHEN type = 'Q' THEN 1
                              ELSE 0
                         END), 0) AS [Average Differential
                                          partial Backup Time] ,
    MAX(CASE WHEN type = 'D' THEN backup_size
                ELSE 0
           END) AS [Database Full Backup Size] ,
```

```
            SUM(CASE WHEN type = 'L' THEN backup_size
                  ELSE 0
               END) / NULLIF(SUM(CASE WHEN type = 'L' THEN 1
                                   ELSE 0
                                   END), 0) AS [Average Transaction Log Backup Size] ,
        --Backup compression?:
            CASE WHEN SUM(backup_size - compressed_backup_size) <> 0 THEN 'yes'
                 ELSE 'no'
            END AS [Backups Compressed]
FROM    master.sys.databases d
            LEFT OUTER JOIN msdb.dbo.backupset b ON d.name = b.database_name
WHERE   d.database_id NOT IN ( 2, 3 )
GROUP BY d.name ,
         is_Password_Protected
--HAVING  MAX(b.backup_finish_date) <= DATEADD(dd, -7, GETDATE()) ;


-- database characteristics
SELECT  d.name ,
        f.NAME ,
        LOWER(f.type_Desc) ,
        physical_Name AS [Physical File Name] ,
        [size] / 64 AS [Database Size (Mb)] ,
        CASE WHEN growth = 0 THEN 'fixed size'
             WHEN is_percent_growth = 0 THEN CONVERT(VARCHAR(10),
                                                         growth / 64)
             ELSE CONVERT(VARCHAR(10), ( [size] * growth / 100 ) / 64)
        END AS [Growth (Mb)] ,
        CASE WHEN max_size = 0 THEN 'No growth allowed'
             WHEN max_size = -1 THEN 'unlimited Growth'
             WHEN max_size = 268435456 THEN '2 TB'
             ELSE CONVERT(VARCHAR(10), max_size / 64) + 'Mb'
        END AS [Max Size] ,
        CASE WHEN growth = 0 THEN 'no autogrowth'
             WHEN is_percent_growth = 0 THEN 'fixed increment'
             ELSE 'percentage'
        END AS [Database Autogrowth Setting]
FROM    master.sys.databases d
            INNER JOIN master.sys.master_files F
                        ON f.database_ID = d.database_ID
ORDER BY f.name ,
         f.file_ID
```

Listing 2-3: Collecting database file and backup file information.

Summary

With the first two chapters complete, the foundation is laid; we've covered database file architecture, the types of backup that are available, and how this, and the overall backup strategy, is affected by the recovery model of the database. We've also considered hardware storage requirements for our database and backup files, the tools available to capture the backups, and how to develop an appropriate Service Level Agreement for a given database, depending on factors such as toleration for data loss, database size, workload, and so on.

We are now ready to move on to the real thing; actually taking and restoring different types of backup. Over the coming chapters, we'll build some sample databases, and demonstrate all the different types of backup and subsequent restore, using both native scripting and a third-party tool (Red Gate SQL Backup).

Chapter 3: Full Database Backups

A full database backup is probably the most common type of backup in the SQL Server world. It is essentially a backup of the data file(s) associated with a database. This chapter will demonstrate how to perform these full database backups, using both GUI-driven and T-SQL techniques.

We'll create and populate a sample database, then demonstrate how to capture a full database backup using both the SQL Server Management Studio (SSMS) GUI, and T-SQL scripts. We'll capture and store some metrics (backup time, size of backup file) for both full backup techniques.

We'll then take a look at the native backup compression feature, which became part of SQL Server Standard edition in SQL Server 2008, and we'll demonstrate how much potential disk storage space (and backup time) can be saved using this feature. By the end of Chapter 3, we'll be ready to restore a full backup file, and so return our sample database to the exact state that it existed at the time the full database backup process was taken.

In Chapter 8, we'll see how to automate the whole process of taking full, as well as differential and transaction log, backups using Red Gate SQL Backup.

What is a Full Database Backup?

As discussed in Chapter 1, a full database backup (herein referred to simply as a "full backup") is essentially an "archive" of your database as it existed at the point in time of the backup operation.

It's useful to know exactly what is contained in this "archive" and a full backup contains:

- a copy of the database at the time of backup creation

- all user objects and data

- system information pertinent to the database

  - user information

  - permissions information

  - system tables and views

- enough of the transaction log to be able to bring the database back online in a consistent state, in the event of a failure.

Why Take Full Backups?

Full backups are the cornerstone of a disaster recovery strategy for any user database, in the event of data corruption, or the loss of a single disk drive, or even a catastrophic hardware failure, where all physical media for a server is lost or damaged. In such cases, the availability of a full backup file, stored securely in a separate location, may be the only route to getting an online business back up and running on a new server, with at least most of its data intact. If there are also differential backups (Chapter 7) and log backups (Chapter 5), then there is a strong chance that we can recover the database to a state very close to that in which it existed shortly before the disaster. If a full backup for a database has never been taken then, by definition, there also won't be any differential or log backups (a full backup is a prerequisite for both), and there is very little chance of recovering the data.

In the event of accidental data loss or data corruption, where the database is still operational, then, again, the availability of a full backup (in conjunction with other backup types, if appropriate) means we can restore a secondary copy of the database to a previous point in time, where the data existed, and then transfer that data back into the live database, using a tool such as SSIS or T-SQL (we cover this in detail in Chapter 6, *Log Restores*).

It is important to stress that these methods, i.e. recovering from potential data loss by restoring backup files, represent the *only* sure way to recover all, or very nearly all, of the lost data. The alternatives, such as use of specialized log recovery tools, or attempting to recover data from secondary or replica databases, offer relatively slim chances of success.

Aside from disaster recovery scenarios, there are also a few day-to-day operations where full backups will be used. Any time that we want to replace an entire database or create a new database containing the entire contents of the backup, we will perform a full backup restore. For example:

- **moving a development project database into production for the first time**; we can restore the full backup to the production server to create a brand new database, complete with any data that is required.

- **refreshing a development or quality assurance system with production data** for use in testing new processes or process changes on a different server; this is a common occurrence in development infrastructures and regular full backup restores are often performed on an automated schedule.

Full Backups in the Backup and Restore SLA

For many databases, an agreement regarding the frequency and scheduling of full database backups will form only one component of a wider Backup and Restore SLA, which also covers the need for other backup types (differential, log, and so on).

However, for certain databases, the SLA may well specify a need for *only* full backups. These full backups will, in general, be taken either nightly or weekly. If a database is subject to a moderate level of data modification, but the flexibility of full point-in-time restore, via log backups, is not required, then the Backup SLA can stipulate simply that nightly full database backups should be taken.

The majority of the development and testing databases that I look after receive only a nightly full database backup. In the event of corruption or data loss, I can get the developers and testers back to a good working state by restoring the previous night's full backup. In theory, these databases are exposed to a maximum risk of losing just less than 24 hours of data changes. However, in reality, the risk is much lower since most development happens during a much narrower daytime window. This risk is usually acceptable in development environments, but don't just assume this to be the case; make sure you get sign-off from the project owners.

For a database subject only to very infrequent changes, it may be acceptable to take only a weekly full backup. Here the risk of loss is just under seven days, but if the database really is only rarely modified then the overall risk is still quite low.

Remember that the whole point of a Backup SLA is to get everyone with a vested interest to "sign off" on acceptable levels of data loss for a given database. Work with the database owners to determine the backup strategy that works best for their databases and for you as the DBA. You don't ever want to be caught in a situation where you assumed a certain level of data loss was acceptable and it turned out you were wrong.

Preparing for Full Backups

We're going to run through examples of how to take full backups only, using both SSMS and T-SQL scripts. Chapter 4 will show how to restore these backups, and then Chapters 5 and 6 will show how to take and restore log backups, and Chapter 7 will cover differential backup and restore. In Chapter 8, we'll show how to manage full, differential and log backups, using a third-party tool (Red Gate SQL Backup) and demonstrate some of the advantages that such tools offer.

Before we get started taking full backups, however, we need to do a bit of preparatory work, namely choosing an appropriate recovery model for our example database, and then creating that database along with some populated sample tables.

Choosing the recovery model

For the example database in this chapter, we're going to assume that our Backup SLA expresses a tolerance to potential data loss of 24 hours, as might be appropriate for a typical development database. We can satisfy this requirement using just full database backups, so differential and log backups will not form part of our backup strategy, at this stage. Full database backups can be taken in any one of the three supported recovery models; SIMPLE, FULL or BULK LOGGED (see Chapter 1 for details).

Given all this, it makes strategic and administrative sense to operate this database in the SIMPLE recovery model. This will enable us to take the full backups we need, and will also greatly simplify the overall management of this database, since in SIMPLE recovery the transaction log is automatically truncated upon CHECKPOINT (see Chapter 1), and so space in the log is regularly made available for reuse. If we operated the database in FULL recovery, then we would end up taking log backups just to control the size of the log file, even though we don't need those log backups for database recovery purposes. This would generate a needless administrative burden, and waste system resources.

Database creation

The sample database for this chapter will be about as simple as it's possible to get. It will consist of a single data (mdf) file contained in a single filegroup; there will be no secondary data files or filegroups. This one data file will contain just a handful of tables where we will store a million rows of data. Listing 3-1 shows our fairly simple database creation script. Note that in a production database the data and log files would be placed on separate drives.

```
CREATE DATABASE [DatabaseForFullBackups] ON PRIMARY
(    NAME = N'DatabaseForFullBackups'
   , FILENAME = N'C:\SQLData\DatabaseForFullBackups.mdf'
   , SIZE = 512000KB
   , FILEGROWTH = 102400KB
)
LOG ON
(    NAME = N'DatabaseForFullBackups_log'
   , FILENAME = N'C:\SQLData\DatabaseForFullBackups_log.ldf'
   , SIZE = 102400KB
   , FILEGROWTH = 10240KB
)
GO
```

Listing 3-1: Creating the DatabaseForFullBackups sample database.

This is a relatively simple CREATE DATABASE statement, though even it is not quite as minimal as it could be; CREATE DATABASE [DatabaseForFullBackups] would work, since all the arguments are optional in the sense that, if we don't provide explicit values for them, they will take their default values from whatever is specified in the model database. Nevertheless, it's instructive, and usually advisable, to explicitly supply values for at least those parameters shown here.

We have named the database **DatabaseForFullBackups**, which is a clear statement of the purpose of this database. Secondly, via the NAME argument, we assign logical names to the physical files. We are adopting the default naming convention for SQL Server 2008, which is to use the database name for logical name of the data file, and append _log to the database name for the logical name of the log file.

File size and growth characteristics

The FILENAME argument specifies the path and file name used by the operating system. Again, we are using the default storage path, storing the files in the default data directory, and the default file name convention, which is to simply append .MDF and .LDF to the logical file names.

The optional SIZE and FILEGROWTH arguments are the only cases where we use some non-default settings. The default initial SIZE settings for the data and log files, inherited from the model database properties, are too small (typically, 3 MB and 1 MB respectively) for most databases. Likewise the default FILEGROWTH settings (typically 1 MB increments for the data files and 10% increments for the log file) are also inappropriate. In busy databases, they can lead to fragmentation issues, as the data and log files grow in many small increments.

The first problem is physical file fragmentation, which occurs when a file's data is written to non-contiguous sectors of the physical hard disk (SQL Server has no knowledge of this). This physical fragmentation is greatly exacerbated if the data and log files are allowed to grow in lots of small auto-growth increments, and it can have a big impact on the performance of the database, especially for sequential write operations.

As a best practice it's wise, when creating a new database, to defragment the disk drive (if necessary) and then create the data and log files pre-sized so that they can accommodate, without further growth in file size, the current data plus estimated data growth over a reasonable period. In a production database, we may want to size the files to accommodate, say, a year's worth of data growth.

There are other reasons to avoid allowing your database files to grow in multiple small increments. Each growth event will incur a CPU penalty. This penalty can be mitigated for data files by instant file initialization (enabled by granting the **perform volume maintenance tasks** right to the SQL Server service account). However, the same optimization does not apply to log files.

Furthermore, growing the log file in many small increments can cause **log fragmentation**, which is essentially the creation of a very large number of small VLFs, which can deteriorate the performance of crash recovery, restores, and log backups (in other words, operations that read the log file). We'll discuss this in more detail in Chapter 5.

In any event, in our case, we're just setting the SIZE and FILEGROWTH settings such that SQL Server doesn't have to grow the files while we pump in our test data. We've used an initial data files size of 500 MB, growing in 100 MB increments, and an initial size for the log file of 100 MB, growing in 10 MB increments.

When you're ready, execute the script in Listing 3-1, and the database will be created. Alternatively, if you prefer to create the database via the SSMS GUI, rather than using a script, simply right-click on the **Databases** node in SSMS, select **New Database...**, and fill out the **General** tab so it looks like that shown in Figure 3-1.

Database name:	DatabaseForFullBackups						
Owner:	<default>						

☑ Use full-text indexing

Database files:

Logical Name	File Type	Filegroup	Initial Size (MB)	Autogrowth		Path
DatabaseForFullBackups	Rows ...	PRIMARY	500	By 100 MB, unrestricted growth	...	C:\SQLData
DatabaseForFullBackups_log	Log	Not Applicable	100	By 10 MB, unrestricted growth	...	C:\SQLData

Figure 3-1: Creating a database via SSMS.

Setting database properties

If, via SSMS, we generate a CREATE script for an existing database, it will contain the expected CREATE DATABASE section, specifying the values for the NAME, FILENAME, SIZE, MAXSIZE and FILEGROWTH arguments. However, this will be followed by a swathe of ALTER DATABASE commands that set various other database options. To see them all, simply browse the various **Properties** pages for any database. All of these options are, under the covers, assigned default values according to those specified by the model system database; hence the name model, since it is used as a model from which to create all user databases. Listing 3-2 shows a script to set six of the more important options.

```
ALTER DATABASE [DatabaseForFullBackups] SET COMPATIBILITY_LEVEL = 100
GO
ALTER DATABASE [DatabaseForFullBackups] SET AUTO_SHRINK OFF
GO
ALTER DATABASE [DatabaseForFullBackups] SET AUTO_UPDATE_STATISTICS ON
GO
ALTER DATABASE [DatabaseForFullBackups] SET READ_WRITE
GO
ALTER DATABASE [DatabaseForFullBackups] SET RECOVERY SIMPLE
GO
ALTER DATABASE [DatabaseForFullBackups] SET MULTI_USER
GO
```

Listing 3-2: Various options of the ALTER DATABASE command.

The meaning of each of these options is as follows:

- **COMPATIBILITY_LEVEL**
  This lets SQL Server know with which version of SQL Server to make the database compatible. In all of our examples, we will be using 100, which signifies SQL Server 2008.

- **AUTO_SHRINK**
  This option either turns on or off the feature that will automatically shrink your database files when free space is available. In almost all cases, this should be set to OFF.

- **AUTO_UPDATE_STATISTICS**
  When turned ON, as it should be in most cases, the optimizer will automatically keep statistics updated, in response to data modications.

- **READ_WRITE**
  This is the default option and the one to use if you want users to be able to update the database. We could also set the database to READ_ONLY to prevent any users making updates to the database.

- **RECOVERY SIMPLE**
  This tells SQL Server to set the recovery model of the database to SIMPLE. Other options are FULL (the usual default) and BULK_LOGGED.

- **MULTI_USER**

  For the database to allow connections for multiple users, we need to set this option. Our other choice is SINGLE_USER, which allows only one connection to the database at a time.

The only case where we are changing the usual default value is the command to set the recovery model to SIMPLE; in most cases, the model database will, by default, be operating in the FULL recovery model and so this is the recovery model that will be conferred on all user databases. If the default recovery model for the model database is already set to SIMPLE, for your instance, then you won't need to execute this portion of the ALTER script.

If you do need to change the recovery model, just make sure you are in the correct database before running this command, to avoid changing another database's recovery model. Alternatively, simpy pull up the **Properties** for our newly created database and change the recovery model manually, on the **Options** page, as shown in Figure 3-2.

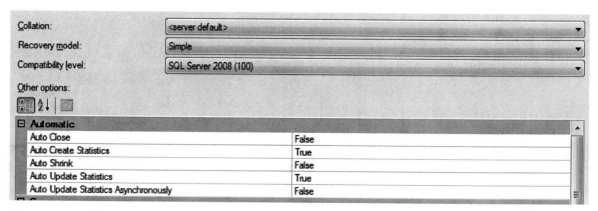

Figure 3-2:   The **Options** page for a database, in SSMS.

Creating and populating the tables

Now that we have a brand new database created on our instance, we need to create a few sample tables. Listing 3-3 shows the script to create two message tables, each with the same simple structure.

```
USE [DatabaseForFullBackups]
GO

SET ANSI_NULLS ON
GO

SET QUOTED_IDENTIFIER ON
GO

CREATE TABLE [dbo].[MessageTable1]
    (
        [MessageData] [nvarchar](200) NOT NULL ,
        [MessageDate] [datetime2] NOT NULL
    )
ON  [PRIMARY]
GO

CREATE TABLE [dbo].[MessageTable2]
    (
        [MessageData] [nvarchar](200) NOT NULL ,
        [MessageDate] [datetime2] NOT NULL
    )
ON  [PRIMARY]
GO
```

Listing 3-3: Table creation script.

MessageTable1 and MessageTable2 are both very simple tables, comprised of only two columns each. The MessageData column will contain a static character string, mainly to fill up data space, and the MessageDate will hold the date and time that the message was inserted.

Now that we have our tables set up, we need to populate them with data. We want to pack in a few hundred thousand rows so that the database will have a substantial size. However, we won't make it so large that it will risk filling up your desktop/laptop drive. Normally, a DBA tasked with pumping several hundred thousand rows of data into a table would reach for the BCP tool and a flat file, which would be the fastest way to achieve this goal. However, since coverage of BCP is out of scope for this chapter, we'll settle for a simpler, but much slower, T-SQL method, as shown in Listing 3-4.

```
USE [DatabaseForFullBackups]
GO

DECLARE @messageData    NVARCHAR(200)

SET @messageData = 'This is the message we are going to use to fill
                    up the first table for now.  We want to get this
                    as close to 200 characters as we can to fill up
                    the database as close to our initial size as we can!!'

INSERT INTO dbo.MessageTable1 VALUES (@messageData, GETDATE())
GO 1000000
```

Listing 3-4: Populating MessageTable1.

The code uses a neat GO trick that allows us to INSERT the same data into the MessageTable1 table multiple times, without using a looping mechanism. The GO statement is normally used as a batch separator, but in this case we pass it a parameter defining the number of times to run the code in the batch.

So, our database is now at a decent size, somewhere around 500 MB. This is not a large database by any stretch of the imagination, but it is large enough that it will take more than a few seconds to back up.

Generating testing data

Getting a decent amount of testing data into a database can be a daunting task, especially when the database becomes much more complex than our example. Red Gate offers a product, SQL Data Generator, which will scan your database and table structure to give you a very robust set of options for automatically generating test data. You can also write custom data generators for even the most specific of projects. See www.red-gate.com/products/SQL_Data_Generator/.

Taking Full Backups

We are now set to go and we're going to discuss taking full backups the "GUI way," in SSMS, and by using native T-SQL Backup commands.

As you work through the backup examples in this chapter, and throughout the book, for learning purposes, you may occasionally want to start again from scratch, that is, to drop the example database, re-create it, and retake the backups. The best way to do this is to delete the existing backup files for that database, and then drop the database in a way that also clears out the backup history for that database, which is stored in the msdb database. This will prevent SQL Server from referencing any old backup information. Listing 3-5 shows how to do this.

```
EXEC msdb.dbo.sp_delete_database_backuphistory
                    @database_name = N'DatabaseName'
GO
USE [master]
GO
DROP DATABASE [DatabaseName]
GO
```

Listing 3-5: Dropping a database and deleting backup history.

Alternatively, using the SSMS GUI, simply right-click on the database, and select **Delete**; by default, the option to **Delete backup and restore history information for databases** will be checked and this will clear out the msdb historical information.

Native SSMS GUI method

Taking full backups using the SSMS GUI is a fairly straightforward process. I use this technique mainly to perform a one-time backup, perhaps before implementing some heavy data changes on the database. This provides an easy way to revert the database to the state it was in before the change process began, should something go wrong.

We're going to store the backup files on local disk, in a dedicated folder. So go ahead now and create a new folder on the root of the **C:** drive of the SQL Server instance, called **SQLBackups** and then create a subfolder called **Chapter3** where we'll store all the full backup files in this chapter. Again, we use the same drive as the one used to store the online data and log files purely as a convenience; in a production scenario, we'd stored the backups on a separate drive!

The Backup Database wizard

We are now ready to start the full backup process. Open SQL Server Management Studio, connect to your server, expand the Databases node and then right-click on the **DatabaseForFullBackups** database, and navigate **Tasks | Backup...**, as shown in Figure 3-3.

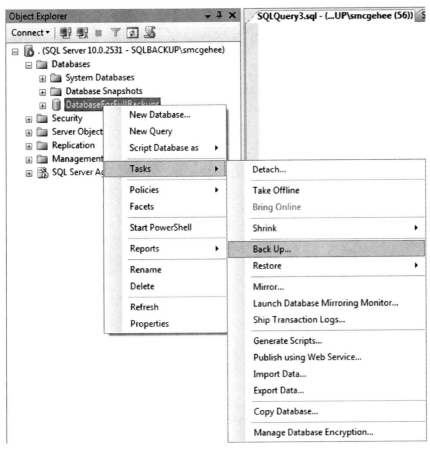

Figure 3-3: Back Up Database menu option.

This will start the backup wizard and bring up a dialog box titled **Back Up Database –
DatabaseForFullBackups**, shown in Figure 3-4, with several configuration options that
are available to the T-SQL BACKUP DATABASE command. Don't forget that all we're really
doing here is using a graphical interface to build and run a T-SQL command.

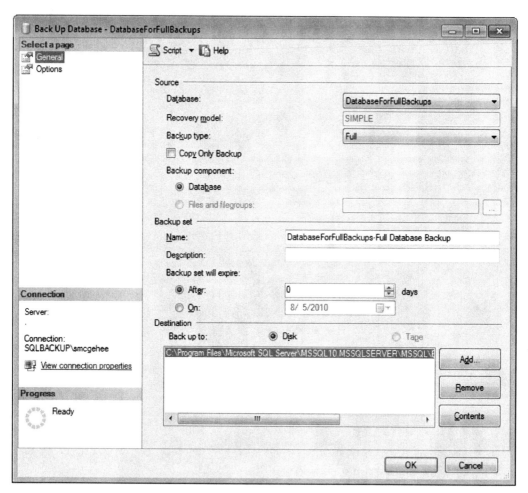

Figure 3-4: Back Up Database wizard.

The **General** page comprises three major sections: **Source**, **Backup set** and **Destination**. In the **Source** section, we specify the database to be backed up and what type of backup to perform. The **Backup type** drop-down list shows the types of backup that are available to your database. In our example we are only presented with two options, **Full** and **Differential**, since our database is in SIMPLE recovery model.

You will also notice a check box with the label **Copy-only backup**. A copy-only full backup is one that does not affect the normal backup operations of a database and is used when a full backup is needed outside of a normal scheduled backup plan. When a normal full database backup is taken, SQL Server modifies some internal archive points in the database, to indicate that a new base file has been created, for use when restoring subsequent differential backups. Copy-only full backups preserve these internal archive points and so cannot be used as a differential base. We're not concerned with copy-only backups at this point.

The **Backup component** section is where we specify either a database or file/filegroup backup. The latter option is only available for databases with more than one filegroup, so it is deactivated in this case. We will, however, talk more about this option when we get to Chapter 9, on file and filegroup backups.

In the **Backup set** section, there are name and description fields used to identify the backup set, which is simply the set of data that was chosen to be backed up. The information provided here will be used to tag the backup set created, and record its creation in the MSDB backup history tables.

There is also an option to set an expiration date on our backup set. When taking SQL Server backups, it is entirely possible to store multiple copies of a database backup in the same file or media. SQL Server will just append the next backup to the end of the backup file. This expiration date lets SQL Server know how long it should keep this backup set in that file before overwriting it. Most DBAs do not use this "multiple backups per file" feature. There are only a few benefits, primarily a smaller number of files to manage, and many more drawbacks: larger backup files and single points of failure, to name only two. For simplicity and manageability, throughout this book, we will only deal with backups that house a single backup per file.

The **Destination** section is where we specify the backup media and, in the case of disk, the location of the file on this disk. The **Tape** option button will be disabled unless a tape drive device is attached to the server.

As discussed in Chapter 1, even if you still use tape media, as many do, you will almost never back up directly to tape; instead you'll back up to disk and then transfer older backups to tape.

When using disk media to store backups, we are offered three buttons to the right of the file listing window, for adding and removing disk destinations, as well as looking at the different backup sets that are already stored in a particular file. The box will be pre-populated with a default file name and destination for the default SQL Server backup folder. We are not going to be using that folder (simply because we'll be storing our backups in separate folders, according to chapter) so go ahead and use the **Remove** button on that file to take it out of the list. Now, use the only available button, the **Add...** button to bring up the **Select Backup Destination** window. Make sure you have the **File name** option selected, click the browse (...) button to bring up the **Locate Database Files** window. Locate the **SQLBackups\Chapter3** directory that you created earlier, on the machine and then enter a name for the file, DatabaseForFullBackups_Full_Native_1.bak as shown in Figure 3-5.

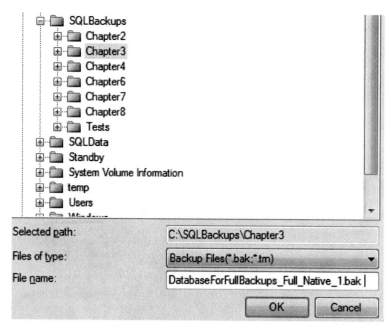

Figure 3-5: Backup file configuration.

Once this has been configured, click **OK** to finalize the new file configuration and click **OK** again on the **Select Backup Destination** dialog box to bring you back to the **Back Up Database** page. Now that we are done with the **General** page of this wizard, let's take a look at the **Options** Page, shown in Figure 3-6.

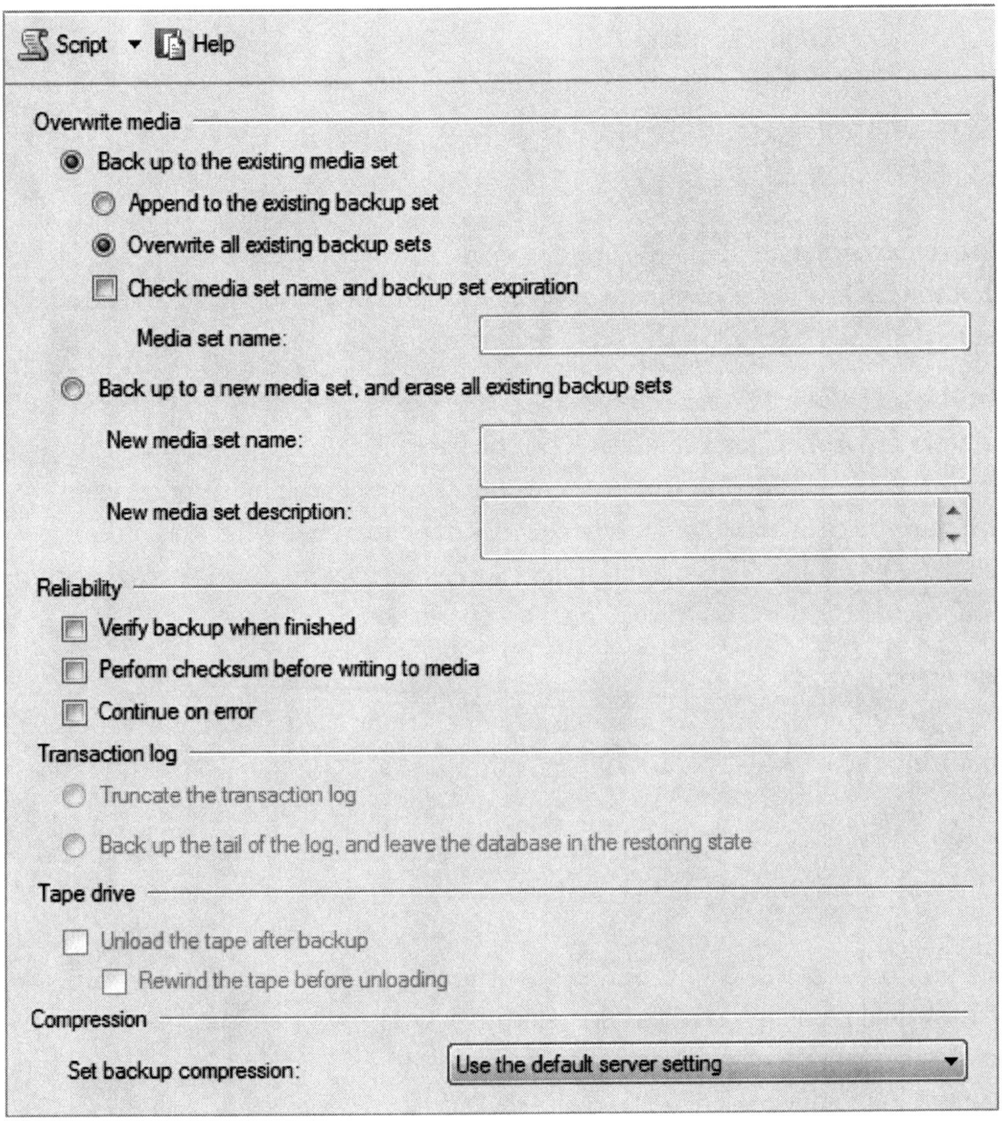

Figure 3-6: Configuration options for backups.

The **Overwrite media** section is used in cases where a single file stores multiple backups and backup sets. We can set the new backup to append to the existing backup set or to overwrite the specifically named set that already exists in the file. We can also use this section to overwrite an existing backup set and start afresh. We'll use the option of **Overwrite all existing backup sets** since we are only storing one backup per file. This will make sure that, if we were to run the same command again in the event of an issue, we would wind up with just one backup set in the file.

The **Reliability** section provides various options that can be used to validate the backup, as follows:

- **Verify backup when finished**
  Validates that the backup set is complete, after the backup operation has completed. It will make sure that each backup in the set is readable and ready for use.

- **Perform checksum before writing to media**
  SQL Server performs a checksum operation on the backup data before writing it to the storage media. As discussed in Chapter 2, a checksum is a special function used to make sure that the data being written to the disk/tape matches what was pulled from the database or log file. This option makes sure your backup data is being written correctly, but might also slow down your backup operation.

- **Continue on error**
  Instructs SQL Server to continue with all backup operations even after an error has been raised during the backup operation.

The **Transaction log** section offers two important configuration options for transaction log backups, and will be covered in Chapter 5.

The **Tape Drive** section of the configuration is only applicable if you are writing your backups directly to tape media. We have previously discussed why this is not the best way for backups to be taken in most circumstances, so we will not be using these options (and they aren't available here anyway, since we've already elected to back up to disk).

The final **Compression** configuration section deals with SQL Server native backup compression, which is an option that we'll ignore for now, but come back to later in the chapter.

Having reviewed all of the configuration options, go ahead and click **OK** at the bottom of the page to begin taking a full database backup of the `DatabaseForFullBackups` database. You will notice the progress section begin counting up in percentage. Once this reaches 100%, you should receive a dialog box notifying you that your backup has completed. Click **OK** on this notification and that should close both the dialog box and the **Back Up Database** wizard.

Gathering backup metrics, Part 1

That wasn't so bad! We took a full backup of our database that has one million rows of data in it. On a reasonably laptop or desktop machine, the backup probably would have taken 30–60 seconds. On a decent server, it will have been much quicker. However, it's useful to have slightly more accurate timings so that we can compare the performance of the various methods of taking full backups. We also need to check out the size of the backup file, so we can see how much storage space it requires and, later, compare this to the space required for compressed backup files.

To find out the size of the backup file, simple navigate to the **SQLBackups\Chapter2** folder in Windows Explorer and check out the size of the `DatabaseForFullBackups_Full_Native_1.bak` file.

You should find that it's roughly the same size as the data (**mdf**) file, i.e. about 500 MB, or half of a gigabyte. This doesn't seem bad now, but given that some databases are over 1 TB in size, you can begin to appreciate the attraction of backup compression.

Checking the exact execution time for the backup process is a little trickier. If we don't want to use a stopwatch to measure the start and stop of the full backup, we can use the `backupset` system table in `MSDB` to give us a more accurate backup time. Take a look at Listing 3-6 for an example of how to pull this information from your system. I'm only returning a very small subset of the available columns, so examine the table more closely, to find more information that you might find useful.

```
USE msdb
GO

SELECT
    database_name
    , DATEDIFF(SS, backup_start_date, backup_finish_date) AS [RunTImeSec]
    , database_creation_date
FROM
    dbo.backupset
ORDER BY
    database_creation_date DESC
```

Listing 3-6: Historical backup runtime query.

Figure 3-7 shows some sample output.

	database_name	RunTImeSec	database_creation_date
1	DatabaseForFullBackups	49	2010-08-03 20:42:40.000

Figure 3-7: Historical backup runtime results.

On my machine the backup takes 49 seconds. That seems fairly good, but we have to consider the size of the test database. It is only 500 MB, which is not a typical size for most production databases.

In the next section, we'll pump more data into the database and take another full backup (this time using T-SQL directly), and we'll get to see how the backup execution time varies with database size.

Native T-SQL method

Every DBA needs to know how to write a backup script in T-SQL. Scripting is our route to backup automation and, in cases where we don't have access to a GUI, it may be the only option available; we can simply execute our backups scripts via the **osql** or **sqlcmd** command line utilities. Here, however, for general readability, we'll execute the scripts via SSMS. Remember that the commands in this section are essentially the same ones that the GUI is generating and executing against the server when we use the Backup wizard.

Before we move on to take another full backup of our DatabaseForFullBackups database, this time using T-SQL, we're first going add a bit more data. Let's put a new message into our second table with a different date and time stamp.

We are going to use the same method to fill the second table as we did for the first. The only thing that is going to change is the text that we are entering. Take a look at Listing 3-7 and use this to push another million rows into the database.

```
USE [DatabaseForFullBackups]
GO

DECLARE @messageData NVARCHAR(200)

SET @messageData = 'This is a different message we are going to
                    use to fill up the second table.  We want to get
                    this as close to 200 characters as we can to
                    fill up the database as close to our initial
                    size as we can.'

INSERT  INTO dbo.MessageTable2
VALUES  ( @messageData, GETDATE() )
GO 1000000
```

Listing 3-7: Populating the MessageTable2 table.

This script should take about a few minutes to fill the secondary table. Once it is populated with another million rows of the same size and structure as the first, our database file should be hovering somewhere around 1 GB in size, most likely just slightly under. Now that we have some more data to work with, let's move on to taking native SQL Server backups using T-SQL only.

A simple T-SQL script for full backups

Take a look at Listing 3-8, which shows a script that can be used to take a full backup of the newly populated DatabaseForFullBackups database.

```
USE master
GO
BACKUP DATABASE [DatabaseForFullBackups] TO
DISK = N'C:\SQLBackups\Chapter3\DatabaseForFullBackups_Full_Native_2.bak'
WITH FORMAT, INIT,  NAME = N'DatabaseForFullBackups-Full Database Backup',
SKIP, NOREWIND, NOUNLOAD,  STATS = 10
GO
```

Listing 3-8: Native full backup T-SQL script.

This script may look like it has some extra parameters, compared to the native GUI backup that we did earlier, but this is the scripted output of that same backup, with only the output file name modified, and a few other very minor tweaks. So what do each of these parameters mean?

The meaning of the first line should be fairly obvious; it is instructing SQL Server to perform a full backup of the DatabaseForFullBackups database. This leads into the second line where we have chosen to back up to disk, and given a complete file path to the resulting backup file. The remainder of the parameters are new, so let's go through each one.

- **FORMAT**

  This option tells SQL Server whether or not to overwrite the media header information. The FORMAT option will erase any information in a backup set that already
  exists when the backup is initialized (NOFORMAT will preserve it).

- **INIT**

  By default, when scripting a backup generated by the Backup wizard, this parameter
  will be set to NOINIT, which lets SQL Server know *not* to initialize a media set when
  taking the backup and instead append any new backup data to the existing backup set.
  However, since we adopt the rule of one backup per backup set, it's useful to use INIT
  instead, to make sure that, if a command gets run twice, we overwrite the existing set
  and still end up with only one backup in the set.

- **NAME**

  The NAME parameter is simply used to identify the backup set. If it is not supplied, the
  set will not record a name.

- **SKIP**

  Using the SKIP parameter will cause SQL Server to skip the expiration check that it
  normally does on the backup set. It doesn't care if any backups existing in the backup
  set have been marked for availability to be overwritten.

- **NOREWIND**

  This parameter will cause SQL Server to keep a tape device open and ready for use
  when the backup operation is complete. This is a performance boost to users of tape
  drives since the tape is already at the next writing point instead of having to search for
  the correct position. This is obviously a tape-only option.

- **NOUNLOAD**

  When backing up to a tape drive, this parameter instructs SQL Server not to unload
  the tape from the drive when the backup operation is completed.

- **STATS**

  This option may prove useful to you when performing query-based backups. The STATS parameter defines the time intervals on which SQL Server should update the "backup progress" messages. For example, using stats=10 will cause SQL Server to send a status message to the query output for each 10 percent of the backup completion.

As noted, if we wished to overwrite an existing backup set, we'd want to specify the INIT parameter but, beyond that, none of these secondary parameters, including the backup set NAME descriptor, are required. As such, we can actually use a much simplified BACKUP command, as shown in Listing 3-9.

```
BACKUP DATABASE [DatabaseForFullBackups] TO
DISK = N'C:\SQLBackups\Chapter3\DatabaseForFullBackups_Full_Native_2.bak'
GO
```

Listing 3-9: Slimmed-down native T-SQL backup code.

Go ahead and start Management Studio and connect to your test server. Once you have connected, open a new query window and use either Listing 3-8 or 3-9 to perform this backup in SSMS. Once it is done executing, do not close the query, as the query output contains some metrics that we want to record.

Gathering backup metrics, Part 2

Now that the backup has completed, let's take a look at the query output window to see if we can gather any information about the procedure. Unlike the native GUI backup, we are presented with a good bit of status data in the messages tab of the query window. The post-backup message window should look as shown in Figure 3-8 (if you ran Listing 3-8, it will also contain ten "percent processed" messages, which are not shown here).

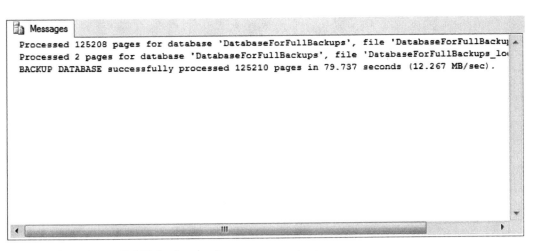

Figure 3-8: Native T-SQL backup script message output.

This status output shows how many database pages the backup processed as well as how quickly the backup was completed. On my machine, the backup operation completed in just under 80 seconds. Notice here that that the backup processes all the pages in the data file, plus two pages in the log file; the latter is required because a full backup needs to include enough of the log that the backup can produce a consistent database, upon restore.

When we ran our first full backup, we had 500 MB in our database and the backup process took 49 seconds to complete. Why didn't it take twice as long this time, now that we just about doubled the amount of data? The fact is that the central process of writing data to the backup file probably did take roughly twice as long, but there are other "overhead processes" associated with the backup task that take roughly the same amount of time regardless of how much data is being backed up. As such, the time to take backups will not increase linearly with increasing database size.

But does the size of the resulting backup file increase linearly? Navigating to our SQL Server backup files directory, we can see clearly that the size is nearly double that of the first backup file (see Figure 3-9). The file size of your native SQL Server backups will grow at nearly the same rate as the database data files grow.

Name	Type	Size
DatabaseForFullBackups_Full_Native_1.bak	BAK File	501,847 KB
DatabaseForFullBackups_Full_Native_2.bak	BAK File	1,002,583 KB
DatabaseForFullBackups_Full_RG_1.sqb	SQL Backup file	3,777 KB

Figure 3-9: Comparing native SQL Server backup file sizes.

We will compare these metrics against the file sizes and speeds we get from backing up the same files using Red Gate's SQL Backup in Chapter 8.

Native Backup Compression

In SQL Server 2008 and earlier versions, backup compression was a feature only available in the Enterprise Edition (or Developer Edition) of SQL Server. However, starting with SQL Server 2008 R2, backup compression has been made available in all editions, so let's take a quick look at what savings it can offer over non-compressed backups, in terms of backup file size and the speed of the backup operation. Generally speaking, third-party backup tools still offer a better compression ratio, better speed and more options (such as compressed and encrypted backups) than native backup compression. However, we'll put that to the test in Chapter 8.

All we're going to do is perform a compressed backup of the `DatabaseForFull-Backups`, using the script shown in Listing 3-10.

```
USE [master]
GO


BACKUP DATABASE [DatabaseForFullBackups]
TO DISK = N'C:\SQLBackups\Chapter3\SQLNativeCompressionTest.bak'
WITH COMPRESSION,  STATS = 10
GO
```

Listing 3-10: SQL native compression backup test.

The only difference between this and our backup script in Listing 3-9, is the use here of the COMPRESSION keyword, which instructs SQL Server to make sure this database is compressed when written to disk. If you prefer to run the compressed backup using the GUI method, simply locate the **Compression** section, on the **Options** page of the Backup Wizard, and change the setting from **Use the default server setting** to **Compress backup**. Note that, if desired, we can use the sp_configure stored procedure to make backup compression the default behavior for a SQL Server instance.

On completion of the backup operation, the query output window will display output similar to that shown in Figure 3-10.

```
Messages
40 percent processed.
50 percent processed.
60 percent processed.
70 percent processed.
80 percent processed.
90 percent processed.
Processed 125208 pages for database 'DatabaseForFullBackups', file 'DatabaseForFullBackups' on file 1.
100 percent processed.
Processed 1 pages for database 'DatabaseForFullBackups', file 'DatabaseForFullBackups_log' on file 1.
BACKUP DATABASE successfully processed 125209 pages in 31.690 seconds (30.867 MB/sec).
```

Figure 3-10: Compressed backup results.

If you recall, a non-compressed backup of the same database took close to 80 seconds and resulted in a backup file size of just over 1 GB. Here, we can see that use of compression has reduced the backup time to about 32 seconds, and it results in a backup file size, shown in Figure 3-11, of only 13 KB!

Name	Date modified	Type	Size
SQLNativeCompressionTest.bak	12/4/2011 6:42 PM	BAK File	13,007 KB

Figure 3-11: Compressed backup file size.

These results represent a considerable saving, in both storage space and processing time, over non-compressed backups.

If you're wondering whether or not the compression rates should be roughly consistent across all your databases, then the short answer is no. Character data, such as that stored in our DatabaseForFullBackups database compresses very well. However, some databases may contain data that doesn't compress as readily such as FILESTREAM and image data, and so space savings will be less.

Verifying Backups

Having discussed the basic concepts of backup verification in Chapter 2, Listing 3-11 shows a simple script to perform a checksum during a backup of our DatabaseForFullBackups database, followed by a RESTORE VERIFYONLY, recalculating the checksum.

```
BACKUP DATABASE [DatabaseForFullBackups]
TO DISK = N'C:\SQLBackups\Chapter3\DatabaseForFullBackups_Full_Native_Checksum.bak'
 WITH CHECKSUM
GO


RESTORE VERIFYONLY
FROM DISK = N'C:\SQLBackups\Chapter3\DatabaseForFullBackups_Full_Native_Checksum.bak'
WITH CHECKSUM
```

Listing 3-11: Backup verification examples.

Hopefully you'll get output to the effect that the backup is valid!

Building a Reusable and Schedulable Backup Script

Ad hoc database and transaction log backups can be performed via simple T-SQL scripts or the GUI, in SQL Server Management Studio. However, for production systems, the DBA will need a way to automate these backups, verify that the backups are valid, schedule and monitor them, and so on. Some of the options for automating backups are listed below.

- **SSMS Maintenance Plans Wizard and Designer** – two tools, built into SSMS, which allow you to configure and schedule a range of core database maintenance tasks, including full database backups and transaction log backups. The DBA can also run DBCC integrity checks, schedule jobs to remove old backup files, and so on. An excellent description of these tools, and their limitations, can be found in Brad McGehee's book, BRAD'S SURE GUIDE TO SQL SERVER MAINTENANCE PLANS.

- **T-SQL scripts** – you can write custom T-SQL scripts to automate your backup tasks. A well established and respected set of maintenance scripts is provided by Ola Hallengren (HTTP://OLA.HALLENGREN.COM/). His scripts create a variety of stored procedures, each performing a specific database maintenance task, including backups, and automated using SQL Agent jobs.

- **PowerShell / SMO scripting** – more powerful and versatile than T-SQL scripting, but with a steeper learning curve for many DBAs, PowerShell can be used to script and automate almost any maintenance task. There are many available books and resources for learning PowerShell. See, for example, WWW.SQLSERVERCENTRAL.COM/ARTICLES/ POWERSHELL/64316/.

- **Third-party backup tools** – several third-party tools exist that can automate backups, as well as verify and monitor them. Most offer backup compression and encryption as well as additional features to ease backup management, verify backups, and so on. Examples include Red Gate's SQL Backup, and Quest's LiteSpeed.

In my role as a DBA, I use a third-party backup tool, namely SQL Backup, to manage and schedule all of my backups. Chapter 8 will show how to use this tool to build a script that can be used in a SQL Agent job to take scheduled backups of databases.

Summary

This chapter explained in detail how to capture full database backups using either SSMS Backup Wizard or T-SQL scripts. We are now ready to move on to the restoration piece of the backup and restore jigsaw. Do not to remove any of the backup files we have captured; we are going to use each of these in the next chapter to restore our DatabaseForFullBackups database.

Chapter 4: Restoring From Full Backup

In the previous chapter, we took two full backups of our `DatabaseForFullBackups` database, one taken when the database was about 500 MB in size and the second when it was around 1 GB. In this chapter, we're going to restore those full backup files, to re-create the databases as they existed at the point in time that the respective backup processes were taken. In both of our examples we will be restoring over existing databases in order to demonstrate some of the issues that may arise in that situation. In Chapter 6, we'll look at some examples that restore a new copy of a database.

Full database restores are the cornerstone of our disaster recovery strategy, but will also be required as part of our regular production and development routines, for example, when restoring to development and test instances. However, for large databases, they can be a time- and disk space-consuming task, as well as causing the DBA a few strategic headaches, which we'll discuss as we progress through the chapter.

Full Restores in the Backup and Restore SLA

For a database that requires only full backups, the restore process is relatively straight-forward, requiring only the relevant full backup file, usually the most recent backup. However, as discussed in Chapter 2, we still need to take into consideration the size of the database being restored, and the location of the backup files, when agreeing an appropriate maximum amount of time that the crash recovery process should take.

For example, let's say someone accidentally deleted some records from a table and they need to be recovered. However, by the time the application owner has been notified of the issue, and in turn notified you, five days have passed since the unfortunate event. If local backup files are retained for only three days, then recovering the lost data will involve retrieving data from tape, which will add time to the recovery process. The SLA needs to stipulate file retention for as long as is reasonably necessary for such data loss or data integrity issues to be discovered. Just don't go overboard; there is no need to keep backup files for 2 weeks on local disk, when 3–5 days will do the trick 99.9% of the time.

Possible Issues with Full Database Restores

When we restore a database from a full backup file, it's worth remembering that this backup file includes all the objects, data and information that were present in the database at that time, including:

- all user-defined objects, including stored procedures, functions, views tables, triggers, database diagrams and the rest

- all data contained in each user-defined table

- system objects that are needed for regular database use and maintenance

- all data contained in the system tables

- user permissions for all objects on the database, including not only default and custom database roles, but also extended object permissions for all explicit permissions that have been set up for any user

- log file information that is needed to get the database back online, including size, location, and some internal information that is required.

In other word, the backup file contains everything needed to re-create an exact copy of the database, as it existed when the backup was taken. However, there may be times when we might not want *all* of this data and information to be present in the restored database. Let's look at a few examples.

Large data volumes

As noted previously, full database restores can be a time-consuming process for large databases, and can quickly eat away at disk space, or even fill up a disk completely. In disaster recovery situations where only a small subset of data has been lost, it often feels frustrating to have to go through a long, full restore process in order to extract what might be only a few rows of data. However, when using only native SQL Server tools, there is no real alternative.

If you have licenses for third-party backup and/or data comparison tools, it's worth investigating the possibility of performing what is termed **object-level restore**. In the case of Red Gate tools, the ones with which I am familiar, their backup products (both SQL Backup and Hyperbac), and SQL Data Compare, offer this functionality. With them, you can compare a backup file directly to a live database, and then restore only the missing object and data, rather than the whole database.

Furthermore, Red Gate also offers a different kind of tool to accommodate these large database restore situations, namely SQL Virtual Restore. This tool allows you to mount compressed backups as databases without going through the entire restore process. Since I've yet to use this tool in a production scenario, I won't be including any examples in this book. However, to learn more, check out Brad McGehee's article on Simple Talk, at WWW.SIMPLE-TALK.COM/SQL/SQL-TOOLS/BRADS-SURE-GUIDE-TO-SQL-VIRTUAL-RESTORE-/.

Restoring databases containing sensitive data

If we simply go ahead and perform a full database restore of a production database onto one of our development or testing instances, we could inadvertently be breaking a lot of rules. It's possible that the production instance stores sensitive data and we do not want every developer in the company accessing social security numbers and bank account information, which would be encrypted in production, on their development machines!

It would only take one rogue employee to steal a list of all clients and their sensitive information to sell to a competitor or, worse, a black market party.

If you work at a financial institution, you may be dealing on a daily basis with account numbers, passwords and financial transaction, as well as sensitive user information such as social security numbers and addresses. Not only will this data be subject to strict security measures in order to keep customers' information safe, it will also be the target of government agencies and their compliance audits.

More generally, while the production servers receive the full focus of attempts to deter and foil hackers, security can be a little lacking in non-production environments. This is why development and QA servers are a favorite target of malicious users, and why having complete customer records on such servers can cause big problems, if a compromise occurs.

So, what's the solution? Obviously, for development purposes, we need the database schemas in our development and test servers to be initially identical to the schema that exists in production, so it's common practice, in such situations, to copy the schema but not the data. There are several ways to do this.

- **Restore the full database backup, but immediately truncate** all tables, purging all sensitive data. You may then need to shrink the development copy of your database; you don't want to have a 100 GB database shell if that space is never going to be needed. Note that, after a database shrink, you should always rebuild your indexes, as they will get fragmented as a result of such an operation.

- **Use a schema comparison tool**, to synch only the objects of the production and development databases.

- **Wipe the database of all user tables** and use SSIS to perform a database object transfer of all required user objects. This can be set up to transfer objects only and to ignore any data included in the production system.

Of course, in each case, we will still need a complete, or at least partial, set of data in the development database, so we'll need to write some scripts, or use a data generation tool, such as SQL Data Generator, to establish a set of test data that is realistic but doesn't flout regulations for the protection of sensitive data.

Too much permission

Imagine now a situation where we are ready to push a brand new database into production, to be exposed to the real world. We take a backup of the development database, restore it on the production machine, turn on the services and website, and let our end-users go wild.

A few weeks later, a frantic manager bursts through the door, screaming that the database is missing some critical data. It was there yesterday, but is missing this morning!

Some detective work reveals that one of the developers accidentally dropped a table, after work hours the night before. How did this happen? At most, the developer should have had read-only access (via the db_datareader role) for the production machine! Upon investigation of the permissions assigned to that user for the production database, it is revealed that the developer is actually a member of the db_owner database role. How did the user get such elevated permissions? Well, the full database backup includes the complete permission set for the database. Each user's permissions are stored in the database and are associated to the login that they use on that server. When we restore the database from development to production, all database internal permissions are restored as well.

If the developer login was assigned db_owner on the development machine, then this permission level will exist on production too, assuming the login was also valid for the production SQL Server. Similarly, if the developer login had db_owner in development but only db_datareader in production, then restoring the development database over the existing production database will effectively elevate the developer to db_owner in production. Even if a user doesn't have a login on the production database server, the restored database still holds the permissions. If that user is eventually given access to the production machine, he or she will automatically have that level of access, even if it wasn't explicitly given by the DBA team.

The only case when this may not happen is when the user is using SQL Server authentication and the internal SID, a unique identifying value, doesn't match on the original and target server. If two SQL logins with the same name are created on different machines, the underlying SIDs will be different. So, when we move a database from Server A to Server B, a SQL login that has permission to access Server A will also be moved to Server B, but the underlying SID will be invalid and the database user will be "orphaned." This database user will need to be "de-orphaned" (see below) before the permissions will be valid. This will never happen for matching Active Directory accounts since the SID is always the same across a domain.

In order to prevent this from happening in our environments, every time we restore a database from one environment to another we should:

- **audit each and every login** – never assume that if a user has certain permissions in one environment they need the same in another; fix any internal user mappings for logins that exist on both servers, to ensure no one gets elevated permissions

- **perform orphaned user maintenance** – remove permissions for any users that do not have a login on the server to which we are moving the database; the `sp_change_users_login` stored procedure can help with this process, reporting all orphans, linking a user to its correct login, or creating a new login to which to link:

  - `EXEC sp_change_users_login 'Report'`

  - `EXEC sp_change_users_login 'Auto_Fix', 'user'`

  - `EXEC sp_change_users_login 'Auto_Fix', 'user', 'login', 'password'`

Don't let these issues dissuade you from performing full restores as and when necessary. Diligence is a great trait in a DBA, especially in regard to security. If you apply this diligence, keeping a keen eye out when restoring databases between mismatched environments, or when dealing with highly sensitive data of any kind, then you'll be fine.

Performing Full Restores

We are now ready to jump in and start restoring databases! This chapter will mimic the structure of Chapter 3, in that we'll first perform a full restore the "GUI way," in SSMS, and then by using native T-SQL **RESTORE** commands. In Chapter 8, we'll perform full restores using the Red Gate SQL Backup tool.

Native SSMS GUI full backup restore

Using the SSMS GUI, we're going to restore the first of the two full backups (`Database-ForFullBackups_Full_Native_1.bak`) that we took in Chapter 3, which was taken when the database contained about 500 MB of data. First, however, we need to decide whether we are going to restore this file over the current "live" version of the `Database-ForFullBackups` database, or simply create a new database. In this case, we are going to restore over the existing database, which is a common requirement when, for example, providing a weekly refresh of a development database.

But wait, you might be thinking, the current version of `DatabaseForFullBackups` contains about 1 GB of data. If we do this, aren't we going to lose half that data? Indeed we are, but rest assured that all of those precious rows of data are safe in our second full database backup file, and we'll be bringing that data backup to life later in this chapter.

So, go ahead and start SSMS, connect to your test instance, and then expand the databases tree menu as shown in Figure 4-1.

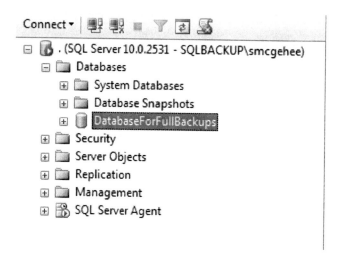

Figure 4-1: Getting SSMS prepared for restoration.

To start the restore process, right-click on the database in question, `DatabaseForFull-Backups`, and navigate **Tasks | Restore | Database...**, as shown in Figure 4-2. This will initiate the Restore wizard.

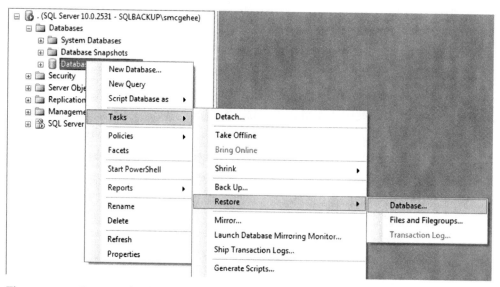

Figure 4-2: Starting the database restore wizard.

The **Restore Database** window appears, with some options auto-populated. For example, the name of the database we're restoring to is auto-filled to be the same as the source database that was backed up. Perhaps more surprisingly, the backup set to restore is also auto-populated, as shown in Figure 4-3. What's happened is that SQL Server has inspected some of the system tables in the msdb database and located the backups that have already been taken for this database. Depending on how long ago you completed the backups in Chapter 3, the window will be populated with the backup sets taken in that chapter, letting us choose which set to restore.

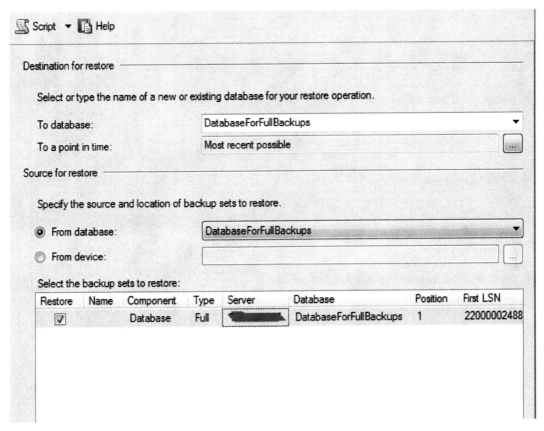

Figure 4-3:   The Restore Database screen.

We are not going to be using this pre-populated form, but will instead configure the restore process by hand, so that we restore our first full backup file. In the **Source for restore** section, choose the **From device** option and then click the ellipsis button (**…**). In the **Specify Backup** window, make sure that the media type shows **File**, and click the **Add** button. In the **Locate Backup File** window, navigate to the **C:\SQLBackups\Chapter3** folder and click on the `DatabaseForFullBackups_Full_Native_1.bak` backup file. Click OK twice to get back to the **Restore Database** window. We will now be able to see which backups are contained in the selected backup set. Since we only ever stored one backup per file, we only see one backup. Tick the box under the **Restore** column to select that backup file as the basis for the restore process, as shown in Figure 4-4.

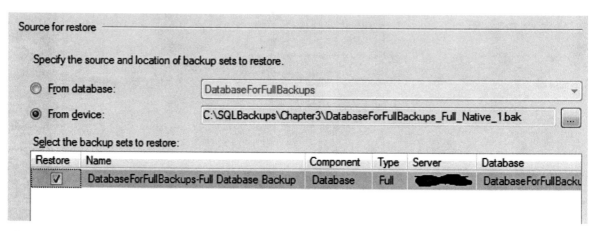

Figure 4-4:   General configurations for full native restore.

Next, click to the **Options** page on the left side of the restore configuration window. This will bring us to a whole new section of options to modify and validate (see Figure 4-5).

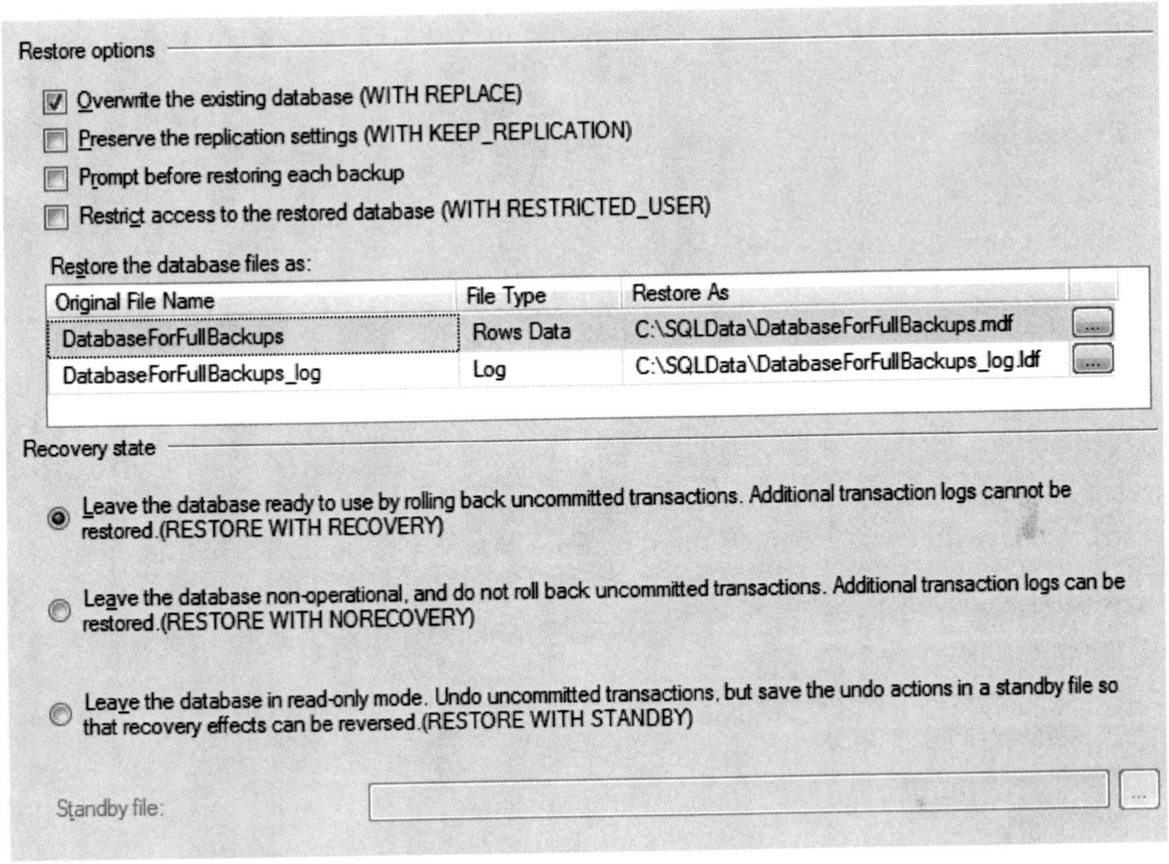

Figure 4-5: The options page configurations for a full database restore.

The top of the screen shows four **Restore options** as shown below.

- **Overwrite the existing database** – the generated T-SQL command will include the REPLACE option, instructing SQL Server to overwrite the currently existing database information. Since we are overwriting an existing database, in this example we want to check this box. Note that it is advised to use the REPLACE option with *care*, due to the potential for overwriting a database with a backup of a different database. See HTTP://MSDN.MICROSOFT.COM/EN-US/LIBRARY/MS191315.ASPX.

- **Preserve the replication settings** – only for use in a replication-enabled environment. Basically allows you to re-initialize replication, after a restore, without having to reconfigure all the replication settings.

- **Prompt before restoring each backup** – receive a prompt before each of the backup files is processed. We only have one backup file here, so leave this unchecked.

- **Restrict access to the restored database** – restricts access to the restored database to only members of the database role db_owner and the two server roles sysadmin and dbcreator. Again, don't select this option here.

The next portion of the **Options** page is the **Restore the database files as:** section, where we specify the location for the data (**mdf**) and log (**ldf**) files for the restored database. This will be auto-populated with the location of the original files, on which the backup was based. We have the option to move them to a new location on our drives but, for now, let's leave them in their original location, although it's wise to double-check that this location is correct for your system.

Finally, we have the **Recovery state** section, where we specify the state in which the database should be left once the current backup file has been restored. If there are no further files to restore, and we wish to return the database to a useable state, we pick the first option, **RESTORE WITH RECOVERY**. When the restore process is run, the backup file will be restored and then the final step of the restore process, database recovery (see Chapter 1), will be carried out. This is the option to choose here, since we're restoring just a single full database backup. We'll cover the other two options later in the book, so we won't consider them further here.

Our restore is configured and ready to go, so click **OK** and wait for the progress section of the restore window to notify us that the operation has successfully completed. If the restore operating doesn't show any progress, the probable reason is that there is another active connection to the database, which will prevent the restore operation from starting. Stop the restore, close any other connections and try again. A convenience of scripting, as we'll see a little later, is that we can check for, and close, any other connections before we attempt the restore operation.

How do we know it worked?

Let's run a few quick queries, shown in Listing 4-1, against our newly restored
DatabaseForFullBackups database to verify that the data that we expect to be here is
actually here.

```
USE [DatabaseForFullBackups]
GO

SELECT   MessageData ,
         COUNT(MessageData) AS MessageCount
FROM     MessageTable1
GROUP BY MessageData

SELECT   MessageData ,
         COUNT(MessageData) AS MessageCount
FROM     MessageTable2
GROUP BY MessageData
```

Listing 4-1:   Checking our restored data.

The first query should return a million rows, each containing the same message. The
second query, if everything worked in the way we intended, should return no rows.

Collecting restore metrics

Having run the full backup, in Chapter 3, we were able to interrogate msdb to gather
some metrics on how long the backup process took. Unfortunately, when we run a restore
process using SSMS, there is no record of the length of the operation, not even in the SQL
Server log files.

The only way to capture the time is to script out the RESTORE command and run the
T-SQL. I won't show this script here, as we're going to run a T-SQL RESTORE command
very shortly, but if you want to see the stats for yourself, right now, you'll need to

re-create the **Restore Database** pages as we had them configured in Figures 4.3–4.5, and then click the **Script** drop-down button, and select **Script Action to New Query Window**. This will generate the T-SQL RESTORE command that will be the exact equivalent of what would be generated under the covers when running the process through the GUI.

When I ran this T-SQL command on my test system, the restore took just under 29 seconds and processed 62,689 pages of data, as shown in Figure 4-6.

```
Messages
Processed 62688 pages for database 'DatabaseForFullBackups', file 'DatabaseForFullBackups' on file 1.
Processed 1 pages for database 'DatabaseForFullBackups', file 'DatabaseForFullBackups_log' on file 1.
RESTORE DATABASE successfully processed 62689 pages in 28.695 seconds (17.067 MB/sec).
```

Figure 4-6:   Full native restore output.

Native T-SQL full restore

We are now going to perform a second full database restore, this time using a T-SQL script, and the second full backup file from Chapter 3 (DatabaseForFullBackups_ Full_Native_2.bak), which was taken after we pushed another 500 MB of data into the database, bringing the total size of the database to just under 1 GB. You may recall from Chapter 3 that doubling the size of the database did increase the backup time, but it was not a linear increase. We'll see if we get similar behavior when performing restores.

Once again, we are going to overwrite the existing DatabaseForFullBackups database. This means that we want to kill all connections that are open before we begin our RESTORE operation, which we can do in one of two ways. The first involves going through the list of processes in master.sys.sysprocesses and killing each SPID associated with the database in question. However, this doesn't always do the trick, since it won't kill connections that run on a different database, but access tables in the database we wish to restore. We need a global way to stop any user process that accesses the database in question.

For this reason, the second and most common way is to place the database into OFFLINE mode for a short period. This will drop all connections and terminate any queries currently processing against the database, which can then immediately be switched back to ONLINE mode, for the restore process to begin. Just be sure not to kill any connections that are processing important data. Even in development, we need to let users know before we just go wiping out currently running queries.

Here, we'll be employing the second technique and so, in Listing 4-2, you'll see that we set the database to OFFLINE mode and use option, WITH ROLLBACK IMMEDIATE, which instructs SQL Server to roll those processes back immediately, without waiting for them to COMMIT. Alternatively, we could have specified WITH ROLLBACK AFTER XX SECONDS, where XX is the number of seconds SQL Server will wait before it will automatically start rollback procedures. We can then return the database to ONLINE mode, free of connections and ready to start the restore process.

```
USE [master]
GO


ALTER DATABASE [DatabaseForFullBackups]
SET OFFLINE WITH ROLLBACK IMMEDIATE
GO


ALTER DATABASE [DatabaseForFullBackups]
SET ONLINE
GO
```

Listing 4-2: Dropping all user connections before a restore.

Go ahead and give this a try. Open two query windows in SSMS; in one of them, start the long-running query shown in Listing 4-3 then, in the second window, run Listing 4-2.

```
USE [DatabaseForFullBackups]
GO


WAITFOR DELAY '00:10:00'
GO
```

Listing 4-3: A long-running query.

You'll see that the session with the long-running query was terminated, reporting a severe error and advising that any results returned be discarded. In the absence of a third-party tool, which will automatically take care of existing sessions before performing a restore, this is a handy script. You can include it in any backup scripts you use or, perhaps, convert it into a stored procedure which is always a good idea for reusable code.

Now that we no longer have to worry about pesky user connections interfering with our restore process, we can go ahead and run the T-SQL **RESTORE** command in Listing 4-4.

```
USE [master]
GO


RESTORE DATABASE [DatabaseForFullBackups] FROM
DISK = N'C:\SQLBackups\Chapter3\DatabaseForFullBackups_Full_Native_2.bak'
WITH FILE = 1, STATS = 25
GO
```

Listing 4-4:   Native SQL Server full backup restore.

The **RESTORE DATABASE** command denotes that we wish to restore a full backup file for the **DatabaseForFullBackups** database. The next portion of the script configures the name and location of the backup file to be restored. If you chose a different name or location for this file, you'll need to amend this line accordingly. Finally, we specify a number of **WITH** options. The **FILE** argument identifies the backup set to be restored, within our backup file. As discussed in Chapter 2, backup files can hold more than one backup set, in which case we need to explicitly identify the number of the backup set within the file. Our policy in this book is "one backup set per file," so we'll always set **FILE** to a value of 1. The **STATS** argument is also one we've seen before, and specifies the time intervals at which SQL Server should update the "backup progress" messages. Here, we specify a message at 25% completion intervals.

Notice that even though we are overwriting an existing database without starting with a tail log backup, we do not specify the **REPLACE** option here, since **DatabaseForFull-Backups** is a **SIMPLE** recovery model database, so the tail log backup is not possible. SQL

Server will still overwrite any existing database on the server called `DatabaseForFull-Backups`, using the same logical file names for the data and log files that are recorded within the backup file.

In such cases, we don't need to specify any of the file names or paths for the data or log files. Note, though, that this only works if the file structure is the same! The backup file contains the data and log file information, including the location to which to restore the data and log files so, if we are restoring a database to a different machine from the original, and the drive letters, for instance, don't match up, we will need to use the `WITH MOVE` argument to point SQL Server to a new location for the data and log files. This will also be a necessity if we need to restore the database on the same server with a different name. Of course, SQL Server won't be able to overwrite any data or log files if they are still in use by the original database. We'll cover this topic in more detail later in this chapter, and again in Chapter 6.

Go ahead and run the `RESTORE` command. Once it is done executing, do not close the query session, as the query output contains some metrics that we want to record.

We can verify that the restore process worked, at this point, by simply opening a new query window and executing the code from Listing 4-1. This time the first query should return a million rows containing the same message, and the second query should also return a million rows containing the same, slightly different, message.

Collecting restore metrics, Part 2

Let's take a look at the Message window, where SQL Server directs non-dataset output, to view some metrics for our native T-SQL restore process, as shown in Figure 4-7. The first full restore of the 500 MB database processed 62,689 pages and took almost 29 seconds, on my test server. This restore, of the 1 GB database, processed roughly double the number of pages (125,201) and took roughly twice as long (almost 67 seconds). So, our database restore timings seem to exhibit more linear behavior than was observed for backup time.

```
Native Restore.sq...P\smcgehee (55))*
  USE [master]
  GO

  RESTORE DATABASE [DatabaseForFullBackups] FROM
  DISK = N'C:\SQLBackups\Chapter2\DatabaseForFullBackups_Full_Native_2.bak'
  WITH FILE = 1, STATS = 25
  GO
```

```
Messages
25 percent processed.
50 percent processed.
75 percent processed.
100 percent processed.
Processed 125208 pages for database 'DatabaseForFullBackups', file 'DatabaseForFullBackups' on file 1.
Processed 2 pages for database 'DatabaseForFullBackups', file 'DatabaseForFullBackups_log' on file 1.
RESTORE DATABASE successfully processed 125210 pages in 66.761 seconds (14.652 MB/sec).
```

Figure 4-7:   Results from the second native full backup restore.

Before we move on, you may be wondering whether any special options or commands are necessary if restoring a native SQL Server backup file that is compressed. The answer is "No;" it is exactly the same process as restoring a normal backup file.

Forcing Restore Failures for Fun

The slight problem with the friendly demos found in most technical books is that the reader is set up for success, and often ends up bewildered when errors start occurring. As such, through this book, we'll be looking at common sources of error when backing up and restoring databases, and how you can expect SQL Server to respond. Hopefully this will better arm you to deal with such unexpected errors, as and when they occur in the real world.

Here, we're going to start with a pretty blatant mistake, but nevertheless one that I've seen novices make. The intent of the code in Listing 4-5 is, we will assume, to create a copy of DatabaseForFullBackups as it existed when the referenced backup file was taken, and name the new copy DatabaseForFullBackups2.

```
RESTORE DATABASE [DatabaseForFullBackups2]
FROM DISK = N'C:\SQLBackups\Chapter3\DatabaseForFullBackups_Full_Native_2.bak'
WITH RECOVERY
GO
```

Listing 4-5   A RESTORE command that will fail.

Assuming you have not deleted the `DatabaseForFullBackups` database, attempting to run Listing 4-5 will result in the following error message (truncated for brevity; basically the same messages are repeated for the log file):

```
Msg 1834, Level 16, State 1, Line 2
The file 'C:\SQLData\DatabaseForFullBackups.mdf' cannot be overwritten.  It is being used by
database 'DatabaseForFullBackups'.

Msg 3156, Level 16, State 4, Line 2
File 'DatabaseForFullBackups' cannot be restored to ' C:\SQLData\DatabaseForFullBackups.mdf'.
Use WITH MOVE to identify a valid location for the file.
...
```

The problem we have here, and even the solution, is clearly stated by the error messages. In Listing 4-5, SQL Server attempts to use, for the `DatabaseForFullBackups2` database being restored, the same file names and paths for the data and log files as are being used for the existing `DatabaseForFullBackups` database, which was the source of the backup file. In other words, it's trying to create data and log files for the `DatabaseForFullBackups2` database, by overwriting data and log files that are being used by the `DatabaseForFullBackups` database. We obviously can't do that without causing the `DatabaseForFullBackups` database to fail.

We will have to either drop the first database to free those file names or, more likely, and as the second part of the error massage suggests, identify a valid location for the log and data files for the new, using `WITH MOVE`, as shown in Listing 4-6.

```
RESTORE DATABASE [DatabaseForFullBackups2]
FROM DISK = 'C:\SQLBackups\Chapter3\DatabaseForFullBackups_Full_Native_2.bak'
WITH RECOVERY,
MOVE 'DatabaseForFullBackups'
TO 'C:\SQLData\DatabaseForFullBackups2.mdf',
MOVE 'DatabaseForFullBackups_log'
TO 'C:\SQLData\DatabaseForFullBackups2_log.ldf'
GO
```

Listing 4-6: A RESTORE command that renames the data and log files for the new database.

We had two choices to fix the script; we could either rename the files and keep them in the same directory or keep the file names the same but put them in a different directory. It can get very confusing if we have a database with the same physical file name as another database, so renaming the files to match the database name seems like the best solution.

Let's take a look at a somewhat subtler error. For this example, imagine that we wish to replace an existing copy of the DatabaseForFullBackups2 test database with a production backup of DatabaseForFullBackups. At the same time, we wish to move the data and log files for the DatabaseForFullBackups2 test database over to a new drive, with more space.

```
USE master
go
RESTORE DATABASE [DatabaseForFullBackups2]
FROM DISK = 'C:\SQLBackups\DatabaseForFileBackups_Full_Native_1.bak'
WITH RECOVERY, REPLACE,
MOVE 'DatabaseForFileBackups'
TO 'D:\SQLData\DatabaseForFileBackups2.mdf',
MOVE 'DatabaseForFileBackups_log'
TO 'D:\SQLData\DatabaseForFileBackups2_log.ldf'
GO
```

Listing 4-7: An "error" while restoring over an existing database.

In fact, no error message at all will result from running this code; it will succeed. Nevertheless, a serious mistake has occurred here: we have inadvertently chosen a backup file for the wrong database, `DatabaseForFileBackups` instead of `DatabaseForFull-Backups`, and used it to overwrite our existing `DatabaseForFullBackups2` database! This highlights the potential issue with misuse of the `REPLACE` option. We can presume a DBA has used it here because the existing database is being replaced, without performing a tail log backup (see Chapter 6 for more details). However, there are two problems with this, in this case. Firstly, `DatabaseForFullBackups2` is a `SIMPLE` recovery model database and so `REPLACE` is not required from the point of view of bypassing a tail log backup, since log backups are not possible. Secondly, use of `REPLACE` has bypassed the normal safety check that SQL Server would perform to ensure the database in the backup matches the database over which we are restoring. If we had run the exact same code as shown in Listing 4-7, but without the `REPLACE` option, we'd have received the following, very useful error message:

```
Msg 3154, Level 16, State 4, Line 1
The backup set holds a backup of a database other than the existing 'DatabaseForFullBackups2'
database.
Msg 3013, Level 16, State 1, Line 1
RESTORE DATABASE is terminating abnormally.
```

Note that we don't have any further use for the `DatabaseForFullBackups2` database, so once you've completed the example, you can go ahead and delete it.

Considerations When Restoring to a Different Location

When restoring a database to a different server or even a different instance on the same server, there are quite a few things to consider, both before starting and after completing the restore operation.

- Version/edition of SQL Server used in the source and destination
  You may receive a request to restore a SQL Server 2008 R2 database backup to a SQL Server 2005 server, which is not a possibility. Likewise, it is not possible to restore a backup of a database that is using enterprise-only options (CDC, transparent data encryption, data compression, partitioning) to a SQL Server Standard Edition instance.

- What SQL Server agent jobs or DTS/DTSX packages might be affected?
  If you are moving the database permanently to a new server, you need to find which jobs and packages that use this database will be affected and adjust them accordingly. Also, depending on how you configure your database maintenance jobs, you may need to add the new database to the list of databases to be maintained.

- What orphaned users will need to be fixed? What permissions should be removed?
  There may be SQL Logins with differing SIDs that we need to fix. There may be SQL logins and Active Directory users that don't need access to the new server. You need to be sure to comb the permissions and security of the new location before signing off the restore as complete.

Restoring System Databases

As discussed briefly in Chapter 2, there are occasions when we may need to restore one of the system databases, such as `master`, `model` or `msdb`, either due to the loss of one of these databases or, less tragically, the loss of a SQL agent job, for example.

Restoring system databases in advance of user databases can also be a time saver. Imagine that we need to migrate an entire SQL Server instance to new hardware. We could restore the `master`, `model` and `msdb` databases and already have our permissions, logins, jobs and a lot of other configuration taken care of in advance. In the case of an emergency, of course, knowledge of how to perform system database restores is essential.

In this section, we'll look at how to perform a restore of both the master and the msdb system databases, so the first thing we need to do is make sure we have valid backups of these databases, as shown in Listing 4-8.

```
USE [master]
GO

BACKUP DATABASE [master]
TO DISK = N'C:\SQLBackups\Chapter4\master_full.bak' WITH INIT
GO

BACKUP DATABASE [msdb]
TO DISK = N'C:\SQLBackups\Chapter4\msdb_full.bak' WITH INIT
GO

BACKUP DATABASE [model]
TO DISK = N'C:\SQLBackups\Chapter4\model_full.bak' WITH INIT
GO
```

Listing 4-8: Taking backups of our system databases.

Restoring the msdb database

We can restore the msdb or model database without making any special modifications to the SQL Server engine or the way it is running, which makes it a relatively straight-forward process (compared to restoring the master database). We will work with the msdb database for the examples in this section.

In order to restore the msdb database, SQL Server needs to be able to take an exclusive lock on it, which means that we must be sure to turn off any applications that might be using it; specifically SQL Server Agent. There are several ways to do this, and you can choose the one with which you are most comfortable. For example, we can stop it directly from SSMS, use the NET STOP command in a command prompt, use a command script, or stop it from the services snap-in tool.

We'll choose the latter option, since we can use the services snap-in tool to view and control all of the services running on our test machine. To start up this tool, simply pull up the **Run** prompt and type in **services.msc** while connected locally or through RDP to the test SQL Server machine. This will bring up the services snap-in within the Microsoft Management Console (MMC). Scroll down until you locate any services labeled **SQL Server Agent (instance)**; the **instance** portion will either contain the unique instance name, or contain **MSSQLSERVER**, if it is the default instance. Highlight the agent service, right-click and select **Stop** from the control menu to bring the SQL Server Agent to a halt, as shown in Figure 4-8.

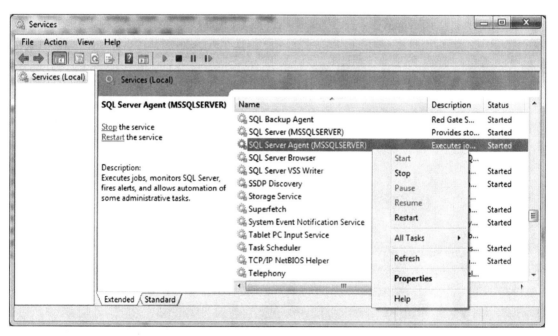

Figure 4-8: Stopping SQL Server Agent with the services snap-in

With the service stopped (the status column should now be blank), the agent is offline and we can proceed with the full database backup restore, as shown in Listing 4-9.

```
USE [master]
GO


RESTORE DATABASE [msdb] FROM
DISK = N'C:\SQLBackups\Chapter4\msdb_full.bak'
GO
```

Listing 4-9: Restoring the msdb database.

With the backup complete, restart the SQL Server Agent service from the services MMC snap-in tool and you'll find that all jobs, schedules, operators, and everything else stored in the msdb database, are all back and ready for use.

This is a very simple task, with only the small change being that we need to shut down a service before performing the restore. Don't close the services tool yet, though, as we will need it to restore the master database.

Restoring the master database

The master database is the control database for a SQL Server instance, and restoring it is a slightly trickier task; we can't just restore master while SQL Server is running in standard configuration.

The first thing we need to do is turn the SQL Server engine service off! Go back to the services management tool, find the service named SQL Server (instance) and stop it, as described previously. You may be prompted with warnings that other services will have to be stopped as well; go ahead and let them shut down.

Once SQL Server is offline, we need to start it again, but using a special startup parameter. In this case, we want to use the —m switch to start SQL Server in single-user mode. This brings SQL Server back online but allows only one user (an administrator) to connect, which is enough to allow the restore of the master database.

To start SQL Server in single-user mode, open a command prompt and browse to the SQL Server installation folder, which contains the **sqlservr.exe** file. Here are the default locations for both SQL Server 2008 and 2008 R2:

- `<Installation Path>`**\MSSQL10.MSSQLSERVER\MSSQL\Binn**

- `<Installation Path>`**\MSSQL10_50.MSSQLSERVER\MSSQL\Binn**

From that location, issue the command **sqlservr.exe —m**. SQL Server will begin the startup process, and you'll see a number of messages to this effect, culminating (hopefully) in a **Recovery is complete** message, as shown in Figure 4-9.

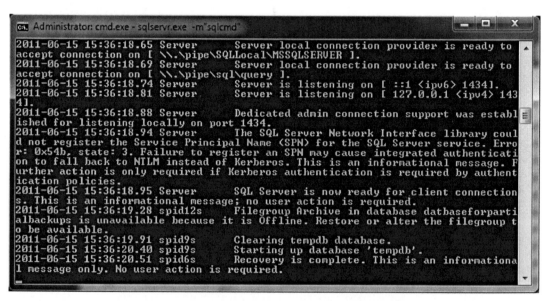

Figure 4-9: Recovery is complete and SQL Server is ready for admin connection.

Once SQL Server is ready for a connection, open a second command prompt and connect to your test SQL Server with **sqlcmd**. Two examples of how to do this are given below, the first when using a trusted connection and the second for a SQL Login authenticated connection.

- **sqlcmd —SYOURSERVER —E**

- **sqlcmd —SYOURSERVER —UloginName —Ppassword**

At the **sqlcmd** prompt, we'll perform a standard restore to the default location for the master database, as shown in Listing 4-10 (if required, we could have used the MOVE option to change the master database location or physical file).

```
RESTORE DATABASE [master] FROM
DISK = 'C:\SQLBackups\Chapter4\master_full.bak'
GO
```

Listing 4-10: Restoring the master database.

In the first **sqlcmd** prompt, you should see a standard restore output message noting the number of pages processed, notification of the success of the operation, and a message stating that SQL Server is being shut down, as shown in Figure 4-10.

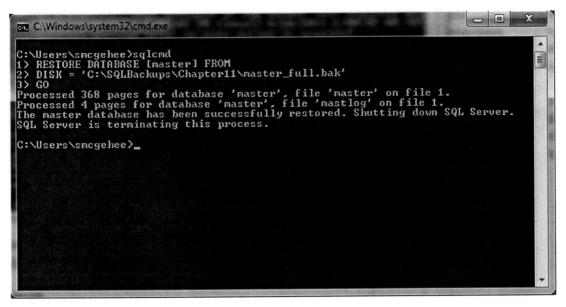

Figure 4-10: Output from restore of master database.

Since we just restored the `master` database, we need the server to start normally to pick up and process all of the internal changes, so we can now start the SQL Server in normal mode to verify that everything is back online and working fine. You have now successfully restored the `master` database!

Summary

Full database backups are the cornerstone of a DBA's backup and recovery strategy. However, these backups are only useful if they can be used successfully to restore a database to the required state in the event of data loss, hardware failure, or some other disaster.

Hopefully, as a DBA, the need to restore a database to recover from disaster will be a rare event, but when it happens, you need to be 100% sure that it's going to work; your organization, and your career as a DBA, my depend on it. Practice test restores for your critical databases on a regular schedule!

Of course, many restore processes won't be as simple as restoring the latest full backup. Log backups will likely be involved, for restoring a database to a specific point in time, and this is where things get more interesting.

Chapter 5: Log Backups

When determining a backup strategy and schedule for a given database, one of the major considerations is the extent to which potential data loss can be tolerated in the event of an errant process, or software or hardware failure. If toleration of data loss is, say, 24 hours, then we need do nothing more than take a nightly full backup. However, if exposure to the risk of data loss is much lower than this for a given database, then it's likely that we'll need to operate that database in FULL recovery model, and supplement those nightly full backups with transaction log backups (and possibly differential database backups – see Chapter 7).

With a log backup, we capture the details of all the transactions that have been recorded for that database since the last log backup (or since the last full backup, if this is the first-ever log backup). In this chapter, we'll demonstrate how to capture these log backups using either the SSMS GUI or T-SQL scripts. However, we'll start by taking a look at how space is allocated and used within a log file; this is of more than academic interest, since it helps a DBA understand and troubleshoot certain common issues relating to the transaction log, such as explosive log growth, or internal log fragmentation.

Capturing an unbroken sequence of log backups means that we will then, in Chapter 6, be able restore a full backup, then apply this series of log backups to "roll forward" the database to the state in which it existed at various, successive points in time. This adds a great deal of flexibility to our restore operations. When capturing only full (and differential) database backups, all we can do is restore one of those backups, in its entirety. With log backups, we can restore a database to the state in which it existed when a given log backup completed, or to the state in which it existed at some point represented *within* that log backup.

A Brief Peek Inside a Transaction Log

A DBA, going about his or her daily chores, ought not to be overly concerned with the internal structure of the transaction log. Nevertheless, some discussion on this topic is very helpful in understanding the appropriate log maintenance techniques, and especially in understanding the possible root cause of problems such as log file fragmentation, or a log file that is continuing to grow and grow in size, despite frequent log backups. However, we will keep this "internals" discussion as brief as possible.

As discussed in Chapter 1, a transaction log stores a record of the operations that have been performed on the database with which it is associated. Each log record contains the details of a specific change, relating to object creation/modification (DDL) operations, as well any data modification (DML) operations. When SQL Server undergoes database recovery (for example, upon start up, or during a RESTORE operation), it, will roll back (undo) or roll forward (redo) the actions described in these log records, as necessary, in order to reconcile the data and log files, and return the database to a consistent state.

Transaction log files are **sequential** files; in other words SQL Server writes to the transaction log sequentially (unlike data files, which tend to be written in a random fashion, as data is modified in random data pages). Each log record inserted into the log file is stamped with a **Log Sequence Number (LSN)**. When a database and its associated log file are first created, the first log record marks the start of the logical file, which at this stage will coincide with the start of the physical file. The LSNs are then ever-increasing; the most recently added log record will always have the highest LSN, and marks the end of the logical file (discussed in more detail shortly). All log records associated with a given transaction are linked in an **LSN chain** with forward and backward pointers to the operation in the transaction that succeeded and preceded the current operation.

Internally, SQL Server divides a transaction log file into a number of sections called **virtual log files** (VLFs). Figure 5-1 depicts a transaction log composed of eight VLFs, and marks the active portion of the log, known as the **active log**.

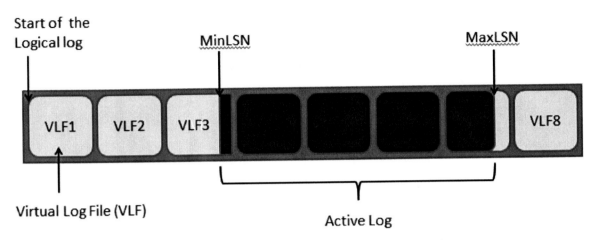

Figure 5-1: A transaction log with 8 VLFs.

The concept of the **active log** is an important one. A VLF can either be "active," if it contains any part of what is termed the **active log**, or "inactive," if it doesn't. Any log record relating to an open transaction is required for possible rollback and so must be part of the active log. In addition, there are various other activities in the database, including replication, mirroring and CDC (Change Data Capture) that use the transaction log and need transaction log records to remain in the log until they have been processed. These records will also be part of the active log.

The log record with the **MinLSN**, shown in Figure 5-1, is defined as the "*oldest log record that is required for a successful database-wide rollback or by another activity or operation in the database.*" This record marks the start of the active log and is sometimes referred to as the "head" of the log. Any more recent log record, regardless of whether it is still open or required, is also part of the active log; this is an important point as it explains why it's a misconception to think of the active portion of the log as containing only records relating to uncommitted transactions. The log record with the highest LSN (i.e. the most recent record added) marks the end of the active log.

Therefore, we can see that a log record is no longer part of the active log only when each of the following three conditions below is met.

1. It relates to a transaction that is committed and so is no longer required for rollback.

2. It is no longer required by any other database process, including a transaction log backup when using **FULL** or **BULK LOGGED** recovery models.

3. It is older (i.e. has a lower LSN) than the **MinLSN** record.

Any VLF that contains any part of the active log is considered active and can never be truncated. For example, VLF3, in Figure 5-1, is an active VLF, even though most of the log records it contains are not part of the active log; it cannot be truncated until the head of the logs moves forward into VLF4.

The operations that will cause the head of the log to move forward vary depending on the recovery model of the database. For databases in the **SIMPLE** recovery model, the head of the log can move forward upon **CHECKPOINT**, when pages are flushed from cache to disk, after first being written to the transaction log. As a result of this operation, many log records would now satisfy the first requirement listed above, for no longer being part of the active log. We can imagine that if, as a result, the **MinLSN** record in Figure 5-1, and all subsequent records in VLF3, satisfied both the first and second criteria, then the head would move forward and VLF3 could now be truncated. Therefore, *generally*, space inside the log is made available for reuse at regular intervals.

Truncation does not reduce the size of the log file

It's worth reiterating that truncation does not affect the physical size of the log; it will still take up the same physical space on the drive. Truncation is merely the act of marking VLFs in the log file as available for reuse, in the recording of subsequent transactions.

For databases using FULL or BULK LOGGED recovery, the head can only move forward as a result of a log backup. Any log record that has not been previously backed up is considered to be still "required" by a log backup operation, and so will never satisfy the second requirement above, and will remain part of the active log. If we imagine that the **MinLSN** record in Figure 5-1 is the first record added to the log after the previous log backup, then the head will remain in that position till the next log backup, at which point it can move forward (assuming the first requirement is also satisfied).

I've stressed this many times, but I'll say it once more for good measure: this is the other reason, in addition to enabling point-in-time restore, why it's so important to **back up the log for any database operating in FULL (or BULK_LOGGED) recovery**; if you don't, the head of the log is essentially "pinned," space will not be reused, and the log will simply grow and grow in size.

The final question to consider is what happens when the active log reaches the end of VLF8. Simplistically, it is easiest to think of space in the log file as being reused in a circular fashion. Once the logical end of the log reaches the end of a VLF, SQL Server will start to reuse the next sequential VLF that is inactive, or the next, so far unused, VLF. In Figure 5-1, this could be VLF8, followed by VLFs 1 and 2, and so on. If no further VLFs were available at all, the log would need to auto-grow and add more VLFs. If this is not possible, due to auto-growth being disabled or the disk housing the log file being full, then the logical end of the active log will meet the physical end of the log file, the transaction log is full, and the 9002 error will be issued.

Three uses for transaction log backups

The primary reason to take log backups is in order to be able to restore them; in other words, during a RESTORE operation, we can restore a full (plus differential) backup, followed by a complete chain of log backup files. As we restore the series of log backups files, we will essentially "replay" the operations described within in order to re-create the database as it existed at a previous point in time.

However, the log backups, and subsequent restores, can also be very useful in reducing the time required for database migrations, and for offloading reporting from the Production environment, via log shipping.

Performing database restores

By performing a series of log backup operations, we can progressively capture the contents of the live log file in a series of log backup files. Once captured in log backup files, the series of log records within these files can, assuming the chain of log records is unbroken, be subsequently applied to full (and differential) database backups as part of a database restore operation. We can restore to the end of one of these backup files, or even to some point in time in the middle of the file, to re-create the database as it existed at a previous point in time, for example, right before a failure.

When operating in SIMPLE recovery model, we can only take full and differential backups *i.e.* we can only back up the data files and not the transaction log. Let's say, for example, we rely solely on full database backups, taken every day at 2 a.m. If a database failure occurs at 1 a.m. one night, all we can do is restore the database as it existed at 2 a.m. the previous day and have lost 23 hours' worth of data. We may be able to reduce the risk of data loss by taking differential backups, in between the nightly full backups. However, both full and differential backups are resource-intensive operations and if you need your risk of data loss to be measured in minutes rather than hours, the only viable option is to operate the database in FULL recovery model and take transaction log backups alongside any full and differential backups.

If we operate the database in FULL recovery, and take transaction log backups, say, every 30 minutes then, in the event of our 2 a.m. disaster, we can restore the previous 2 a.m. full backup, followed by a series of 48 log backup files, in order to restore the database as it existed at 1.30 a.m., losing 30 minutes' worth of data. If the live transaction log were still available we could also perform a tail log backup and restore the database to a time directly before the disaster occurred.

The frequency with which log backups are taken will depend on the tolerable exposure to data loss, as expressed in your Backup and Restore SLA (discussed shortly).

Large database migrations

It is occasionally necessary to move a database from one server to another, and you may only have a short window of time in which to complete the migration. For example, let's say a server has become overloaded, or the server hardware has reached the end of its life, and a fresh system needs to be put in place. Just before we migrate the database to the new server, we need to disconnect all users (so that no data is committed after your final backup is taken), and our SLA dictates a maximum of an hour down-time, so we've got only one hour to get them all connected again on the new server!

Given such constraints, we won't have the time within that window to take a full backup of the database, transfer it across our network, and then restore it on the target server. Fortunately, however, we can take advantage of the small file footprint of the transaction log backup in order to reduce the time required to perform the task.

For example, prior to the migration window, we can transfer, to the target server, a full database backup from the night before. We can restore that file to the new server using the **WITH NORECOVERY** option (discussed in Chapter 6), to put the database into a restoring state and allow transaction log backups to be applied to the database at a later time.

After this, we can take small transaction log backups of the migrating database over the period of time until the migration is scheduled. These log backup files are copied over to the target server and applied to our restoring target database (stipulating **NORECOVERY** as each log backup is applied, to keep the database in a restoring state, so more log backups can be accepted).

At the point the migration window opens, we can disconnect all users from the original database, take a final log backup, transfer that final file to the target server, and apply it to the restoring database, specifying WITH RECOVERY so that the new database is recovered, and comes online in the same state it was in when you disconnected users from the original.

We still need to bear in mind potential complicating factors related to moving databases to different locations, as discussed in Chapter 4. Orphaned users, elevated permissions and connectivity issues would still need to be addressed after the final log was applied to the new database location.

Log shipping

Almost every DBA has to make provision for business reporting. Often, the reports produced have to be as close to real time as possible, *i.e.* they must reflect as closely as possible the data as it currently exists in the production databases. However, running reports on a production machine is never a best practice, and the use of High Availability solutions (real-time replication, CDC solutions, log reading solutions, and so on) to get that data to a reporting instance can be expensive and time consuming.

Log shipping is an easy and cheap way to get near real-time data to a reporting server. The essence of log shipping is to restore a full database to the reporting server using the WITH STANDBY option, then regularly ship log backup files from the production to the reporting server and apply them to the standby database to update its contents. The STANDBY option will keep the database in a state where more log files can be applied, but will put the database in a read-only state, so that it always reflects the data in the source database at the point when the last applied log backup was taken.

This means that the reporting database will generally lag behind the production database by 15–30 minutes or more. This sort of lag is usually not a big problem and, in many cases, log shipping is an easy way to satisfy, not only the production users, but the reporting users as well.

Practical log shipping

It is out of scope to get into the full details of log shipping here, but the following article offers a practical guide to the process: WWW.SIMPLE-TALK.COM/SQL/BACKUP-AND-RECOVERY/ POP-RIVETTS-SQL-SERVER-FAQ-NO.4-POP-DOES-LOG-SHIPPING/.

Log Backups in the Backup and Restore SLA

As discussed in detail in Chapter 2, determining whether or not log backups are required for a database and, if so, how frequently, will require some conversations with the database owners.

The first rule is not to include log backups in the SLA for a given database, unless they are really required. Log backups bring with them considerable extra administrative overhead, with more files to manage, more space required to store them, more jobs to schedule, and so on. While we need to make sure that these operations are performed for every database that needs them, we definitely don't want to take them on all databases, regardless of need.

If it's a development database, we most likely won't need to take transaction log backups, and the database can be operated in `SIMPLE` recovery model. If it's a production database, then talk to the project manager and developers; ask them questions about the change load on the data; find out how often data is inserted or modified, how much data is modified, at what times of the day these modifications take place, and the nature of the data load/modification processes (well defined or ad hoc).

If it's a database that's rarely, if ever, modified by end-users, but is subject to daily, well-defined data loads, then it's also unlikely that we'll need to perform log backups, so we can operate the database in SIMPLE recovery model. We can take a full database backup after each data load, or simply take a nightly full backup and then, if necessary, restore it, then replay any data load processes that occurred subsequently.

If a database is modified frequently by ad hoc end-user processes, and toleration of data loss is low, then it's very likely that transaction log backups will be required. Again, talk with the project team and find out the acceptable level of data loss. You will find that, in most cases, taking log backups once per hour will be sufficient, meaning that the database could lose up to 60 minutes of transactional data. For some databases, an exposure to the risk of data loss of more than 30 or 15 minutes might be unacceptable. The only difference here is that we will have to take, store, and manage many more log backups, and more backup files means more chance of something going wrong; losing a file or having a backup file become corrupted. Refer back to the *Backup scheduling* section of Chapter 2 for considerations when attempting to schedule all the required backup jobs for a given SQL Server instance.

Whichever route is the best for you, the most important thing is that you are taking transaction log backups for databases that require them, and *only* for those that required them.

Preparing for Log Backups

In this chapter, we'll run through examples of how to take log backups using both SSMS and T-SQL scripts. In Chapter 8, we'll show how to manage your log and other backups, using a third-party tool (Red Gate SQL Backup) and demonstrate some of the advantages that such tools offer.

Before we get started taking log backups, however, we need to do a bit of prep work, namely choosing an appropriate recovery model for our example database, and then creating that database along with some populated sample tables.

Choosing the recovery model

We're going to assume that the Service Level Agreement for our example database expresses a tolerance to potential data loss of no more than 60 minutes. This immediately dictates a need to take log backups at this interval (or shorter), in order that we can restore a database to a state no more than 60 minutes prior to the occurrence of data being lost, or the database going offline.

This rules out **SIMPLE** as a potential recovery model for our database since, as discussed, in this model a database operates in "auto-truncate" mode and any inactive VLFs are made available for reuse whenever a database **CHECKPOINT** operation occurs. With the inactive VLFs being continuously overwritten, we cannot capture a continuous chain of log records into our log backups, and so can't use these log backups as part of a database **RESTORE** operation. In fact, it isn't even possible to take log backups for a database that is operating in **SIMPLE** recovery.

This leaves us with a choice of two recovery models: **FULL** or **BULK LOGGED**. All databases where log backups are required should be operating in the **FULL** recovery model, and that's the model we're going to use. However, a database operating in **FULL** recovery may be switched temporarily to the **BULK LOGGED** model in order to maximize performance, and minimize the growth of the transaction log, during bulk operations, such as bulk data loads or certain index maintenance operations. When a database is operating in **BULK LOGGED** model, such operations are only minimally logged, and so require less space in the log file. This can save a DBA the headache of having log files growing out of control, and can save a good deal of time when bulk loading data into your database.

However, use of BULK LOGGED has implications that make it unsuitable for long-term use in a database where point-in-time restore is required, since it is not possible to restore a database to a point in time within a log file that contains minimally logged operations.

We'll discuss this in more detail in the next chapter, along with the best approach to minimizing risk when a database does need to be temporarily switched to BULK LOGGED model. For now, however, we're going to choose the FULL recovery model for our database.

Creating the database

Now that we know that FULL recovery is the model to use, let's go ahead and get our new database created so we can begin taking some log backups. We are going to stick with the naming convention established in previous chapters, and call this new database DatabaseForLogBackups. We can either create the database via the SSMS GUI or use the script shown in Listing 5-1.

```
USE [master]
GO

CREATE DATABASE [DatabaseForLogBackups] ON PRIMARY
(      NAME = N'DatabaseForLogBackups'
   , FILENAME = N'C:\SQLData\DatabaseForLogBackups.mdf'
   , SIZE = 512000KB
   , FILEGROWTH = 51200KB ) LOG ON
( NAME = N'DatabaseForLogBackups_log'
     , FILENAME = N'C:\SQLData\DatabaseForLogBackups_log.ldf'
   , SIZE = 51200KB
   , FILEGROWTH = 51200KB )
GO
ALTER DATABASE [DatabaseForLogBackups] SET RECOVERY FULL
GO
```

Listing 5-1: Creating our new DatabaseForLogBackups database.

This script will create for us a new `DatabaseForLogBackups` database, with the data and log files for this database stored in the **C:\SQLData** directory. Note that, if we didn't specify the `FILENAME` option, then the files would be auto-named and placed in the default directory for that version of SQL Server (for example, in SQL Server 2008, this is `\Program Files\Microsoft SQL Server\MSSQL10.MSSQLSERVER\MSSQL\DATA`).

We have assigned some appropriate values for the initial sizes of these files and their file growth characteristics. As discussed in Chapter 3, it's generally not appropriate to accept the default file size and growth settings for a database, and we'll take a deeper look at the specific problem that can arise with a log file that grows frequently in small increments, later in this chapter. For each database, we should size the data and log files as appropriate for their current data requirements, plus predicted growth over a set period.

In the case of our simple example database, I know how exactly much data I plan to load into our tables (you'll find out shortly!), so I have chosen an initial data file size that makes sense for that purpose, 500 MB. We don't want the file to grow too much but if it does, we want it to grow in reasonably sized chunks, so I've chosen a growth step of 50 MB. Each time the data file needs to grow, it will grow by 50 MB, which provides enough space for extra data, but not so much that we will have a crazy amount of free space after each growth. For the log file, I've chosen an initial size of 50 MB, and I am allowing it to grow by an additional 50 MB whenever it needs more room to store transactions.

Immediately after creating the database, we run an `ALTER DATABASE` command to ensure that our database is set up to use our chosen recovery mode, namely `FULL`. This is very important, especially if the `model` database on the SQL Server instance is set to a different recovery model, since all users' databases will inherit that setting.

Now that we have a new database, set to use the `FULL` recovery model, we can go ahead and start creating and populating the tables we need for our log backup tests.

Creating and populating tables

We are going to use several simple tables that we will populate with a small initial data load. Subsequently, we'll take a full database backup and then perform another data load. This will make it possible to track our progress as we restore our log backups, in the next chapter.

```
USE [DatabaseForLogBackups]
GO

SET ANSI_NULLS ON
GO
SET QUOTED_IDENTIFIER ON
GO
CREATE TABLE [dbo].[MessageTable1]
    (
        [Message] [nvarchar](100) NOT NULL ,
        [DateTimeStamp] [datetime2] NOT NULL
    )
ON  [PRIMARY]
GO
CREATE TABLE [dbo].[MessageTable2]
    (
        [Message] [nvarchar](100) NOT NULL ,
        [DateTimeStamp] [datetime2] NOT NULL
    )
ON  [PRIMARY]
GO
CREATE TABLE [dbo].[MessageTable3]
    (
        [Message] [nvarchar](100) NOT NULL ,
        [DateTimeStamp] [datetime2] NOT NULL
    )
ON  [PRIMARY]
GO
```

Listing 5-2:   Creating the tables.

Listing 5-2 creates three simple message tables, each of which will store simple text messages and a time stamp so that we can see exactly when each message was inserted into the table.

Having created our three tables, we can now pump a bit of data into them. We'll use the same technique as in Chapter 3, *i.e.* a series of INSERT commands, each with the GO X batch separator, to insert ten rows into each of the three tables, as shown in Listing 5-3.

```
USE [DatabaseForLogBackups]

INSERT INTO dbo.MessageTable1
    VALUES ('This is the initial data for MessageTable1', GETDATE())
GO 10

INSERT INTO dbo.MessageTable2
    VALUES ('This is the initial data for MessageTable2', GETDATE())
GO 10

INSERT INTO dbo.MessageTable3
    VALUES ('This is the initial data for MessageTable3', GETDATE())
GO 10
```

Listing 5-3: Initial population of tables.

We'll be performing a subsequent data load shortly, but for now we have a good base of data from which to work, and we have a very important step to perform before we can even think about taking log backups. Even though we set the recovery model to FULL, we won't be able to take log backups (in other words, the database is still effectively in auto-truncate mode) until we've first performed a full backup.

Before we do that, however, let's take a quick look at the current size of our log file, and its space utilization, using the DBCC SQLPERF (LOGSPACE); command. This will return results for all databases on the instance, but for the DatabaseForLogBackups we should see results similar to those shown in Figure 5-2.

Backup Stage	Log Size	Space Used
Before full backup	50 MB	0.65 %

Figure 5-2: DBCC SQLPERF (LOGSPACE) output before full backup.

This shows us that we have a 50 MB log file and that it is only using a little more than one half of one percent of that space.

Taking a base full database backup

Before we can even take log backups for our `DatabaseForLogBackups` database, we need to take a base full backup of the data file. We've covered all the details of taking full backups in Chapter 3, so simply run Listing 5-4 to take a full backup of the database, placing the backups in a central folder location, in this case **C:\SQLBackups\Chapter5** so they are readily available for restores. You've probably noticed that, for our simple example, the backup files are being stored on the same drive as the data and log files. In the real world, you'd store the data, log, and backup files on three separate disk drives.

```
USE [master]
GO


BACKUP DATABASE [DatabaseForLogBackups]
TO DISK = N'C:\SQLBackups\Chapter5\DatabaseForLogBackups_Native_Full.bak'
WITH NAME = N'DatabaseForLogBackups-Full Database Backup', STATS = 10, INIT
GO
```

Listing 5-4: Taking a native full backup.

So, at this stage, we've captured a full backup of our new database, containing three tables, each with ten rows of data. We're ready to start taking log backups now, but let's run the DBCC SQLPERF(LOGSPACE) command again, and see what happened to our log space.

Backup Stage	Log Size	Space Used
Before full backup	50 MB	0.65 %
After full backup	50 MB	0.73%

Figure 5-3: DBCC SQLPERF (LOGSPACE) output after full backup.

What's actually happened here isn't immediately apparent from these figures, so it needs a little explanation. We've discussed earlier how, for a FULL recovery model database, only a log backup can free up log space for reuse. This is true, but the point to remember is that such a database is actually operating in auto-truncate mode until the first full backup of that database completes. The log is truncated as a result of this first-ever full backup and, from that point on, the database is truly in FULL recovery, and a full backup will *never* cause log truncation. So, hidden in our figures is the fact that the log was truncated as a result of our first full backup, and the any space taken up by the rows we added was made available for reuse. Some space in the log would have been required to record the fact that a full backup took place, but overall the space used shows very little change.

Later in the chapter, when taking log backups with T-SQL, we'll track what happens to these log space statistics as we load a large amount of data into our tables, and then take a subsequent log backup.

Taking Log Backups

We're going to discuss taking log backups the "GUI way," in SSMS, and by using native T-SQL Backup commands. However, before taking that elusive first log backup, let's quickly insert ten new rows of data into each of our three tables, as shown in Listing 5-5. Having done so, we'll have ten rows of data for each table that is captured in a full database backup, and another ten rows for each table that is not in the full database backup, but where the details of the modifications are recorded in the live transaction log file.

```
USE [DatabaseForLogBackups]
GO
INSERT INTO MessageTable1
    VALUES ('Second set of data for MessageTable1', GETDATE())
GO 10
INSERT INTO MessageTable2
    VALUES ('Second set of data for MessageTable2', GETDATE())
GO 10
INSERT INTO MessageTable3
    VALUES ('Second set of data for MessageTable3', GETDATE())
GO 10
```

Listing 5-5:   A second data load.

The GUI way: native SSMS log backups

Open SSMS, connect to your test server, locate the `DatabaseForLogBackups` database, right-click on it and select the **Tasks | Back Up...** option. Select the **Back Up...** menu item to bring up the **General** page of the **Back Up Database** window, with which you should be familiar from Chapter 3, when we performed full database backups. The first set of configurable options is shown in Figure 5-4.

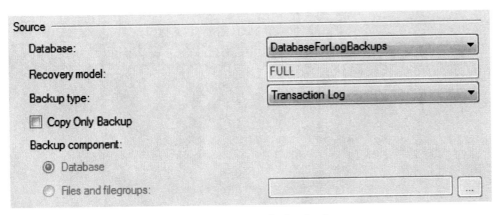

Figure 5-4: The Source section configuration for log backup.

Notice that we've selected the `DatabaseForLogBackups` database and, this time, we've changed the **Backup type** option to **Transaction Log**, since we want to take log backups. Once again, we leave the **Copy-only backup** option unchecked.

COPY_ONLY backups of the log file

When this option is used, when taking a transaction log backup, the log archiving point is not affected and does not affect the rest of our sequential log backup files. The transactions contained within the log file are backed up, but the log file is not truncated. This means that the special COPY_ONLY log backup can be used independently of conventional, scheduled log backups, and would not be needed when performing a restore that included the time span where this log backup was taken.

The **Backup component** portion of the configuration is used to specify full database backup versus file or filegroup backup; we're backing up the transaction log here, not the data files, so these options are disabled.

The second set of configurable options for our log backup, shown in Figure 5-5, is titled **Backup set** and deals with descriptions and expiration dates. The name field is auto-filled and the description will be left blank. The backup set expiration date can also be left with the default values. As discussed in Chapter 3, since we are only storing one log backup set per file, we do not need to worry about making sure backup sets expire at a given time. Storing multiple log backups would reduce the number of backup files that we need to manage, but it would cause that single file to grow considerably larger with each backup stored in it. We would also run the risk of losing more than just one backup if the file were to become corrupted or was lost.

Figure 5-5: The Backup set section configuration for log backups.

The final section of the configuration options is titled **Destination**, where we specify where to store the log backup file and what it will be called. If there is a file already selected for use, click the **Remove** button because we want to choose a fresh file and location.

Now, click the **Add** button to bring up the backup destination selection window. Click the browse (**...**) button and navigate to our chosen backup file location (**C:\SQLBackups\ Chapter5**) and enter the file name **DatabaseForLogBackups_Native_Log_1.trn** at the bottom, as shown in Figure 5-6.

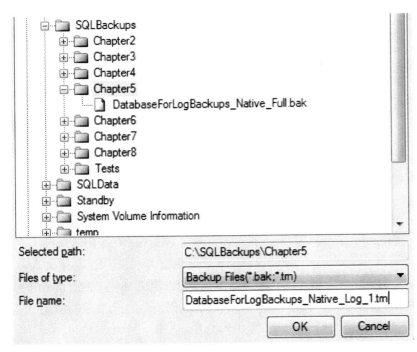

Figure 5-6: Selecting the path and filename for your log backup file.

Note that, while a full database backup file is identified conventionally by the `.BAK` extension, most DBAs identify log backup files with the `.TRN` extension. You can use whatever extension you like, but this is the standard extension for native log backups and it makes things much less confusing if everyone sticks to a familiar convention.

When you're done, click the **OK** buttons on both the **Locate Database Files** and **Select Backup Destination** windows to bring you back to the main backup configuration window. Once here, select the **Options** menu on the upper left-hand side of the window to bring up the second page of backup options. We are going to focus here on just the **Transaction log** section of this **Options** page, shown in Figure 5-7, as all the other options on this page were covered in detail in Chapter 3.

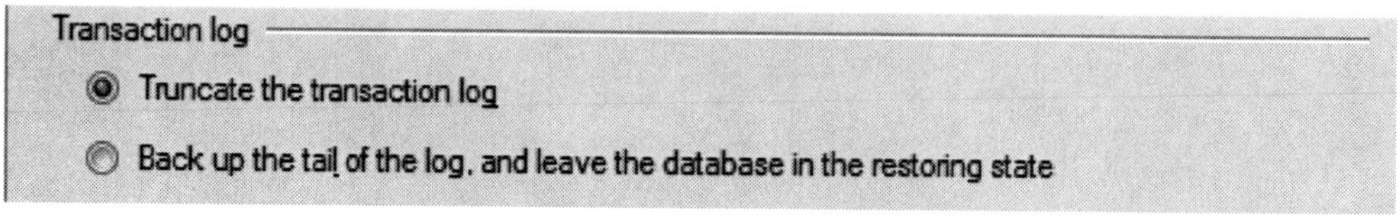

Transaction log

◉ Truncate the transaction log

◎ Back up the tail of the log, and leave the database in the restoring state

Figure 5-7:   Configuration options for transaction log backup.

The **Transaction log** section offers two important configuration option configurations. For all routine, daily log backups, the default option of **Truncate the transaction log** is the one you want; on completion of the log backup the log file will be truncated, if possible (*i.e.* space inside the file will be made available for reuse). The second option, **Back up the tail of the log...**, is used exclusively in response to a disaster scenario; you've lost data, or the database has become corrupt in some way, and you need to restore it to a previous point in time. Your last action before attempting a RESTORE operation should be to back up the tail of the log, *i.e.* capture a backup of the remaining contents (those records added since the last log backup) of the live transaction log file, assuming it is still available. This will put the database into a restoring state, and assumes that the next action you wish to perform is a RESTORE. This is a vital option in database recovery, and we'll demonstrate it in Chapter 6, but it won't be a regular maintenance task that is performed.

Having reviewed all of the configuration options, go ahead and click **OK**, and the log backup will begin. A progress meter will appear in the lower left-hand side of the window but since we don't have many transactions to back up, the operation will probably complete very quickly and you'll see a notification that your backup has completed and was successful. If, instead, you receive an error message, you'll need to check your configuration settings and to attempt to find what went wrong.

We have successfully taken a transaction log backup! As discussed in Chapter 3, various metrics are available regarding these log backups, such as the time it took to complete, and the size of the log backup file. In my test, the backup time was negligible in this case (measured in milliseconds). However, for busy databases, handling hundreds or thousands of transactions per second, the speed of these log backups can be a very important consideration and, as was demonstrated for full backups in Chapter 3, use of backup compression can be beneficial. In Chapter 8, we'll compare the backup speeds and compression ratios obtained for native log backups, versus log backups with native compression, versus log backups with SQL Backup compression.

Right now, though, we'll just look at the log backup size. Browse to the **C:\SQLBackups\ Chapter5** folder, or wherever it is that you stored the log backup file and simply note the size of the file. In my case, it was 85 KB.

T-SQL log backups

Now that we have taken a log backup using the GUI method, we'll insert some new rows into our `DatabaseForLogBackups` table and then take a second log backup, this time using a T-SQL script. Rerun `DBCC SQLPERF(LOGSPACE)`before we start. Since we've only added a small amount of data, and have performed a log backup, the live log file is still 50 MB in size, and less than 1% full.

Listing 5-6 shows the script to insert our new data; this time we're inserting considerably more rows into each of the three tables (1,000 into the first table, 10,000 into the second and 100,000 into the third) and so our subsequent transaction log backup should also be much larger, as a result.

Notice that we print the date and time after inserting the rows into `MessageTable2`, and then use the `WAITFOR DELAY` command before proceeding with the final `INSERT` command; both are to help us when we come to perform some point-in-time restores, in Chapter 6.

```
USE [DatabaseForLogBackups]
GO
INSERT  INTO dbo.MessageTable1
VALUES  ( 'Third set of data for MessageTable1', GETDATE() )
GO 1000
INSERT  INTO dbo.MessageTable2
VALUES  ( 'Third set of data for MessageTable2', GETDATE() )
GO 10000

-- Note this date down as we'll need it in the next chapter
PRINT GETDATE()
GO
WAITFOR DELAY '00:02:00'
GO

INSERT  INTO dbo.MessageTable3
VALUES  ( 'Third set of data for MessageTable3', GETDATE() )
GO 100000
```

Listing 5-6: Third data insert for `DatabaseForLogBackups` (with 2-minute delay).

Go ahead and run this script in SSMS (it will take several minutes). Before we perform a T-SQL log backup, let's check once again on the size of the log file and space usage for our `DatabaseForLogBackups` database.

Backup Stage	Log Size	Space Used
Initial stats	50 MB	0.8 %
After third data data load	100 MB	55.4%

Figure 5-8: DBCC SQLPERF (LOGSPACE) output after big data load.

We now see a more significant portion of our log being used. The log actually needed to grow above its initial size of 50 MB in order to accommodate this data load, so it jumped in size by 50 MB, which is the growth rate we set when we created the database. 55% of that space is currently in use.

When we used the SSMS GUI to build our first transaction log backup, a T-SQL BACKUP LOG command was constructed and executed under the covers. Listing 5-7 simply creates directly in T-SQL a simplified version of the backup command that the GUI would have generated.

```
USE [master]
GO

BACKUP LOG [DatabaseForLogBackups]
TO DISK = N'C:\SQLBackups\Chapter5\DatabaseForLogBackups_Native_Log_2.trn'
WITH NAME = N'DatabaseForLogBackups-Transaction Log Backup', STATS = 10
GO
```

Listing 5-7: Native T-SQL transaction log backup code.

The major difference between this script, and the one we saw for a full database backup in Chapter 3, is that the BACKUP DATABASE command is replaced by the BACKUP LOG command, since we want SQL Server to back up the transaction log instead of the data files.

We use the TO DISK parameter to specify the backup location and name of the file. We specify our central **SQLBackups** folder and, once again, apply the convention of using .TRN to identify our log backup. The WITH NAME option allows us to give the backup set an appropriate set name. This is informational only, especially since we are only taking one backup per file/set. Finally, we see the familiar STATS option, which dictates how often the console messages will be updated during the operation. With the value set to 10, a console message should display when the backup is (roughly) 10%, 20%, 30% complete, and so on, as shown in Figure 5-9, along with the rest of the statistics from the successful backup.

```
🔳 Messages
   10 percent processed.
   20 percent processed.
   31 percent processed.
   40 percent processed.
   50 percent processed.
   61 percent processed.
   71 percent processed.
   80 percent processed.
   90 percent processed.
   100 percent processed.
   Processed 7033 pages for database 'DatabaseForLogBackups', file 'DatabaseForLogBackups_log' on file 1.
   BACKUP LOG successfully processed 7033 pages in 3.562 seconds (15.424 MB/sec).
```

Figure 5-9:   Successful transaction log backup message.

Notice that this log backup took about 3.5 seconds to complete; still not long, but much longer than our first backup took. Also, Figure 5-10 shows that the size of our second log backup file weighs in at 56 MB. This is even larger than our full backup, which is to be expected since we just pumped in 3,700 times more records into the database than were there during the full backup.

The log backup file size is also broadly consistent with what we would have predicted, given the stats we got from DBCC SQLPERF (LOGSPACE), which indicated a 100 MB log which was about 55% full.

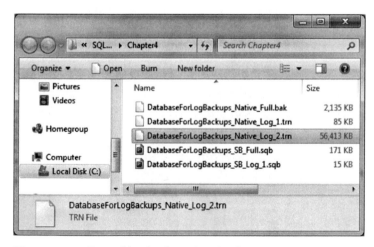

Figure 5-10:   Second log backup size check.

Let's check the log utilization one last time with the
DBCC SQLPERF (LOGSPACE) command.

Backup Stage	Log Size	Space Used
Initial stats	50 MB	0.8 %
After third data data load	100 MB	55.4%
After T-SQL log backup	100 MB	5.55%

Figure 5-11: DBCC SQLPERF (LOGSPACE) output after big data load.

This is exactly the behavior we expect; as a result of the backup operation, the log has
been truncated, and space in inactive VLFs made available for reuse, so only about 5% of
the space is now in use. As discussed earlier, truncation does not affect the physical size of
the log, so it remains at 100 MB.

Forcing Log Backup Failures for Fun

Having practiced these log backups a few times, it's rare for anything to go wrong with
the actual backup process itself. However, it's still possible to stumble into the odd
gotcha. Go ahead and run Listing 5-8 in an SSMS query window; try to work out what the
error is going to be before you run it.

```
CREATE DATABASE [ForceFailure]
-- Using the NO_WAIT option so no rollbacks
-- of current transactions are attempted
ALTER  DATABASE [ForceFailure] SET RECOVERY SIMPLE WITH NO_WAIT
GO


BACKUP DATABASE [ForceFailure] TO DISK = 'C:\SQLBackups\Chapter5\ForceFailure_Full.bak'
GO


BACKUP LOG [ForceFailure] TO DISK = 'C:\SQLBackups\Chapter5\ForceFailure_Log.trn'
GO


--Tidy up once we're done as we no longer need this database
DROP DATABASE ForceFailure
GO
```

Listing 5-8:   Forcing a backup failure.

You should see the message output shown in Figure 5-12.

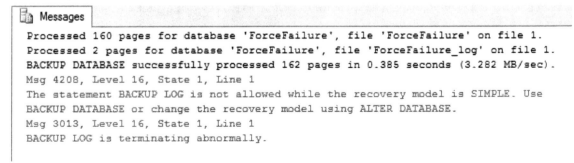

Figure 5-12:   Running a log backup on a SIMPLE model database.

We can see that the database was successfully created, the BACKUP DATABASE operation was fine, but then we hit a snag with the log backup operation:


```
Msg 4208, Level 16, State 1, Line 1
The statement BACKUP LOG is not allowed while the recovery model is SIMPLE. Use BACKUP
DATABASE or change the recovery model using ALTER DATABASE.
```

The problem is very clear: we are trying to perform a log backup on a database that is operating in the SIMPLE recovery model, which is not allowed.

The exact course of action, on seeing an error like this, depends on the reason why you were trying to perform the log backup. If you simply did not realize that log backups were not possible in this case, then lesson learned. If log backups are required in the SLA for this database, then the fact that the database is in SIMPLE recovery is a serious problem. First, you should switch it to FULL recovery model immediately, and take another full database backup, to restart the log chain. Second, you should find out when and why the database got switched to SIMPLE, and report what the implications are for point-in-time recovery over that period.

An interesting case where a DBA might see this error is upon spotting that a log file for a certain database is growing very large, and assuming that the cause is the lack of a log backup. Upon running the BACKUP LOG command, the DBA is surprised to see the database is in fact in SIMPLE recovery. So, why would the log file be growing so large? Isn't log space supposed to be reused after each CHECKPOINT, in this case? We'll discuss possible reasons why you still might see log growth problems, even for databases in SIMPLE recovery, in the next section.

Troubleshooting Log Issues

The most common problem that DBAs experience with regard to log management is rapid, uncontrolled (or even uncontrollable) growth in the size of the log. In the worst case, a transaction log can grow until there is no further available space on its drive and so it can grow no more. At this point, you'll encounter Error 9002, the "transaction log full" error, and the database will become read-only. If you are experiencing uncontrolled growth of the transaction log, it is due, either to a very high rate of log activity, or to factors that are preventing space in the log file from being reused, or both.

As a log file grows and grows, a related problem is that the log can become "internally fragmented," if the growth occurs in lots of small increments. This can affect the performance of any operation that needs to read the transaction log (such as database restores).

Failure to take log backups

Still the most common cause of a rapidly growing log, sadly, is simple mismanagement; in other words failure to take log backups for a database operating in FULL recovery. Since log backups are the only operation that truncates the log, if they aren't performed regularly then your log file may grow rapidly and eat up most or all of the space on your drive. I rest more peacefully at night in the knowledge that, having read this chapter, this is a trap that won't catch you out.

If you're asked to troubleshoot a "runaway" transaction log for a FULL recovery model database, then a useful first step is to interrogate the value of the log_reuse_wait_desc column in sys.databases, as shown in Listing 5-9.

```
USE master
GO
SELECT name ,
        recovery_model_desc ,
        log_reuse_wait_desc
FROM    sys.databases
WHERE   name = 'MyDatabase'
```

Listing 5-9: Finding possible causes of log growth.

If the value returned for the log_reuse_wait_desc column is LOG BACKUP, then the reason for the log growth is the lack of a log backup. If this database requires log backups, start taking them, at a frequency that will satisfy the terms of the SLA, and control the growth of the log from here in. If the database doesn't require point-in-time recovery, switch the database to SIMPLE recovery.

In either case, if the log has grown unacceptably large (or even full) in the meantime, refer to the forthcoming section on *Handling the 9002 Transaction Log Full error*.

Other factors preventing log truncation

There are a few factors, in addition to a lack of log backups, which can "pin" the head of the log, and so prevent space in the file from being reused. Some of these factors can cause the size of the log to grow rapidly, or prevent the log file from being truncated, even when operating in SIMPLE recovery model.

The concept of the active log, and the criteria for log truncation, as discussed earlier in the chapter, also explains why a "rogue" long-running transaction, or a transaction that never gets committed, can cause very rapid log growth, regardless of the recovery model in use. If we have a single, very long-running transaction, then any log records that relate to transactions that started and committed after this transaction must still be part of the active log. This can prevent large areas of the log from being truncated, either by a log backup or by a CHECKPOINT, even though the vast majority of the log records are no longer required.

Such problems manifest in a value of ACTIVE TRANSACTION for the log_reuse_wait_desc column. The course of action in the short term is to discover which transaction is causing the problem and find out if it's possible to kill it. In the longer term, you need to work out how to tune very long-running transactions or break them down into smaller units, and to find out what application issues are causing transactions to remain uncommitted.

DBCC OPENTRAN

A tool that is useful in tracking down rogue transactions is DBCC OPENTRAN(DatabaseName). *It will report the oldest active transaction for that database, along with its start time, and the identity of the session that started the transaction.*

There are several other issues that can be revealed through the `log_reuse_wait_desc` column, mainly relating to various processes, such as replication, which require log records to remain in the log until they have been processed. We haven't got room to cover them here, but Gail Shaw offers a detailed description of these issues in her article, *Why is my transaction log full?* at WWW.SQLSERVERCENTRAL.COM/ARTICLES/TRANSACTION+LOG/72488/.

Excessive logging activity

If no problems are revealed by the `log_reuse_wait_desc` column then the log growth may simply be caused by a very high rate of logging activity. For a database using the FULL recovery model, all operations are fully logged, including bulk data imports, index rebuilds, and so on, all of which will write heavily to the log file, causing it to grow rapidly in size.

It is out of scope for this book to delve into the full details of bulk operations but, essentially, you need to find a way to either minimize the logging activity or, if that's not possible, then simply plan for it accordingly, by choosing appropriate initial size and growth settings for the log, as well as an appropriate log backup strategy.

As noted in Chapter 1, certain bulk operations can be minimally logged, by temporarily switching the database from FULL to BULK_LOGGED recovery, in order to perform the operation, and then back again. Assuming your SLA will permit this, it is worth considering, given that any bulk logged operation will immediately prevent point-in-time recovery to a point within any log file that contains records relating to the minimally logged operations. We'll cover this option in a little more detail in Chapter 6.

Handling the 9002 Transaction Log Full error

As noted earlier, in the worst case of uncontrolled log growth you may find yourself facing down the dreaded "9002 Transaction Log Full" error. There is no more space within the log to write new records, there is no further space on the disk to allow the log file to grow, and so the database becomes read-only until the issue is resolved.

Obviously the most pressing concern in such cases is to get SQL Server functioning normally again, either by making space in the log file, or finding extra disk space. If the root cause of the log growth turns out to be no log backups (or insufficiently frequent ones), then perform one immediately. An even quicker way to make space in the log, assuming you can get permission to do it, is to temporarily switch the database to SIMPLE recovery to force a log truncation, then switch it back to FULL and perform a full backup.

The next step is to investigate all possible causes of the log growth, as discussed in the previous sections, and implement measures to prevent its recurrence.

Having done so, however, you may still be left with a log file that has ballooned to an unacceptably large size. As a one-off operation, in such circumstances, it's acceptable to use DBCC SHRINKFILE to reclaim space in the log and reduce its physical size.

The recommended way to do this is to disconnect all users from the database (or wait for a time when there is very low activity), take a log backup or just force a CHECKPOINT if the database is in SIMPLE recovery, and then perform the DBCC SHRINKFILE operation, as follows: DBCC SHRINKFILE(<logical name of log file>,TRUNCATEONLY);. This will shrink the log to its smallest possible size. You can then resize the log appropriately, via an ALTER DATABASE command. This technique, when performed in this manner as a one-off operation, should resize the log and remove any fragmentation that occurred during its previous growth.

Finally, before moving on, it's worth noting that there is quite a bit of bad advice out there regarding how to respond to this transaction log issue. The most frequent offenders are suggestions to force log truncation using BACKUP LOG WITH TRUNCATE_ONLY (deprecated in SQL Server 2005) or its even more disturbing counterpart, BACKUP LOG TO DISK='NUL', which takes a log backup and discards the contents, without SQL Server having any knowledge that the log chain is broken. Don't use these techniques. The only correct way to force log truncation is to temporarily switch the database to SIMPLE recovery.

Likewise, you should never schedule regular DBCC SHRINKFILE tasks as a means of controlling the size of the log as it can cause terrible log fragmentation, as discussed in the next section.

Log fragmentation

A fragmented log file can dramatically slow down any operation that needs to read the log file. For example, it can cause slow startup times (since SQL Server reads the log during the database recovery process), slow RESTORE operations, and more. Log size and growth should be planned and managed to avoid excessive numbers of growth events, which can lead to this fragmentation.

A log is fragmented if it contains a very high number of VLFs. In general, SQL Server decides the optimum size and number of VLFs to allocate. However, a transaction log that auto-grows frequently in small increments, will suffer from log fragmentation. To see this in action, let's simply re-create our previous ForceFailure database, withal its configuration settings set at whatever the model database dictates, and then run the **DBCC LogInfo** command, which is an undocumented and unsupported command (at least there is very little written about it by Microsoft) but which will allow us to interrogate the VLF architecture.

```
CREATE DATABASE [ForceFailure]
ALTER  DATABASE [ForceFailure] SET RECOVERY FULL WITH NO_WAIT
GO


DBCC Loginfo;
GO
```

Listing 5-10: Running DBCC Loginfo on the ForceFailure database.

The results are shown in Figure 5-13. The **DBCC LogInfo** command returns one row per VLF and, among other things, indicates the Status of that VLF. A Status value of 2 indicates a VLF is active and cannot be truncated; a Status value of 0 indicates an inactive VLF.

	FileId	FileSize	StartOffset	FSeqNo	Status	Parity	CreateLSN
1	2	253952	8192	300	2	128	0
2	2	262144	262144	299	2	64	0
3	2	262144	524288	296	0	64	185000000005600308
4	2	262144	786432	297	0	64	185000000016800336
5	2	262144	1048576	298	0	64	185000000043200267

Figure 5-13: Five VLFs for our empty ForceFailure database.

Five rows are returned, indicating five VLFs (two of which are currently active). We are not going to delve any deeper here into the meaning of any of the other columns returned.

Now let's insert a large number of rows (one million) into a VLFTest table, in the ForceFailure database, using a script reproduced by kind permission of Jeff Moden (www.sqlservercentral.com/Authors/Articles/Jeff_Moden/80567/), and then rerun the DBCC LogInfo command, as shown in Listing 5-11.

```
USE ForceFailure ;
GO
IF OBJECT_ID('dbo.VLFTest', 'U') IS NOT NULL
    DROP TABLE dbo.VLFTest ;
--===== AUTHOR: Jeff Moden
--===== Create and populate 1,000,000 row test table.
-- "SomeID" has range of 1 to 1000000 unique numbers
-- "SomeInt" has range of 1 to 50000 non-unique numbers
-- "SomeLetters2";"AA"-"ZZ" non-unique 2-char strings
-- "SomeMoney"; 0.0000 to 99.9999 non-unique numbers
-- "SomeDate" ; >=01/01/2000 and <01/01/2010 non-unique
-- "SomeHex12"; 12 random hex characters (ie, 0-9,A-F)
SELECT TOP 1000000
        SomeID = IDENTITY( INT,1,1 ),
        SomeInt = ABS(CHECKSUM(NEWID())) % 50000 + 1 ,
        SomeLetters2 = CHAR(ABS(CHECKSUM(NEWID())) % 26 + 65)
        + CHAR(ABS(CHECKSUM(NEWID())) % 26 + 65) ,
        SomeMoney = CAST(ABS(CHECKSUM(NEWID())) % 10000 / 100.0 AS MONEY) ,
        SomeDate = CAST(RAND(CHECKSUM(NEWID())) * 3653.0 + 36524.0 AS DATETIME) ,
        SomeHex12 = RIGHT(NEWID(), 12)
INTO    dbo.VLFTest
FROM    sys.all_columns ac1
        CROSS JOIN sys.all_columns ac2 ;

DBCC Loginfo;
GO

--Tidy up once you're done as we no longer need this database
DROP DATABASE ForceFailure
GO
```

Listing 5-11: Inserting one million rows and interrogating DBCC Loginfo.

This time, the DBCC LogInfo command returns 131 rows, indicating 131 VLFs, as shown in Figure 5-14.

	FileId	FileSize	StartOffset	FSeqNo	Status	Parity	CreateLSN
1	2	253952	8192	24	2	64	0
2	2	327680	262144	25	2	64	0
3	2	262144	589824	26	2	64	25000000013300327
4	2	262144	851968	27	2	64	26000000001800261
5	2	262144	1114112	28	2	64	27000000002300201
6	2	262144	1376256	29	2	64	28000000002400204
7	2	262144	1638400	30	2	64	29000000001800262
8	2	262144	1900544	31	2	64	30000000002400188
9	2	262144	2162688	32	2	64	31000000002400210

Query executed successfully.   tonytest.testnet (10.0 SP1) sa (53) ForceFailure 00:00:00 131 rows

Figure 5-14: 131 VLFs for our `ForceFailure` database, with one million rows.

The growth properties inherited from the `model` database dictate a small initial size for the log files, then growth in relatively small increments. These properties are inappropriate for a database subject to this sort of activity and lead to the creation of a large number of VLFs. By comparison, try re-creating `ForceFailure`, but this time with some sensible initial size and growth settings (such as those shown in Listing 5-1). In my test, this resulted in an initial 4 VLFs, expanding to 8 VLFs after inserting a million rows.

The "right" number of VLFs for a given database depends on a number of factors, including, of course, the size of the database. Clearly, it is not appropriate to start with a very small log and grow in small increments, as this leads to fragmentation. However, it might also cause problems to go to the opposite end of the scale and start with a huge (tens of GB) log, as then SQL Server would create very few VLFs, and this could affect log space reuse. Further advice on how to achieve a reasonable number of VLFs can be found in Paul Randal's TechNet article *Top Tips for Effective Database Maintenance*, at HTTP://TECHNET.MICROSOFT.COM/EN-US/MAGAZINE/2008.08.DATABASE.ASPX.

If you do diagnose a very fragmented log, you can remedy the situation using DBCC SHRINKFILE, as described in the previous section. Again, never use this as a general means of controlling log size; instead, ensure that your log is sized, and grows, appropriately.

Summary

This chapter explained in detail how to capture log backups using either SSMS Backup Wizard or T-SQL scripts. We also explored, and discussed, how to avoid certain log-related issues such as explosive log growth and log fragmentation.

Do not to remove any of the backup files we have captured; we are going to use each of these in the next chapter to perform various types of restore operation on our `DatabaseForLogBackups` database.

Chapter 6: Log Restores

Whereas log backups will form a routine part of our daily maintenance tasks on a given database, log restores, at least in response to an emergency, will hopefully be a much rarer occurrence. However, whenever they need to be performed, it's absolutely vital the job is done properly.

In this chapter, we're going to restore the full backup of our `DatabaseForLogBackups` database from Chapter 5, and then apply our series of log backups in order to return our databases to various previous states. We'll demonstrate how to perform a complete transaction log restore, and how to restore to a point in time within a log file.

Log Restores in the SLA

With an appropriate backup schedule in place, we know that with the right collection of files and enough time we can get a database back online and, with a point-in-time restore, get it back to a state fairly close to the one it was in before whatever unfortunate event befell it.

However, as discussed in Chapter 2, the SLA needs to clearly stipulate an agreed maximum time for restoring a given database, which takes sensible account of the size of the database, where the necessary files are located, and the potential complexity of the restore.

Possible Issues with Log Restores

There are several factors that could possibly affect our ability to perform a point-in-time log restore successfully or at least cause some disruption to the process:

- an incomplete series of log backup files

- a missing full backup database file

- minimally logged transactions in a log file.

Let's take a look at each in turn.

Missing or corrupt log backup

A restore operation to a particular point will require an unbroken log backup chain; that is, we need to be able to apply each and every backup file, in an unbroken sequence, up to the one that contains the log records covering the time to which we wish to restore the database. If we don't have a complete sequence of log files describing a complete LSN chain right up to the point we wish to restore, then we will only be able to restore to the end of the last file before the sequence was broken. The most common cause of a broken log file sequence is a missing or corrupted backup file. However, another possibility is that someone manually forced a truncation of the log without SQL Server's knowledge (see the *Handling the 9002 Transaction Log Full error* section in Chapter 5).

This could prove disastrous, especially in the case of a failure very late in a day. For example, if we are taking log backups each hour, but somehow lose the transaction log backup file that was taken at 1 p.m., a failure that happens at 8 p.m. will cost us eight full hours of data loss.

Missing or corrupt full backup

If we find that the latest full backup file, on which we planned to base a RESTORE operation, is missing or corrupt, then there is still hope that we can perform our point-in-time restore. Full backups do not break the log chain, and each log backup contains all the log records since the last log backup, so we can restore the previous good full backup and then restore the full chain of log files extending from this full backup up to the desired point of recovery.

However, this is not a reason to skip full backups, or to adopt a cavalier attitude towards full backup failures. When performing a restore operation, the greatest chance of success comes when that operation involves the smallest number of files possible. The more files we have to restore, the greater the chance of failure.

Minimally logged operations

In Chapter 5, we discussed briefly the fact that it is not possible to restore a database to a point in time within a log file that contains minimally logged operations, recorded while the database was operating in the BULK_LOGGED recovery model. In order to visualize this, Figure 6-1 depicts an identical backup timeline for two databases, each of which we wish to restore to the same point in time (represented by the arrow). The green bar represents a full database backup and the yellow bars represent a series of log backups. The only difference between the two databases is that the first is operating in FULL recovery model, and the second in BULK LOGGED.

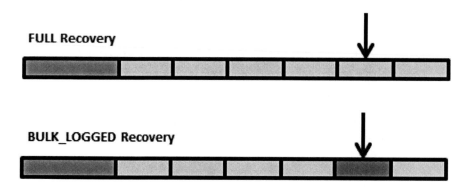

Figure 6-1:   Database backup timeline.

During the time span of the fifth log backup of the day, a **BULK INSERT** command was performed on each database, in order to load a set of data. This bulk data load completed without a hitch but, in an unrelated incident, within the time span of the fifth log backup, a user ran a "rogue" transaction and crucial data was lost. The project manager informs the DBA team and requests that the database is restored to a point just where the transaction that resulted in data loss started.

In the **FULL** recovery model database this is not an issue. The bulk data load was fully logged and we can restore the database to any point in time within that log file. We simply restore the last full database backup, without recovery, and apply the log files to the point in time right before the unfortunate data loss incident occurred (we'll see how to do this later in the chapter).

In the **BULK LOGGED** database, we have a problem. We can restore to any point in time within the first four log backups, but not to any point in time within the fifth log backup, which contains the minimally logged operations. For that log file, we are in an "all or nothing" situation; we must apply none of the operations in this log file, so stopping the restore at the end of the fourth file, or we must apply all of them, proceeding to restore to any point in time within the sixth log backup.

In other words, we can restore the full database backup, again without recovery, and apply the first four log backups to the database. Unfortunately, we will not have the option to restore to any point in time within the fifth log. If we apply the whole of the fifth log file backup, this would defeat the purpose of the recovery, since the errant process committed its changes somewhere inside of that log backup file, so we'd simply be removing the data we were trying to get back! We have little choice but to restore up to the end of the fourth log, enter database recovery, and report the loss of any data changes that were made after this time.

Hopefully, this will never happen to you and, unless your SLA adopts a completely "zero tolerance" attitude towards any risk of data loss, it is not a reason to avoid BULK_LOGGED recovery model altogether. There are valid reasons using this recovery model in order to reduce the load on the transaction log, and if we follow best practices, we should not find ourselves in this type of situation.

```
USE [master]
GO


BACKUP LOG [SampleDB] TO DISK = '\\path\example\filename.trn'
GO


ALTER DATABASE [SampleDB] SET RECOVERY BULK_LOGGED WITH NO_WAIT
GO


-- Perform minimally logged transactions here
-- Stop minimally logged transactions here

ALTER DATABASE [SampleDB] SET RECOVERY FULL WITH NO_WAIT
GO


BACKUP LOG [SampleDB] TO DISK = '\\path\example\filename.trn'
GO
```

Listing 6-1: A template for temporarily switching a database to BULK_LOGGED recovery model.

If we do need to perform maintenance operations that can be minimally logged and we wish to switch to BULK_LOGGED model, the recommended practice is to take a log backup immediately before switching to BULK_LOGGED, and immediately after switching the database back to FULL recovery, as demonstrated in Listing 6-1. This will, as far as possible, isolate the minimally logged transactions in a single log backup file.

Performing Log Restores

Being prepared to restore your database and log backups is one of the DBAs most important jobs. All DBAs are likely, eventually, to find themselves in a situation where a crash recovery is required, and it can be a scary situation. However, the well-prepared DBA will know exactly where the required backup files are stored, will have been performing backup verification and some random test restores, and can exude a calm assurance that this database will be back online as quickly as possible.

As we did for log backups, we're going to discuss how to perform log restores the "GUI way," in SSMS, and then by using native T-SQL Backup commands. We're going to be restoring to various states the DatabaseForLogBackups database from Chapter 5, so before we start, let's review, pictorially, our backup scheme for that database, and what data is contained within each backup file.

With our first example, using the GUI, we'll restore the DatabaseForLogBackups database to the state in which it existed at the point after the first log backup was taken; in other words, we'll restore right to the end of the transaction log DatabaseForLog-Backups_Native_Log_1.trn, at which point we should have 20 rows in each of our three message tables.

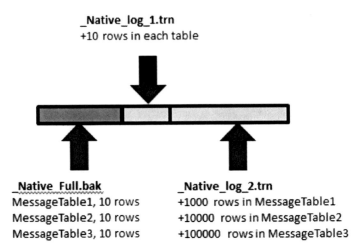

Figure 6-2: Backup scheme for `DatabaseForLogBackups`.

In our second example, using a T-SQL script, we'll restore to a specific point in time within the second log backup, just before the last 100,000 records were inserted into `MessageTable3`. This will leave the first two tables with their final row counts (1,020 and 10,020, respectively), but the third with just 20 rows.

As discussed in Chapter 1, there are several different ways to restore to a particular point inside a log backup; in this case, we'll demonstrate the most common means, which is to use the `STOPAT` parameter in the `RESTORE LOG` command to restore the database to a state that reflects all transactions that were committed at the specified time.

GUI-based log restore

We will begin by using the native SQL Server backup files that we took in Chapter 5 to restore our database to the state that it was in after the first transaction log backup was taken. We are going to restore the entire transaction log backup in this example. Go ahead and get SSMS started and connected to your test SQL Server.

Right-click on `DatabaseForLogBackups` in the object explorer and select **Tasks |
Restore | Database...** to begin the restore process and you'll see the **Restore Database**
screen, which we examined in detail in Chapter 4.

This time, rather than restore directly over an existing database, we'll restore to a new
database, basically a copy of the existing `DatabaseForLogBackups` but as it existed
at the end of the first log backup. So, in the **To database:** section, enter a new database
name, such as `DatabaseForLogBackups_RestoreCopy`.

In the **Source for restore** section of the screen, you should see that the required backup
files are auto-populated (SQL Server can interrogate the `msdb` database for the backup
history). This will only be the case if all the backup files are in their original location (**C:\
SQLBackups\Chapter5**, if you followed through the examples). Therefore, as configured
in Figure 6-3, our new copy database would be restored to the end of the second log
backup, in a single restore operation. Alternatively, by simply deselecting the second log
file, we could restore the database to the end of the first log file.

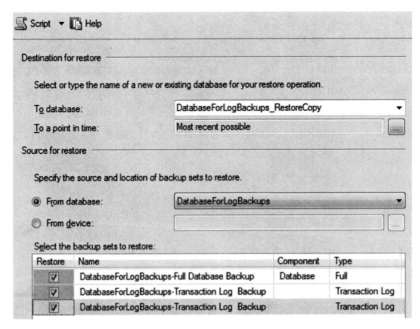

Figure 6-3: Initial **Restore Database** screen for `DatabaseForLogBackups`.

However, if the backup files have been moved to a new location, we'd need to manually locate each of the required files for the restore process, and perform the restore process in several steps (one operation to restore the full backup and another the log file). Since it is not uncommon that the required backups won't still be in their original local folders, and since performing the restore in steps better illustrates the process, we'll ignore this useful auto-population feature for the backup files, and perform the restore manually. Click on **From device:** and choose the browse button to the right of that option, navigate to **C:\SQLBackups\Chapter5** and choose the full backup file. Having done so, the relevant section of the **Restore Database** page should look as shown in Figure 6-4.

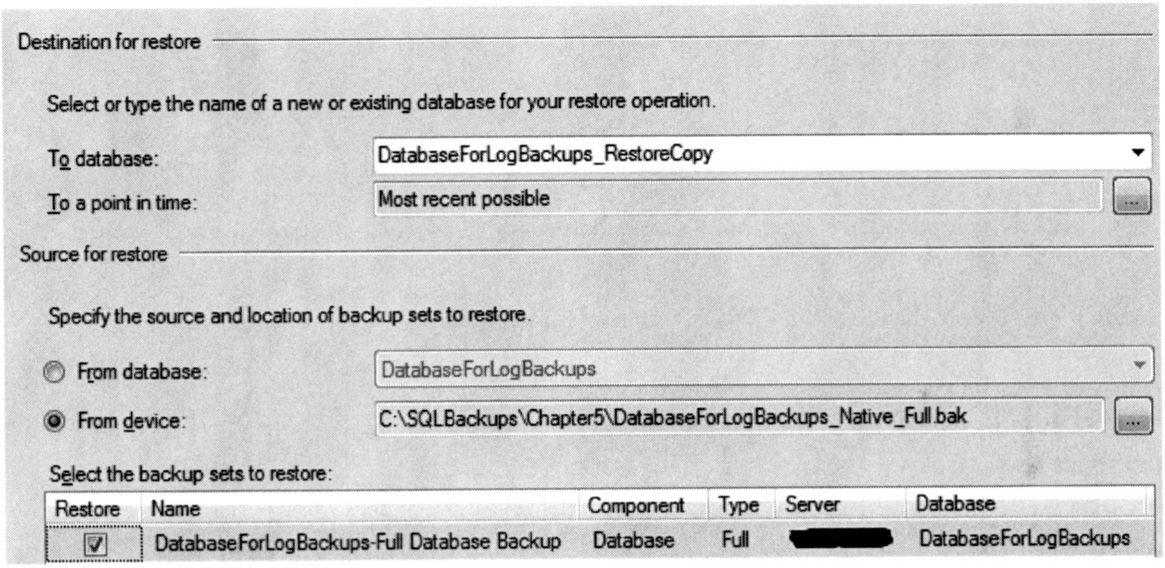

Figure 6-4: Restore the full backup file.

Next, click through to the **Options** page. We know that restoring the full backup is only the first step in our restore process, so once the full backup is restored we need the new `DatabaseForLogBackups_RestoreCopy` database to remain in a restoring state, ready to accept further log files. Therefore, we want to override the default restore state (RESTORE WITH RECOVERY) and choose instead RESTORE WITH NORECOVERY, as shown in Figure 6-5.

Restore options

- ☐ Overwrite the existing database (WITH REPLACE)
- ☐ Preserve the replication settings (WITH KEEP_REPLICATION)
- ☑ Prompt before restoring each backup
- ☐ Restrict access to the restored database (WITH RESTRICTED_USER)

Restore the database files as:

Original File Name	File Type	Restore As	
DatabaseForLogBackups	Rows Data	C:\SQLData\DatabaseForLogBackups_RestoreCopy.mdf	...
DatabaseForLogBackups_log	Log	C:\SQLData\DatabaseForLogBackups_RestoreCopy_1.ldf	...

Recovery state

- ○ Leave the database ready to use by rolling back uncommitted transactions. Additional transaction logs cannot be restored.(RESTORE WITH RECOVERY)

- ◉ Leave the database non-operational, and do not roll back uncommitted transactions. Additional transaction logs can be restored.(RESTORE WITH NORECOVERY)

- ○ Leave the database in read-only mode. Undo uncommitted transactions, but save the undo actions in a standby file so that recovery effects can be reversed.(RESTORE WITH STANDBY)

Figure 6-5: Restore the full backup file while leaving the database in a restoring state.

Note that SQL Server has automatically renamed the data and log files for the new database so as to avoid clashing with the existing `DatabaseForLogBackups` database, on which the restore is based. Having done this, we're ready to go. First, however, you might want to select the **Script** menu option, from the top of the **General** Page, and take a quick look at the script that has been generated under the covers. I won't show it here, as we'll get to these details in the next example, but you'll notice use of the MOVE parameter, to rename the data and log files, and the NORECOVERY parameter, to leave the database in a restoring state. Once the restore is complete, you should see the new `DatabaseForLogBackups_RestoreCopy` database in your object explorer, but with a green arrow on the database icon, and the word "**Restoring...**" after its name.

We're now ready to perform the second step, and restore our first transaction log. Right-click on the new `DatabaseForLogBackups_RestoreCopy` database and select **Tasks**

| **Restore** | **Transaction Log....** In the **Restore source** section, we can click on **From previous backups of database:**, and then select DatabaseForLogBackups database. SQL Server will then retrieve the available log backups for us to select. Alternatively, we can manually select the required log backup, which is the route we'll choose here, so click on **From file or tape:** and select the first log backup file from its folder location (**C:\ SQLBackups\Chapter5\DatabaseForLogBackups_Native_Log_1.trn**). The screen should now look as shown in Figure 6-6.

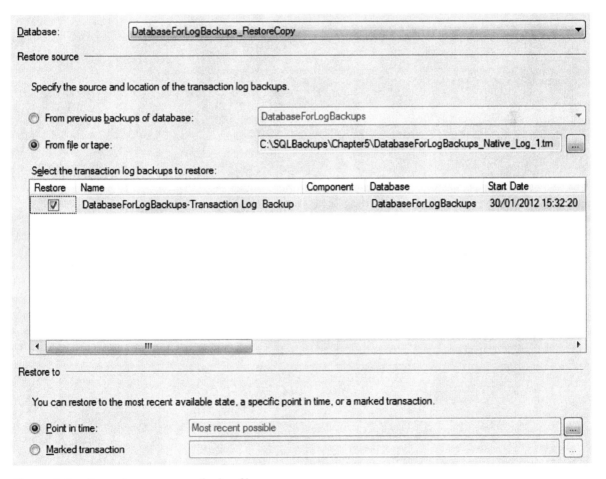

Figure 6-6: Preparing to restore the log file.

195

Now switch to the **Options** page and you should see something similar to Figure 6-7.

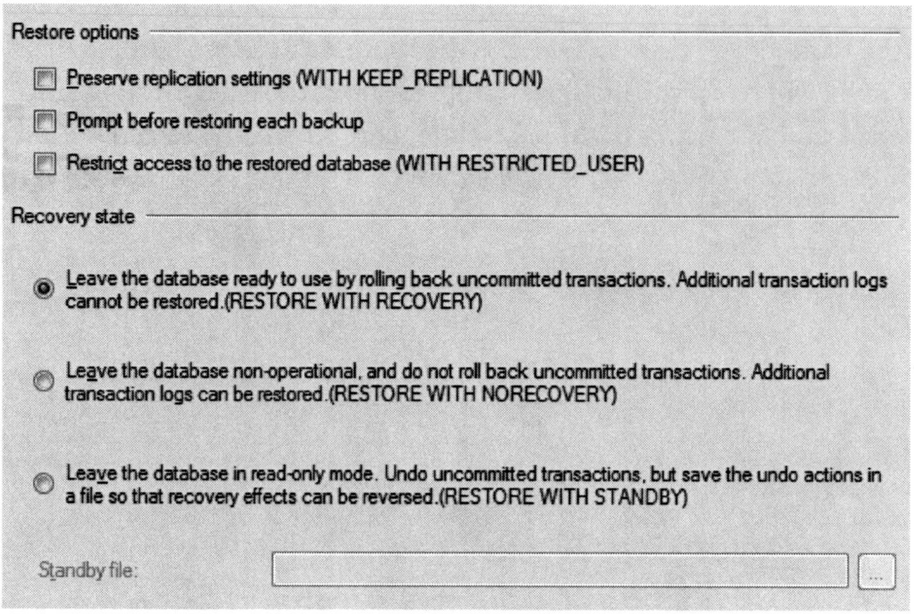

Figure 6-7: Configuring the data and log files for the target database.

This time we want to complete the restore and bring the database back online, so we can leave the default option, `RESTORE WITH RECOVERY` selected. Once you're ready, click **OK** and the log backup restore should complete and the `DatabaseForLogBackups_RestoreCopy` database should be online and usable.

As healthy, paranoid DBAs, our final job is to confirm that we have the right rows in each of our tables, which is easily accomplished using the simple script shown in Listing 6-2.

```
USE DatabaseForLogBackups_RestoreCopy
SELECT   COUNT(*) FROM    dbo.MessageTable1
SELECT   COUNT(*) FROM    dbo.MessageTable2
SELECT   COUNT(*) FROM    dbo.MessageTable3
```

Listing 6-2: Checking our row counts.

If everything ran correctly, there should be 20 rows of data in each table. We can also run a query to return the columns from each table, to make sure that the data matches what we originally inserted.

As is hopefully clear, GUI-based restores, when all the required backup files are still available in their original local disk folders, can be quick, convenient, and easy. However, if they are not, for example due to the backup files being moved, after initial backup, from local disk to network space, or after a backup has been brought back from long-term storage on tape media, then these GUI restores can be quite clunky, and the process is best accomplished by script.

T-SQL point-in-time restores

In this section, we will be performing a point-in-time restore. This operation will use all three of the backup files (one full, two log) to restore to a point in time somewhere before we finalized the last set of INSERT statements that were run against the DatabaseFor-LogBackups database.

When doing a point-in-time restore, we are merely restoring completely all of the log backup files after the full database backup, except the very last log file, where we'll stop at a certain point and, during database recovery, SQL Server will only roll forward the transactions up to that specified point. In order to restore to the right point, in this example you will need to refer back to the timestamp value you saw in the output of Listing 5-6, the third data load for the DatabaseForLogBackups database.

Hopefully, you will rarely be called upon to perform these types of restore but when you are, it's vital that you're well drilled, having practiced your restore routines many times, and confident of success, based on your backup validation techniques and random test restores.

GUI-based point-in-time restore

It's entirely possible to perform point-in-time restores via the GUI. On the **Restore Database** *page, we simply need to configure a specific date and time, in the* **To a point in time:** *option, rather than accept the default setting of* **most recent possible**. *We don't provide a full worked example in the GUI, but feel free to play around with configuring and executing these types of restore in the GUI environment.*

Don't worry; point-in-time restores are not as complicated as they may sound! To prove it, let's jump right into the script in Listing 6-3.

The overall intent of this script is to restore the `DatabaseForLogBackup` full backup file over the top of the `DatabaseForLogBackup_RestoreCopy` database, created in the previous GUI restore, apply the entire contents of the first log backup, and then the contents of the second log backup, up to the point just before we inserted 100,000 rows into `MessageTable3`.

```
USE [master]
GO

--STEP 1: Restore the full backup. Leave database in restoring state
RESTORE DATABASE [DatabaseForLogBackups_RestoreCopy]
FROM DISK = N'C:\SQLBackups\Chapter5\DatabaseForLogBackups_Native_Full.bak'
WITH FILE = 1,  MOVE N'DatabaseForLogBackups' TO N'C:\SQLData\
DatabaseForLogBackups_RestoreCopy.mdf',
MOVE N'DatabaseForLogBackups_log' TO N'C:\SQLData\DatabaseForLogBackups_
RestoreCopy_1.ldf',
NORECOVERY, STATS = 10
GO

--STEP 2: Completely restore 1st log backup. Leave database in restoring state
RESTORE LOG [DatabaseForLogBackups_RestoreCopy]
FROM DISK = N'C:\SQLBackups\Chapter5\DatabaseForLogBackups_Native_Log.trn'
WITH FILE = 1, NORECOVERY, STATS = 10
GO
```

```
--STEP 3: P-I-T restore of 2nd log backup. Recover the database
RESTORE LOG [DatabaseForLogBackups_RestoreCopy]
FROM DISK = N'C:\SQLBackups\Chapter5\DatabaseForLogBackups_Native_Log_2.trn'
WITH FILE = 1,  NOUNLOAD,  STATS = 10,
STOPAT = N'January 30, 2012 3:34 PM' , -- configure your time here
RECOVERY
GO
```

Listing 6-3: T-SQL script for a point-in-time restore of `DatabaseForLogbackups`.

The first section of the script restores the full backup file to the restore copy database. We use the MOVE parameter for each file to indicate that, rather than use the data and log files for `DatabaseForLogBackups` as the target for the restore, we should use those for a different database, in this case `DatabaseForLogBackup_RestoreCopy`. The NORECOVERY parameter indicates that we wish to leave the target database, `Database-ForLogBackup_RestoreCopy`, in a restoring state, ready to accept further log backup files. Finally, we use the REPLACE parameter, since we are overwriting the data and log files that are currently being used by the `DatabaseForLogBackup_RestoreCopy` database.

The second step of the restore script applies the first transaction log backup to the database. This is a much shorter command, mainly due to the fact that we do not have to specify a MOVE parameter for each data file, since we already specified the target data and log files for the restore, and those files will have already been placed in the correct location before this RESTORE LOG command executes. Notice that we again use the NORECOVERY parameter in order to leave the database in a non-usable state so we can move on to the next log restore and apply more transactional data.

The second and final LOG RESTORE command is where you'll spot the brand new STOPAT parameter. We supply our specific timestamp value to this parameter in order to instruct SQL Server to stop applying log records at that point. The supplied timestamp value is important since we are instructing SQL Server to restore the database to the state it was in at the point of the last committed transaction at that specific time. We need to use the date time that was output when we ran the script in Chapter 5 (Listing 5-6). In my case, the time portion of the output was 3.33 p.m.

You'll notice that in Listing 6-3 I added one minute to this time, the reason being that the time output does not include seconds, and the transactions we want to include could have committed at, for example, 2:33:45. By adding a minute to the output and rounding up to 2:34:00, we will capture all the rows we want, but not the larger set of rows that inserted next, after the delay. Note, of course, that the exact format of the timestamp, and its actual value, will be different for you!

This time, we specify the RECOVERY parameter, so that when we execute the command the database will enter recovery mode, and the database will be restored to the point of the last committed transaction at the specified timestamp. When you run Listing 6-3 as a whole, you should see output similar to that shown in Figure 6-8.

```
54 percent processed.
100 percent processed.
Processed 232 pages for database 'DatabaseForLogBackups_RestoreCopy', file
'DatabaseForLogBackups' on file 1.
Processed 5 pages for database 'DatabaseForLogBackups_RestoreCopy', file
'DatabaseForLogBackups_log' on file 1.
RESTORE DATABASE successfully processed 237 pages in 0.549 seconds (3.369 MB/sec).
100 percent processed.
Processed 0 pages for database 'DatabaseForLogBackups_RestoreCopy', file
'DatabaseForLogBackups' on file 1.
Processed 9 pages for database 'DatabaseForLogBackups_RestoreCopy', file
'DatabaseForLogBackups_log' on file 1.
RESTORE LOG successfully processed 9 pages in 0.007 seconds (9.556 MB/sec).
10 percent processed.
20 percent processed.
31 percent processed.
40 percent processed.
50 percent processed.
61 percent processed.
71 percent processed.
80 percent processed.
90 percent processed.
100 percent processed.
```

```
Processed 0 pages for database 'DatabaseForLogBackups_RestoreCopy', file
'DatabaseForLogBackups' on file 1.
Processed 7033 pages for database 'DatabaseForLogBackups_RestoreCopy', file
'DatabaseForLogBackups_log' on file 1.
RESTORE LOG successfully processed 7033 pages in 1.807 seconds (30.403 MB/sec).
```

Figure 6-8: Output from the successful point-in-time restore operation.

We see the typical percentage completion messages as well as the total restore operation metrics after each file is completed. What we might like to see in the message output, but cannot, is some indication that we performed a point-in-time restore with the STOPAT parameter. There is no obvious way to tell if we successfully did that other than to double-check our database to see if we did indeed only get part of the data changes that are stored in our second log backup file.

All we have to do is rerun Listing 6-2 and this time, if everything went as planned, we should have 1,020 rows in MessageTable1, 10,020 rows in MessageTable2, but only 20 rows in MessageTable3, since we stopped the restore just before the final 100,000 rows were added to that table.

Possible difficulties with point-in-time restores

When restoring a database in order to retrieve lost data after, for example, a rogue transaction erroneously deleted it, getting the exact time right can be the difference between stopping the restore just before the data was removed, which is obviously what we want, or going too far and restoring to the point after the data was removed.

The less sure you are of the exact time to which you need to restore, the trickier the process can become. One option, which will be demonstrated in Chapter 8, is to perform a STANDBY restore, which leaves the target database in a restoring state, but keeps it read-only accessible. In this way you can roll forward, query to see if the lost data is still there, roll forward a bit further, and so on.

Aside from third-party log readers (very few of which offer support beyond SQL Server 2005), there are a couple of undocumented and unsupported functions that can be used to interrogate the contents of log files (`fn_dblog`) and log backups (`fn_dump_dblog`). So for example, we can look at the contents of our second log backup files as shown in Listing 6-4.

```
SELECT   *
FROM     fn_dump_dblog(DEFAULT, DEFAULT, DEFAULT, DEFAULT,
         'C:\SQLBackups\Chapter5\DatabaseForLogBackups_Native_Log_2.trn',
                 DEFAULT, DEFAULT, DEFAULT, DEFAULT, DEFAULT, DEFAULT,
                 DEFAULT, DEFAULT, DEFAULT, DEFAULT, DEFAULT, DEFAULT,
                 DEFAULT, DEFAULT, DEFAULT, DEFAULT, DEFAULT, DEFAULT,
                 DEFAULT, DEFAULT, DEFAULT, DEFAULT, DEFAULT, DEFAULT,
                 DEFAULT, DEFAULT, DEFAULT, DEFAULT, DEFAULT, DEFAULT,
                 DEFAULT, DEFAULT, DEFAULT, DEFAULT, DEFAULT, DEFAULT,
                 DEFAULT, DEFAULT, DEFAULT, DEFAULT, DEFAULT, DEFAULT,
                 DEFAULT, DEFAULT, DEFAULT, DEFAULT, DEFAULT, DEFAULT,
                 DEFAULT, DEFAULT, DEFAULT, DEFAULT, DEFAULT, DEFAULT,
                 DEFAULT, DEFAULT, DEFAULT, DEFAULT, DEFAULT, DEFAULT,
                 DEFAULT, DEFAULT, DEFAULT);
```

Listing 6-4:   Exploring log backups with `fn_dump_dblog`.

It's not pretty and it's not supported (so use with caution); it accepts a whole host of parameters, the only one we've defined being the path to the log backup, and it returns a vast array of information that we're not going to begin to get into here...but, it does return the **Begin Time** for each of the transactions contained in the file, and it *may* give you some help in working out where you need to stop.

An alternative technique to point-in-time restores using `STOPAT`, is to try to work out the LSN value associated with, for example, the start of the rogue transaction that deleted your data. We're not going to walk through an LSN-based restore here, but a good explanation of some of the practicalities involved can be found here: HTTP://JANICECLEE. COM/2010/07/25/ALTERNATIVE-TO-RESTORING-TO-A-POINT-IN-TIME/.

Forcing Restore Failures for Fun

After successfully performing two restore operations, let's get some first-hand experience with failure. Understanding how SQL Server responds to certain common mistakes is a great first step to being prepared when tragedy actually strikes. Take a look at the script in Listing 6-5, a restore of a full backup over the top of an existing database, and try to predict what's going to go wrong, and why.

```
USE [master]
GO
RESTORE DATABASE [DatabaseForLogBackups_RestoreCopy]
FROM DISK = N'C:\SQLBackups\Chapter5\DatabaseForLogBackups_Native_Full.bak'
WITH FILE = 1,
MOVE N'DatabaseForLogBackups'
    TO N'C:\SQLData\DatabaseForLogBackups_RestoreCopy.mdf',
MOVE N'DatabaseForLogBackups_log'
    TO N'C:\SQLData\DatabaseForLogBackups__RestoreCopy_1.ldf',
STATS = 10, RECOVERY
GO
```

Listing 6-5: Spot the deliberate mistake, Part 1.

Do you spot the mistake? It's quite subtle, so if you don't manage to, simply run the script and examine the error message:

```
Msg 3159, Level 16, State 1, Line 1
The tail of the log for the database "DatabaseForLogBackups_RestoreCopy" has not been backed
up. Use BACKUP LOG WITH NORECOVERY to backup the log if it contains work you do not want to
lose. Use the WITH REPLACE or WITH STOPAT clause of the RESTORE statement to just overwrite
the contents of the log.
Msg 3013, Level 16, State 1, Line 1
RESTORE DATABASE is terminating abnormally.
```

The script in Listing 6-5 is identical to what we saw in Step 1 of Listing 6-3, except that here we are restoring over an existing database, and receive an error which is pretty descriptive. The problem is that we are about to overwrite the existing log file for the

`DatabaseForLogBackups_RestoreCopy` database, which is a `FULL` recovery model database, and we have not backed up the tail of the log, so we would lose any transactions that were not previously captured in a backup.

This is a very useful warning message to get in cases where we needed to perform crash recovery and had, in fact, forgotten to do a tail log backup. In such cases, we could start the restore process with the tail log backup, as shown in Listing 6-6, and then proceed.

```
USE master
GO
BACKUP LOG DatabaseForLogBackups_RestoreCopy
TO DISK = 'D:\SQLBackups\Chapter5\DatabaseForLogBackups_RestoreCopy_log_tail.trn'
WITH NORECOVERY
```

Listing 6-6: Perform a tail log backup.

In cases where we're certain that our restore operation does not require a tail log backup, we can use `WITH REPLACE` or `WITH STOPAT`. In this case, the error can be removed, without backing up the tail of the log, by adding the `WITH REPLACE` clause to Listing 6-5.

Let's take a look at a second example failure. Examine the script in Listing 6-7 and see if you can spot the problem.

```
--STEP 1: Restore the log backup
USE [master]
GO
RESTORE DATABASE [DatabaseForLogBackups_RestoreCopy]
FROM DISK = N'C:\SQLBackups\Chapter5\DatabaseForLogBackups_Native_Full.bak'
WITH FILE = 1,
MOVE N'DatabaseForLogBackups'
    TO N'C:\SQLData\DatabaseForLogBackups_RestoreCopy.mdf',
MOVE N'DatabaseForLogBackups_log'
    TO N'C:\SQLData\DatabaseForLogBackups__RestoreCopy_1.ldf',
STATS = 10, REPLACE
GO
```

```
--Step 2: Restore to the end of the first log backup
RESTORE LOG [DatabaseForLogBackups_RestoreCopy]
FROM DISK = N'C:\SQLBackups\Chapter5\DatabaseForLogBackups_Native_Log_1.trn'
WITH FILE = 1, RECOVERY, STATS = 10
GO
```

Listing 6-7: Spot the deliberate mistake, Part 2.

Look over each of the commands carefully and then execute this script; you should see results similar to those shown in Figure 6-9.

```
54 percent processed.
100 percent processed.
Processed 232 pages for database 'DatabaseForLogBackups_RestoreCopy', file
'DatabaseForLogBackups' on file 1.
Processed 5 pages for database 'DatabaseForLogBackups_RestoreCopy', file
'DatabaseForLogBackups_log' on file 1.
RESTORE DATABASE successfully processed 237 pages in 1.216 seconds (1.521 MB/sec).
Msg 3117, Level 16, State 1, Line 2
The log or differential backup cannot be restored because no files are ready to rollforward.
Msg 3013, Level 16, State 1, Line 2
RESTORE LOG is terminating abnormally.
```

Figure 6-9: Output from the (partially) failed restore.

We can see that this time the full database backup restore, over the top of the existing database, was successful (note that we remembered to use **REPLACE**). It processed all of the data in what looks to be the correct amount of time. Since that operation completed, it must be the log restore that caused the error. Let's look at the error messages in the second part of the output, which will be in red.

The first error we see in the output is the statement "*The log or differential backup cannot be restored because no files are ready to rollforward.*" What does that mean? If you didn't catch the mistake in the script, it was that we left out an important parameter in the full database restore operation. Take a look again, and you will see that we don't have the **NORECOVERY** option in the command. Therefore, the first restore command finalized the restore and placed the database in a recovered state, ready for user access (with only ten rows in each table!); no log backup files can then be applied as part of the current restore operation. Always specify NORECOVERY if you need to continue further with a log backup restore operation.

Of course, there are many other possible errors that can arise if you're not fully paying attention during the restore process, and we can't cover them all. However, as one final example, take a look at Listing 6-8 and see if you can spot the problem.

```
USE [master]
GO
RESTORE DATABASE [DatabaseForLogBackups_RestoreCopy]
FROM DISK = N'C:\SQLBackups\Chapter5\DatabaseForLogBackups_Native_Full.bak'
WITH FILE = 1,
MOVE N'DatabaseForLogBackups'
    TO N'C:\SQLData\DatabaseForLogBackups_RestoreCopy.mdf',
MOVE N'DatabaseForLogBackups_log'
    TO N'C:\SQLData\DatabaseForLogBackups__RestoreCopy_1.ldf',
NORECOVERY, STATS = 10, REPLACE
GO

RESTORE LOG [DatabaseForLogBackups]
FROM DISK = N'C:\SQLBackups\Chapter5\DatabaseForLogBackups_Native_Log_2.trn'
WITH FILE = 1, NORECOVERY, STATS = 10
GO

RESTORE LOG [DatabaseForLogBackups]
FROM DISK = N'C:\SQLBackups\Chapter5\DatabaseForLogBackups_Native_Log_1.trn'
WITH FILE = 1, RECOVERY, STATS = 10
GO
```

Listing 6-8: Forcing one more fun failure.

Did you catch the problem before you ran the script? If not, take a look at your output, examine the error message you get when the first log file restore is attempted. I'm sure you'll be able to figure out what's wrong in short order!

Summary

After reading and working through this chapter, you should also be fairly comfortable with the basics of log restore operations, and in particular with point-in-time restores. The key to successful restores is to be well organized and well drilled. You should know exactly where the required backup files are stored; you should have confidence the operation will succeed, based on your backup validations, and regular, random "spot-check" restores.

You may be under pressure to retrieve critical lost data, or bring a stricken database back online, as quickly as possible, but it's vital not to rush or panic. Proceed carefully and methodically, and your chances of success are high.

Chapter 7: Differential Backup and Restore

A differential database backup in SQL Server is simply a copy of every page that has had a change made to it since the last full backup was taken. We capture, in a differential backup file, the changed data pages then, during a restore process, apply that differential backup to the last full backup, also known as the base backup, in order to roll the database forward to the state in which it existed at the point the differential backup was taken.

In my experience, opinion is somewhat split within the DBA community as to the value of differential database backups. Some DBAs seem to regard this third type of backup as an unnecessary complication and prefer, where possible, to restrict their backup strategy to two types of backup: full and log. Others, however, find them to be a necessity, and a useful way of reducing the time required to take backups, space required to store local backup files, and the number of log files that may need to be applied during a point-in-time restore. My opinion is that differential backups, used correctly and in the right situations, are a key recovery option in your environment.

The basic structure of this chapter will be familiar, so we'll be moving at a quicker pace; after discussing why and when differential backups can form a useful part of your backup and restore strategy, and some pros and cons in their use, we'll walk through examples of taking and then restoring native differential backups, using the SSMS GUI and T-SQL, gathering metrics as we go. Finally, we'll take a look a few common errors that can arise when taking and restoring differential backups.

Differential Backups, Overview

As noted in the introduction, a differential database backup is a copy of every page that has changed since the *last full backup*. The last part of that sentence is worth stressing. It is not possible to take a differential database backup without first taking a full database backup, known as the **base backup**. Whenever a new full backup is taken, SQL Server will clear any markers in its internal tracking mechanism, which are stored to determine which data pages changed since the last full backup, and so would need to be included in any differential backup. Therefore, each new full backup becomes the base backup for any subsequent differential backups. If we lose a full backup, or it becomes corrupted, any differential backups that rely on that base will be unusable.

This is the significant difference in the relationship between a differential backup and its associated full backup, and the relationship between log backups and their associated full backup. While we always restore a full backup before any log backups, the log backups are not inextricably linked to any single full backup; if a full backup file goes missing, we can still go back to a previous full backup and restore the full chain of log files, since every log backup contains all the log that was entered since the last **log** backup. A full backup resets the log chain, so that we have all the needed information to begin applying subsequent log backups, but doesn't break the chain. A differential backup always contains all changes since the last full backup, and so is tied to one specific full backup.

Because the data changes in any differential backup are cumulative since the base backup, if we take one full backup followed by two differential backups then, during a restore process where we wish to return the database to a state as close as possible to that it was in at the time of the disaster, we only need to restore the full backup and the single, most recent differential backup (plus any subsequent transaction log backups).

Advantages of differential backups

Perhaps the first question to answer is why we would want to capture only the changed data in a backup; why not just take another full backup? The answer is simple: backup time and backup file space utilization. A full database backup process, for a large database, will be a time- and resource-consuming process, and it is usually not feasible to run this process during normal operational hours, due to the detrimental impact it could have on the performance of end-user and business processes. In most cases, a differential database backup will contain much less data, and require much less processing time than a full database backup. For a large database that is not subject to a huge number of changes, a differential backup can execute in 10% of the time it would take for a full backup.

For a real-world example, let's consider one of my moderately-sized production databases. The processing time for a full database backup is usually about 55 minutes. However, the average differential backup takes only about 4 minutes to complete. This is great, since I still have a complete set of backups for recovery, but the processing time is greatly reduced. Remember that the larger a database, the more CPU will be consumed by the backup operation, the longer the backup operation will take, and the greater the risk will be of some failure (e.g. network) occurring during that operation.

The other saving that we get with a differential backup, over a full backup, is the space saving. We are only storing the data pages that have been modified since the last full backup. This is typically a small fraction of the total size, and that will be reflected in the size of the differential backup file on disk. As such, a backup strategy that consists of, say, one daily full backup plus a differential backup, is going to consume less disk space than an equivalent strategy consisting of two full backups.

> **Will differential backups always be smaller than full backups?**
>
> *For the most part, if you refresh your base backup on a regular schedule, you will find that a differential backup should be smaller in size than a full database backup. However, there are situations where a differential backup could become even larger than its corresponding base backup, for example if the base backup is not refreshed for a long period and during that time a large amount of data has been changed or added. We'll discuss this further shortly, in the "Possible issues with differential backups" section.*

Let's assume that the same moderately-sized production database, mentioned above, has a backup strategy consisting of a weekly full backup, hourly transaction log backups and daily differential backups. I need to retain on disk, locally, the backups required to restore the database to any point in the last three days, so that means storing locally the last three differential backups, the last three days' transaction log backups, plus the base full backup. The full backup size is about 22 GB, the log backups are, on average, about 3 GB each, and 3 days' worth of differential backups takes up another 3 GB, giving a total of about 28 GB. If I simply took full backups and log backups, I'd need almost 70 GB of space at any time for one database.

Deciding exactly the right backup strategy for a database is a complex process. We want to strive as far as possible for simplicity, short backup times, and smaller disk space requirements, but at the same time we should never allow such goals to compromise the overall quality and reliability of our backup regime.

Differential backup strategies

In what situations can the addition of differential backups really benefit the overall database recovery scheme? Are there any other cases where they might be useful?

Reduced recovery times

The number one reason that most DBAs and organizations take differential backups is as a way of reducing the number of log files that would need to be restored in the case of an emergency thus, potentially, simplifying any restore process. For example, say we had a backup strategy consisting of a nightly full backup, at 2 a.m., and then hourly log backups. If a disaster occurred at 6.15 p.m., we'd need to restore 17 backup files (1 full backup and 16 log backups), plus the tail log backup, as shown in Figure 7-1.

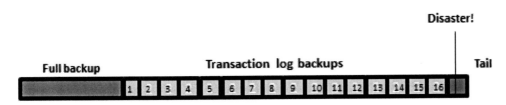

Figure 7-1: A long chain of transaction log backups.

This is a somewhat dangerous situation since, as we have discussed, the more backup files we have to take, store, and manage the greater the chance of one of those files being unusable. This can occur for reasons from disk corruption to backup failure. Also, if any of these transaction log backup files is not usable, we cannot restore past that point in the database's history.

If, instead, our strategy included an additional differential backup at midday each day, then we'd only need to restore eight files: the full backup, the differential backup, and six transaction log backups (11–16), plus a tail log backup, as shown in Figure 7-2. We would also be safe in the event of a corrupted differential backup, because we would still have all of the log backups since the full backup was taken.

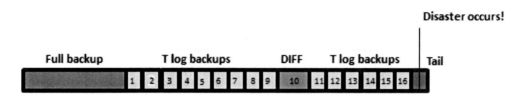

Figure 7-2: Using a differential backup can shorten the number of backup files to restore.

In any situation that requires a quick turnaround time for restoration, a differential backup is our friend. The more files there are to process, the more time it will also take to set up the restore scripts, and the more files we have to work with, the more complex will be the restore operation, and so (potentially) the longer the database will be down.

In this particular situation, the savings might not be too dramatic, but for mission-critical systems, transaction logs can be taken every 15 minutes. If we're able to take one or two differential backups during the day, it can cut down dramatically the number of files involved in any restore process.

Consider, also, the case of a VLDB where full backups take over 15 hours and so nightly full backups cannot be supported. The agreed restore strategy must support a maximum data loss of one hour, so management has decided that weekly full backups, taken on Sunday, will be supplemented with transaction log backups taken every hour during the day. Everything is running fine until one Friday evening the disk subsystem goes out on that machine and renders the database lost and unrecoverable. We are now going to have to restore the large full backup from the previous Sunday, plus well over 100 transaction log files. This is a tedious and long process.

Fortunately, we now know of a better way to get this done, saving a lot of time and without sacrificing too much extra disk space: we take differential database backups each night except Sunday as a supplemental backup to the weekly full one. Now, we'd only need to restore the full, differential and around 20 log backups.

Database migrations

In Chapters 3 and 5, we discussed the role of full and log backups in database migrations in various scenarios. Differential restores give us another great way to perform this common task and can save a lot of time when the final database move takes place.

Imagine, in this example, that we are moving a large database, operating in SIMPLE recovery model, from Server A to Server B, using full backups. We obviously don't want to lose any data during the transition, so we kill any connections to the database and place it into single-user mode before we take the backup. We then start our backup, knowing full well that no new changes can be made to our database or data. After completion, we take the source database offline and begin the restore the database to Server B. The whole process takes 12 hours, during which time our database is down and whatever front-end application it is that uses that database is also offline. No one is happy about this length of down-time. What could we do to speed the process up a bit?

A better approach would be to incorporate differential database backups. 16 hours before the planned migration (allowing a few hours' leeway on the 12 hours needed to perform the full backup and restore), we take a full database backup, not kicking out any users and so not worrying about any subsequent changes made to the database. We restore to Server B the full database backup, using the NORECOVERY option, to leave the database in a state where we can apply more backup files.

Once the time has come to migrate the source database in its final state, we kill any connections, place it in single-user mode and perform a differential backup. We have also been very careful not to allow any other full backups to happen via scheduled jobs or other DBA activity. This is important, so that we don't alter the base backup for our newly created differential backup.

Taking the differential backup is a fast process (10–15 minutes), and the resulting backup file is small, since it only holds data changes made in the last 12 to 16 hours. Once the backup has completed, we take the source database offline and immediately start the differential restore on the target server, which also takes only 10–15 minutes to complete, and we are back online and running.

We have successfully completed the migration, and the down-time has decreased from a miserable 12 hours to a scant 30 minutes. There is a bit more preparation work to be done using this method, but the results are the same and the uptime of the application doesn't need to take a significant hit.

Possible issues with differential backups

In most cases in my experience, the potential issues or downsides regarding differential backups are just minor inconveniences, rather than deal breakers, and usually do not outweigh the savings in disk space usage and backup time, especially for larger databases.

Invalid base backup

The biggest risk with differential backups is that we come to perform a restore, and find ourselves in a situation where our differential backup file doesn't match up to the base backup file we have ready (we'll see this in action later). This happens when a full backup is taken of which we are unaware. Full database backups are taken for many reasons outside of your nightly backup jobs. If, for example, someone takes a full backup in order to restore it to another system, and then deletes that file after they are done, our next differential is not going to be of much use, since it is using that deleted file as its base.

The way to avoid this situation is to ensure that any database backups that are taken for purposes other than disaster recovery are **copy-only backups**. In terms of the data it contains and the manner in which it is restored, a copy-only backup is just like a normal full backup. However, the big difference is that, unlike a regular full backup, with a copy-only backup, SQL Server's internal mechanism for tracking data pages changed since the last full backup is left untouched and so the core backup strategy is unaffected.

However, if this sort of disaster does strike, all we can do is look through the system tables in MSDB to identify the new base full backup file and hope that it will still be on disk or tape and so can be retrieved for use in your restore operation. If it is not, we are out of luck in terms of restoring the differential file. We would need to switch to using the last full backup and subsequent transaction log backups, assuming that you were taking log backups of that database. Otherwise, our only course of action would be to use the last available full database backup.

Bottom line: make sure that a) only those people who need to take backups have the permissions granted to do so, and b) your DBA team and certain administrative users know how and when to use a copy-only backup operation.

Missing or corrupt base backup

Without a base full backup, there is no way to recover any subsequent differential backup files. If we need a base backup that has been archived to offsite tape storage, then there may be a significant delay in starting the restore process. We can prevent this from happening by making sure the mechanism of backup file cleanup leaves those base files on disk until a new one is created. I keep weekly base backups in a specially-named folder that isn't touched for seven days, so that I know the files will be available in that time span.

If a base backup simply goes missing from your local file system, this is an issue that needs careful investigation. Only the DBA team and the Server Administration team should have access to the backup files and they should know much better than to delete files without good cause or reason.

Finally, there is no getting around the fact that every restore operation that involves a differential backup will involve a minimum of two files (the base full and the differential) rather than one. Let's say, just for the sake of illustration, that your SLA dictates a maximum of 12 hours' data loss, so you take backups at midnight and midday. If we only take full backups, then we'll only ever need to restore one full backup file; if our midday backup is a differential, then we'll always need to restore the midnight full, followed by the midday differential. In the event of corruption or loss of a single backup file, the maximum exposure to data loss, in either case, is 24 hours.

This really is a small risk to take for the great rewards of having differential backups in your rotation. I have taken many thousands of database backups and restored thousands of files as well. I have only run into corrupt files a few times and they were never caused by SQL Server's backup routines.

To help alleviate this concern, we should do two things. Firstly, always make sure backups are being written to some sort of robust storage solution. We discussed this in Chapter 2, but I can't stress enough how important it is to have backup files stored on a redundant SAN or NAS system. These types of systems can cut the risk of physical disk corruptions down to almost nothing.

Secondly, as discussed in Chapter 4, we should also perform spot-check restores of files. I like to perform at least one randomly-chosen test restore per week. This gives me even more confidence that my backup files are in good shape without having to perform CHECKSUM tests on each and every backup file.

Infrequent base refresh and/or frequently updated databases

The next possible issue regards the management and timing of the full base backup. If the base backup isn't refreshed regularly, typically on a weekly basis, the differentials will start to take longer to process. If a database is subject to very frequent modification, then differential backups get bigger and more resource-intensive and the benefits of differential over full, in terms of storage space and backup time reduction, will become more marginal. Ultimately, if we aren't refreshing the base backup regularly then the benefits obtained from differentials may not justify the complicating factor of an additional backup type to manage.

Differentials in the backup and restore SLA

So what does all this mean with regard to how differential backups fit into our overall Backup SLA? My personal recommendation is to use differential backups as part of your backup regimen on a SQL Server as often as possible. In the previous sections, we've discussed their reduced file size and faster backup times, compared to taking an additional full backup and the benefits that can bring, especially for large databases. We've also seen how they can be used to reduce the number of transaction log files that need to be processed during point-in-time restores.

For some VLDBs, differential backups may be a necessity. I manage several databases that take 12 or more hours to have a full backup and, in these cases, nightly full backups would place undue strain not only on the SQL Server itself but the underlying file system. I would be wasting CPU, disk I/O and precious disk space every night. Performing a weekly full database backup and nightly differential backups has very little negative impact on our recoverability, compared to nightly full backups, and any concerns in this regard shouldn't stop you from implementing them.

Nevertheless, some database owners and application managers feel skittish about relying on differential backups in the case of a recovery situation, and you may get some push back. They may feel that you are less protected by not taking a full backup each night and only recording the changes that have been made. This is normal and you can easily calm their nerves by explaining exactly how this type of backup works, and how any risks can be mitigated.

Preparing for Differential Backups

Before we get started taking differential backups, we need to do a bit of preparatory work, namely choosing an appropriate recovery model for our database, creating that database along with some populated sample tables, and then taking the base full backup for that database. I could have used the sample database from Chapter 3, plus the latest full backup from that chapter as the base, but I decided to make it easier for people who, for whatever reason, skipped straight to this chapter. Since we've been through this process several times now, the scripts will be presented more or less without commentary; refer back to Chapters 3 and 5 if you need further explanation of any of the techniques.

Recovery model

There are no recovery model limitations for differential backups; with the exception of the `master` database, we can take a differential backup of any database in any recovery model. The only type of backup that is valid for the `master` database is a full backup.

For our example database in this chapter, we're going to assume that, in our Backup SLA, we have a maximum tolerance of 24 hours' potential data loss. However, unlike in Chapter 3, this time, we'll satisfy this requirement using a weekly full backup and nightly differential backups.

Since we don't need to perform log backups, it makes sense, for ease of log management, to operate the database in `SIMPLE` recovery model.

Sample database and tables plus initial data load

Listing 7-1 shows the script to create the sample `DatabaseForDiffBackups` database, plus a very simple table (`MessageTable`), and then load it with an initial 100,000 rows of data. When creating the database, we place the data and log file in a specific, non-default folder, **C:\SQLData**, and set appropriate initial size and growth characteristics for these files. We also set the database recovery model to `SIMPLE`. Feel free to modify the data and log file paths if you need to place them elsewhere on your server.

```
USE [master]
GO
CREATE DATABASE [DatabaseForDiffBackups] ON PRIMARY
(    NAME = N'DatabaseForDiffBackups'
   , FILENAME = N'C:\SQLData\DatabaseForDiffBackups.mdf'
   , SIZE = 102400KB , FILEGROWTH = 10240KB ) LOG ON
(    NAME = N'DatabaseForDiffBackups_log'
   , FILENAME = N'C:\SQLData\DatabaseForDiffBackups_log.ldf'
   , SIZE = 51200KB , FILEGROWTH = 10240KB )
GO
ALTER DATABASE [DatabaseForDiffBackups] SET RECOVERY SIMPLE
GO

USE [DatabaseForDiffBackups]
GO

CREATE TABLE [dbo].[MessageTable]
    (
       [Message] [nvarchar](100) NOT NULL
    )
ON  [PRIMARY]
GO

INSERT  INTO MessageTable
VALUES  ( 'Initial Data Load: This is the first set of data we are populating the table with' )
GO 100000
```

Listing 7-1:   `DatabaseForDiffBackups` database, `MessageTable` table, initial
data load (100,000 rows).

Base backup

As discussed earlier, just as we can't take log backups without first taking a full backup of a database, so we also can't take a differential backup without taking a full base backup. Any differential backup is useless without a base. Listing 7-2 performs the base full backup for our `DatabaseForDiffBackups` database and stores it in the **C:\SQLBackups\Chapter7** folder. Again, feel free to modify this path as appropriate f or your system.

```
USE [master]
GO


BACKUP DATABASE [DatabaseForDiffBackups]
TO DISK = N'C:\SQLBackups\Chapter7\DatabaseForDiffBackups_Full_Native.bak'
WITH NAME = N'DatabaseForDiffBackups-Full Database Backup', STATS = 10
GO
```

Listing 7-2: Base full backup for `DatabaseForDiffBackups`.

We are not going to worry about the execution time for this full backup, so once the backup has completed successfully, you can close this script without worrying about the output. However, we will take a look at the backup size though, which should come out to just over 20 MB. We can take a look at how our differential backup file sizes compare, as we pump more data into the database.

Taking Differential Backups

As per our usual scheme, we're going to demonstrate how to take differential backups the "GUI way," in SSMS, and by using native T-SQL Backup commands. In Chapter 8, you'll see how to perform differential backups, as part of a complete and scheduled backup routine using the Red Gate SQL Backup tool.

Before taking the first differential backup, we'll INSERT 10,000 more rows into MessageTable, as shown in Listing 7-3. This is typical of the type of load that we would typically find in a differential backup.

```
USE [DatabaseForDiffBackups]
GO

INSERT  INTO MessageTable
VALUES  ( 'Second Data Load: This is the second set of data we are populating the table with' )
GO 10000
```

Listing 7-3: Second data load (10,000 rows) for MessageTable.

Native GUI differential backup

We are now ready to take our first differential database backup, via the SSMS GUI backup configuration tool; this should all be very familiar to you by now if you worked through previous chapters, so we're going to move fast!

In SSMS, right-click on the **DatabaseForDiffBackups** database, and navigate **Tasks | Backup...** to reach the familiar Backup Database configuration screen. In the **Source** section, double-check that the correct database is selected (a good DBA always double-checks) and then change the **Backup type** to **Differential**.

Leave the **Backup set** section as-is, and move on to the **Destination** section. Remove the default backup file (which would append our differential backup to the base full backup file) and add a new destination file at **C:\SQLBackups\Chapter7**, called DatabaseForDiffBackups_Diff_Native_1.bak. The screen will look as shown in Figure 7-3.

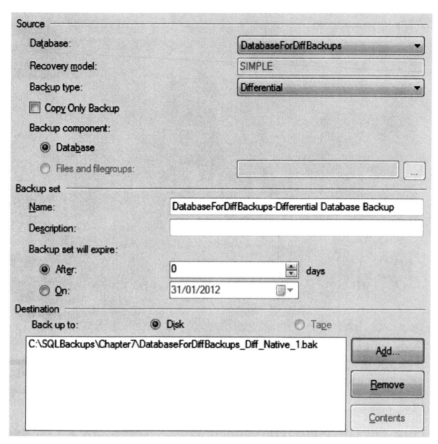

Figure 7-3: Native GUI differential backup configuration.

There's nothing to change on the **Options** page, so we're done. Click **OK** and the differential backup will be performed.

Figure 7-4 summarizes the storage requirements and execution time metrics for our first differential backup. The execution time was obtained by scripting out the equivalent BACKUP command and running the T-SQL, as described in Chapter 3. The alternative method, querying the backupset table in msdb (see Listing 3-5), does not provide sufficient granularity for a backup that ran in under a second.

Differential Backup Name	Number of Rows	Execution Time	Storage Required
DatabaseForDiffBackups_Diff_ Native_1.bak	10000	0.311 Seconds	3.16 MB

Figure 7-4: Differential backup statistics, Part 1.

Native T-SQL differential backup

We are now going to take our second native differential backup using T-SQL code. First, however, let's INSERT a substantial new data load of 100,000 rows into MessageTable, as shown in Listing 7-4.

```
USE [DatabaseForDiffBackups]
GO

INSERT  INTO MessageTable
VALUES  ( 'Third Data Load: This is the third set of data we are populating the table with' )
GO 100000
```

Listing 7-4: Third data load (100,000 rows) for MessageTable.

We're now ready to perform our second differential backup, and Listing 7-5 shows the code to do it. If you compare this script to the one for our base full backup (Listing 7-2), you'll see they are almost identical in structure, with the exception of the WITH DIFFERENTIAL argument that we use in Listing 7-5 to let SQL Server know that we are not going to be taking a full backup, but instead a differential backup of the changes made since the last full backup was taken. Double-check that the path to the backup file is correct, and then execute the script.

```
USE [master]
GO


BACKUP DATABASE [DatabaseForDiffBackups]
TO DISK = N'C:\SQLBackups\Chapter7\DatabaseForDiffBackups_Diff_Native_2.bak'
WITH DIFFERENTIAL,
    NAME = N'DatabaseForDiffBackups-Differential Database Backup',
STATS = 10
GO
```

Listing 7-5:   Native T-SQL differential backup for `DatabaseForDiffBackups`.

Having run the command, you should see results similar to those shown in Figure 7-5.

```
Messages
 12 percent processed.
 22 percent processed.
 32 percent processed.
 42 percent processed.
 52 percent processed.
 62 percent processed.
 72 percent processed.
 82 percent processed.
 92 percent processed.
 Processed 2560 pages for database 'DatabaseForDiffBackups', file 'DatabaseForDiffBackups' on file 1.
 100 percent processed.
 Processed 1 pages for database 'DatabaseForDiffBackups', file 'DatabaseForDiffBackups_log' on file 1.
 BACKUP DATABASE WITH DIFFERENTIAL successfully processed 2561 pages in 1.569 seconds (12.748 MB/sec).
```

Figure 7-5:   Native differential T-SQL backup script message output.

Figure 7-6 summarizes the storage requirements and execution time metrics for our second differential backup, compared to the first differential backup.

Differential Backup Name	Number of Rows	Execution Time (S)	Storage Required (MB)
DatabaseForDiffBackups_Diff_Native_1.bak	10000	0.31	3.2
DatabaseForDiffBackups_Diff_Native_2.bak	110000	1.57	20.6

Figure 7-6: Differential backup statistics, Part 2.

So, compared to the first differential backup, the second one contains 11 times more rows, took about five times longer to execute, and takes up over six times more space. This all seems to make sense; don't forget that backup times and sizes don't grow linearly based on the number of records, since every backup includes in it, besides data, headers, backup information, database information, and other structures.

Compressed differential backups

By way of comparison, I reran the second differential backup timings, but this time using backup compression. Just as for full backups, the only change we need to make to our backup script is to add the COMPRESSION keyword, which will ensure the backup is compressed regardless of the server's default setting. Remember, this example will only work if you are using SQL Server 2008 R2 or above, or the Enterprise edition of SQL Server 2008.

Note that, if you want to follow along, you'll need to restore full and first differential backups over the top of the existing DatabaseForDiffBackups database, and then rerun the third data load (alternatively, you could start again from scratch).

```
USE [master]
GO


BACKUP DATABASE [DatabaseForDiffBackups]
TO DISK = N'C:\SQLBackups\Chapter7\DatabaseForDiffBackups_Diff_Native_Compressed.bak'
WITH NAME = N'DatabaseForDiffBackups-Diff Database Backup', STATS = 10, COMPRESSION
GO
```

Listing 7-6: Compressed differential backup.

In my test, the compressed backup offered very little advantage in terms of execution time, but substantial savings in disk space, as shown in Figure 7-7.

Differential Backup Name	Number of Rows	Execution Time (S)	Storage Required (MB)
DatabaseForDiffBackups_Diff_Native_1. bak	10000	0.31	3.2
DatabaseForDiffBackups_Diff_Native_2. bak	110000	1.57	20.6
DatabaseForDiffBackups_Diff_Native_ Compressed.bak	110000	1.43	0.5

Figure 7-7: Differential backup statistics, Part 3.

Performing Differential Backup Restores

We are now ready to perform a RESTORE on each of our differential backup files, once using the SSMS GUI, and once using a T-SQL script.

Native GUI differential restore

We are going to restore our first differential backup file (_Diff_Native_1.bak) for the DatabaseForDiffBackups database, over the top of the existing database. If you have already removed this database, don't worry; as long as you've still got the backup files, it will not affect the example in this section.

In SSMS, right-click on the DatabaseForDiffBackups database, and navigate **Tasks | Restore | Database** to reach the **General** page of the **Restore Database** configuration screen, shown in Figure 7-8.

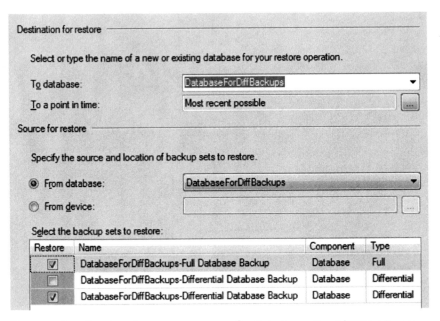

Figure 7-8: Starting the restore process for DatabaseForDiffBackups.

Notice that the base full backup, and the second differential backups have been auto-selected as the backups to restore. Remember that, to return the database to the most recent state possible, we only have to restore the base, plus the most recent differential; we do not have to restore both differentials. However, in this example we do want to restore the first rather than the second differential backup, so deselect the second differential in the list in favor of the first.

Now, click over to the **Options** screen; in the **Restore options** section, select **Overwrite the existing database**. That done, you're ready to go; click **OK**, and the base full backup will be restored, followed by the first differential backup.

Let's query our newly restored database in order to confirm that it worked as expected; if so, we should see a count of 100,000 rows with a message of **Initial Data Load...**, and 10,000 rows with a message of **Second Data Load...**, as confirmed by the output of Listing 7-7 (the message text is cropped for formatting purposes).

```
USE [DatabaseForDiffBackups]
GO

SELECT   Message ,
         COUNT(Message) AS Row_Count
FROM     MessageTable
GROUP BY Message
```

```
Message                                         Row_Count
-----------------------------------------------------------
Initial Data Load: This is the first set of data…    100000
Second Data Load: This is the second set of data…    10000

(2 row(s) affected)
```

Listing 7-7: Query to confirm that the differential restore worked as expected.

Native T-SQL differential restore

We're now going to perform a second differential restore, this time using T-SQL scripts. While we could perform this operation in a single script, we're going to split it out into two scripts so that we can see, more clearly than we could during the GUI restore, the exact steps of the process. Once again, our restore will overwrite the existing DatabaseForDiffBackups database. The first step will restore the base backup, containing 100,000 rows, and leave the database in a "restoring" state. The second step will restore the second differential backup file (_Diff_Native_2.bak), containing all the rows changed or added since the base backup (10,000 rows from the second data load and another 100,000 from the third), and then recover the database, returning it to a usable state.

Without further ado, let's restore the base backup file, using the script in Listing 7-8.

```
USE [master]
GO


RESTORE DATABASE [DatabaseForDiffBackups]
FROM DISK = N'C:\SQLBackups\Chapter7\DatabaseForDiffBackups_Full_Native.bak'
WITH  NORECOVERY,  STATS = 10
GO
```

Listing 7-8: Base full database backup restore.

Notice the **WITH NORECOVERY** argument, meaning that we wish to leave the database in a restoring state, ready to receive further backup files. Also note that we did not specify **REPLACE** since it is not needed here, since **DatabaseForDiffBackups** is a **SIMPLE** recovery model database.

Having executed the script, refresh your object explorer window and you should see that the **DatabaseForDiffBackups** database now displays a **Restoring...** message, as shown in Figure 7-9.

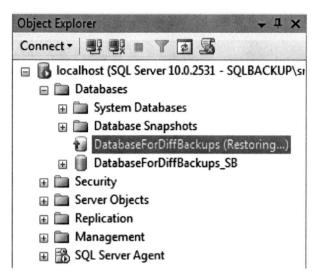

Figure 7-9: The `DatabaseForDiffBackups` database in restoring mode.

We're now ready to run the second **RESTORE** command, shown in Listing 7-9, to get back all the data in the second differential backup (*i.e.* all data that has changed since the base full backup was taken) and bring our database back online.

```
USE [master]
GO


RESTORE DATABASE [DatabaseForDiffBackups]
FROM DISK = N'C:\SQLBackups\Chapter7\DatabaseForDiffBackups_Diff_Native_2.bak'
WITH STATS = 10
GO
```

Listing 7-9: Native T-SQL differential restore.

We don't explicitly state the **WITH RECOVERY** option here, since **RECOVERY** is the default action. By leaving it out of our differential restore we let SQL Server know to recover the database for regular use.

Once this command has successfully completed, our database will be returned to the state it was in at the time we started the second differential backup. As noted earlier, this is actually no reason, other than a desire here to show each step, to run Listings 7-8 and 7-9 separately. We can simply combine them and complete the restores process in a single script. Give it a try, and you should see a **Messages** output screen similar to that shown in Figure 7-10.

```
Messages
10 percent processed.
20 percent processed.
31 percent processed.
41 percent processed.
52 percent processed.
62 percent processed.
72 percent processed.
83 percent processed.
93 percent processed.
100 percent processed.
Processed 2456 pages for database 'DatabaseForDiffBackups', file 'DatabaseForDiffBackups' on file 1.
Processed 2 pages for database 'DatabaseForDiffBackups', file 'DatabaseForDiffBackups_log' on file 1.
RESTORE DATABASE successfully processed 2458 pages in 3.947 seconds (4.863 MB/sec).
14 percent processed.
24 percent processed.
34 percent processed.
44 percent processed.
54 percent processed.
64 percent processed.
74 percent processed.
84 percent processed.
94 percent processed.
100 percent processed.
Processed 2560 pages for database 'DatabaseForDiffBackups', file 'DatabaseForDiffBackups' on file 1.
Processed 1 pages for database 'DatabaseForDiffBackups', file 'DatabaseForDiffBackups_log' on file 1.
RESTORE DATABASE successfully processed 2561 pages in 3.264 seconds (6.128 MB/sec).
```

Figure 7-10: Native differential restore results.

Remember that the differential backup file contained slightly more data than the base full backup, so it makes sense that a few more pages are processed in the second **RESTORE**. The faster backup time for the differential backup compared to the base full backup, even though the former had more data to process, can be explained by the higher overhead attached to a full restore; it must prepare the data and log files and create the space for the restore to take place, whereas the subsequent differential restore only needs to make sure there is room to restore, and start restoring data.

Everything looks good, but let's put on our "paranoid DBA" hat and double-check. Rerunning Listing 7-7 should result in the output shown in Figure 7-11.

	Message	Row_Count
1	Initial Data Load: This is the first set of data we are populating the table with	100000
2	Second Data Load: This is the second set of data we are populating the table with	10000
3	Third Data Load: This is the last set of data we are populating the table with	100000

Figure 7-11: Data verification results from native T-SQL differential restore.

Restoring compressed differential backups

Listing 7-10 shows the script to perform the same overall restore process as the previous section, but using the compressed differential backup file.

```
USE [master]
GO


RESTORE DATABASE [DatabaseForDiffBackups]
FROM DISK='C:\SQLBackups\Chapter7\DatabaseForDiffBackups_Full_Native.bak'
WITH NORECOVERY
GO

RESTORE DATABASE [DatabaseForDiffBackups]
FROM DISK='C:\SQLBackups\Chapter7\DatabaseForDiffBackups_Diff_Native_Compressed.bak'
WITH RECOVERY
GO
```

Listing 7-10: Restoring a compressed native differential backup.

As you can see, it's no different than a normal differential restore. You don't have to include any special options to let SQL Server know the backup is compressed. That information is stored in the backup file headers, and SQL Server will know how to handle the compressed data without any special instructions from you in the script!

You will undoubtedly see that the restore took just a bit longer that the uncompressed backup would take to restore. This is simply because more work is going on to decompress the data and it, and that extra step, cost CPU time, just as an encrypted backup file would also take slightly longer to restore.

Forcing Failures for Fun

Having scored several notable victories with our differential backup and restore processes, it's time to taste the bitter pill of defeat. Think of it as character building; it will toughen you up for when similar errors occur in the real world! We'll start with a possible error that could occur during the backup part of the process, and then look at a couple of possible errors that could plague your restore process.

Missing the base

Go ahead and run the script in Listing 7-11. It creates a brand new database, then attempts to take a differential backup of that database.

```
USE [master]
GO

CREATE DATABASE [ForcingFailures] ON PRIMARY
( NAME = N'ForcingFailures', FILENAME = N'C:\SQLDATA\ForcingFailures.mdf',
   SIZE = 5120KB , FILEGROWTH = 1024KB ) LOG ON
( NAME = N'ForcingFailures_log', FILENAME = N'C:\SQLDATA\ForcingFailures_log.ldf',
   SIZE = 1024KB , FILEGROWTH = 10%)
GO
```

```
BACKUP DATABASE [ForcingFailures]
TO DISK = N'C:\SQLBackups\Chapter7\ForcingFailures_Diff.bak'
WITH DIFFERENTIAL, STATS = 10
GO
```

Listing 7-11: A doomed differential backup.

If you hadn't already guessed why this won't work, the error message below will leave you in no doubt.

```
Msg 3035, Level 16, State 1, Line 2
Cannot perform a differential backup for database "ForcingFailures", because a current
database backup does not exist. Perform a full database backup by reissuing BACKUP DATABASE,
omitting the WITH DIFFERENTIAL option.
Msg 3013, Level 16, State 1, Line 2
BACKUP DATABASE is terminating abnormally.
```

We can't take a differential backup of this database without first taking a full database backup as the base from which to track subsequent changes!

Running to the wrong base

Let's perform that missing full base backup of our ForcingFailures database, as shown in Listing 7-12.

```
USE [master]
GO
BACKUP DATABASE [ForcingFailures]
TO DISK = N'C:\SQLBackups\Chapter7\ForcingFailures_Full.bak'
WITH STATS = 10
GO
```

Listing 7-12: Base full backup for ForcingFailures database.

We are now fully prepared for some subsequent differential backups. However, unbeknown to us, someone sneaks in and performs a second full backup of the database, in order to restore it to a development server.

```
USE [master]
GO
BACKUP DATABASE [ForcingFailures]
TO DISK = N'C:\SQLBackups\ForcingFailures_DEV_Full.bak'
WITH STATS = 10
GO
```

Listing 7-13: A rogue full backup of the ForcingFailures database.

Back on our production system, we perform a differential backup.

```
USE [master]
GO
BACKUP DATABASE [ForcingFailures]
TO DISK = N'C:\SQLBackups\Chapter7\ForcingFailures_Diff.bak'
WITH DIFFERENTIAL, STATS = 10
GO
```

Listing 7-14: A differential backup of the ForcingFailures database.

Some time later, we need to perform a restore process, over the top of the existing (FULL recovery model) database, so prepare and run the appropriate script, only to get a nasty surprise.

```
USE [master]
GO
RESTORE DATABASE [ForcingFailures]
FROM DISK = N'C:\SQLBackups\Chapter7\ForcingFailures_Full.bak'
WITH  NORECOVERY,  REPLACE,  STATS = 10
GO
```

```
RESTORE DATABASE [ForcingFailures]
FROM DISK = N'C:\SQLBackups\Chapter7\ForcingFailures_Diff.bak'
WITH STATS = 10
GO
```

```
Processed 176 pages for database 'ForcingFailures', file 'ForcingFailures' on file 1.
Processed 1 pages for database 'ForcingFailures', file 'ForcingFailures_log' on file 1.
RESTORE DATABASE successfully processed 177 pages in 0.035 seconds (39.508 MB/sec).
Msg 3136, Level 16, State 1, Line 2
This differential backup cannot be restored because the database has not been restored to the
correct earlier state.
Msg 3013, Level 16, State 1, Line 2
RESTORE DATABASE is terminating abnormally.
```

Listing 7-15: A failed differential restore of the ForcingFailures database.

Due to the "rogue" second full backup, our differential backup does not match our base full backup. As a result, the differential restore operation fails and the database is left in a restoring state. This whole mess could have been averted if that non-scheduled full backup had been taken as a copy-only backup, since this would have prevented SQL Server assigning it as the new base backup for any subsequent differentials.

However, what can we do at this point? Well, the first step is to examine the backup history in the msdb database to see if we can track down the rogue backup, as shown in Listing 7-16.

```
USE [MSDB]
GO

SELECT  bs.type ,
        bmf.physical_device_name ,
        bs.backup_start_date ,
        bs.user_name
FROM    dbo.backupset bs
        INNER JOIN dbo.backupmediafamily bmf
                ON bs.media_set_id = bmf.media_set_id
WHERE   bs.database_name = 'ForcingFailures'
ORDER BY bs.backup_start_date ASC
```

Listing 7-16: Finding our rogue backup.

This query will tell us the type of backup taken (D = full database, I = differential database, somewhat confusingly), the name and location of the backup file, when the backup was started, and who took it. We can check to see if that file still exsists in the designated directory and use it to restore our differential backup (we can also roundly castigate whoever was responsible, and give them a comprehensive tutorial on use of copy-only backups).

If the non-scheduled full backup file is no longer in that location and you are unable to track it down, then there is not a lot you can do at this point, unless you are also taking transaction log backups for the database. If not, you'll simply have to recover the database as it exists, as shown in Listing 7-17, and deal with the data loss.

```
USE [master]
GO
RESTORE DATABASE [ForcingFailures] WITH RECOVERY
```

Listing 7-17: Bringing our database back online.

Recovered, already

For our final example, we'll give our beleaguered `ForcingFailures` database a rest and attempt a differential restore on `DatabaseForDiffBackups`, as shown in Listing 7-18. See if you can figure out what is going to happen before executing the command.

```
USE [master]
GO


RESTORE DATABASE [DatabaseForDiffBackups]
FROM DISK = N'C:\SQLBackups\Chapter7\DatabaseForDiffBackups_Full_Native.bak'
WITH REPLACE,  STATS = 10
GO


RESTORE DATABASE [DatabaseForDiffBackups]
FROM DISK = N'C:\SQLBackups\Chapter7\DatabaseForDiffBackups_Diff_Native_2.bak'
WITH STATS = 10
GO
```

Listing 7-18: Spot the mistake in the differential restore script.

This script should look very familiar to you but there is one small omission from this version which will prove to be very important. Whether or not you spotted the error, go ahead and execute it, and you should see output similar to that shown in Figure 7-12.

```
Messages
 10 percent processed.
 20 percent processed.
 31 percent processed.
 41 percent processed.
 52 percent processed.
 62 percent processed.
 72 percent processed.
 83 percent processed.
 93 percent processed.
 100 percent processed.
 Processed 2456 pages for database 'DatabaseForDiffBackups', file 'DatabaseForDiffBackups' on file 1.
 Processed 2 pages for database 'DatabaseForDiffBackups', file 'DatabaseForDiffBackups_log' on file 1.
 RESTORE DATABASE successfully processed 2458 pages in 5.837 seconds (3.288 MB/sec).
 Msg 3117, Level 16, State 4, Line 2
 The log or differential backup cannot be restored because no files are ready to rollforward.
 Msg 3013, Level 16, State 1, Line 2
 RESTORE DATABASE is terminating abnormally.
```

Figure 7-12: No files ready to roll forward.

The first RESTORE completes successfully, but the second one fails with the error message *"The log or differential backup cannot be restored because no files are ready to rollforward."* The problem is that we forgot to include the NORECOVERY argument in the first RESTORE statement. Therefore, the full backup was restored and database recovery process proceeded as normal, to return the database to an online and usable state. At this point, the database is not in a state where it can accept further backups.

If you see this type of error when performing a restore that takes more than one backup file, differential, or log, you now know that there is a possibility that a previous RESTORE statement on the database didn't include the NORECOVERY argument that would allow for more backup files to be processed.

Summary

We have discussed when and why you should be performing differential backups. Differential backups, used properly, can help a DBA make database restores a much simpler and faster process than they would be with other backup types. In my opinion, differential backups should form an integral part of the daily backup arsenal.

If you would like more practice with these types of backups, please feel free to modify the database creation, data population and backup scripts provided throughout this chapter. Perhaps you can try a differential restore of a database and move the physical data and log files to different locations.

Finally, we explored some of the errors that can afflict differential backup and restore; if you know, up front, the sort of errors you might see, you'll be better armed to deal with them when they pop up in the real world. We couldn't cover every possible situation, of course, but knowing how to read and react to error messages will save you time and headaches in the future.

Chapter 8: Database Backup and Restore with SQL Backup

This chapter will demonstrate how to perform each of the types of database backup we've discussed in previous chapters (namely full and differential database backups and log backups), using Red Gate's SQL Backup Pro tool. At this stage, knowledge of the basic characteristics of each type of backup is assumed, based on prior chapters, in order to focus on the details of capturing the backups using either the SQL Backup GUI or SQL Backup scripts.

One of the advantages of using such a tool is the relative ease with which backups can be automated – a vital task for any DBA. We'll discuss a basic SQL Backup script that will allow you to take full, log, or differential backups of all selected databases on a SQL Server instance, store those backups in a central location, and receive notifications of any failure in the backup operation.

Preparing for Backups

As usual, we need to create our sample database, tables, and data. Listing 8-1 shows the script to create a `DatabaseForSQLBackups` database.

```
USE master
go

CREATE DATABASE [DatabaseForSQLBackups] ON PRIMARY (
    NAME = N'DatabaseForSQLBackups'
  , FILENAME = N'C:\SQLData\DatabaseForSQLBackups.mdf'
  , SIZE = 512000KB
  , FILEGROWTH = 102400KB ) LOG ON (
    NAME = N'DatabaseForSQLBackups_log'
```

```
    , FILENAME = N'C:\SQLData\DatabaseForSQLBackups_log.ldf'
    , SIZE = 102400KB
    , FILEGROWTH = 10240KB )
GO
ALTER DATABASE [DatabaseForSQLBackups] SET RECOVERY SIMPLE
GO
```

Listing 8-1: Creating `DatabaseForSQLBackups`.

Notice that we set the database, initially at least, to `SIMPLE` recovery model. Later we'll want to perform both differential database backups and log backups, so our main, operational model for the database will be `FULL`. However, as we'll soon be performing two successive data loads of one million rows each, and we don't want to run into the problem of bloating the log file (as described in the *Troubleshooting Log Issues* section of Chapter 5), we're going to start off in `SIMPLE` model, where the log will be auto-truncated, and only switch to `FULL` once these initial "bulk loads" have been completed.

Listing 8-2 shows the script to create our two, familiar, sample tables, and then load `MessageTable1` with 1 million rows.

```
USE [DatabaseForSQLBackups]
GO
CREATE TABLE [dbo].[MessageTable1]
    (
        [MessageData] [nvarchar](200) NOT NULL ,
        [MessageDate] [datetime2] NOT NULL
    )
ON   [PRIMARY]
GO

CREATE TABLE [dbo].[MessageTable2]
    (
        [MessageData] [nvarchar](200) NOT NULL ,
        [MessageDate] [datetime2] NOT NULL
    )
ON   [PRIMARY]
GO

USE [DatabaseForSQLBackups]
```

```
GO
DECLARE @messageData NVARCHAR(200)

SET @messageData = 'This is the message we are going to use to fill
                    up the first table for now.  We want to get this
                    as close to 200 characters as we can to fill up
                    the database as close to our initial size as we
                    can!!'

INSERT  INTO MessageTable1
VALUES  ( @messageData, GETDATE() )
GO 1000000
```

Listing 8-2:   Creating sample tables and initial million row data load for `MessageTable1`.

Take a look in the **C:\SQLData** folder, and you should see that our data and log files are still at their initial sizes; the data file is approximately 500 MB in size (and is pretty much full), and the log file is still 100 MB in size. Therefore we have a total database size of about 600 MB.

It's worth noting that, even if we'd set the database in FULL recovery model, the observed behavior would have been the same, up to this point. Don't forget that a database is only fully engaged in FULL recovery model *after* the first full backup, so the log may still have been truncated during the initial data load.

If we'd performed a full backup *before* the data load, the log would not have been truncated and would now be double that of our data file, just over 1 GB. Of course, this means that the log file would have undergone many auto-growth events, since we only set it to an initial size of 100 MB and to grow in 10 MB steps.

Full Backups

In this section, we'll walk through the process of taking a full backup of the example `DatabaseForSQLBackups` database, using both the SQL Backup GUI, and SQL Backup T-SQL scripts. In order to follow through with the examples, you'll need to have installed the Red Gate SQL Backup Pro GUI on your client machine, registered your test SQL Server instances, and installed the server-side components of SQL Backup. If you've not yet completed any part of this, please refer to Appendix A, for installation and configuration instructions.

SQL Backup full backup GUI method

Open the SQL Backup management GUI, expand the server listing for your test server, in the left pane, right-click the `DatabaseForSQLBackups` database and select **Back Up...** from the menu to enter Step 1 (of 5) in the **Back Up** wizard. The left pane lets you select the server to back up (which will be the test server housing our database) and the right pane allows you to select a backup template that you may have saved on previous runs through the backup process (at Step 5). Since this is our first backup, we don't yet have any templates, so we'll discuss this feature later.

Step 2 is where we specify the database(s) to back up (`DatabaseForSQLBackups` will be preselected) and the type of backup to be performed (by default, **Full**). In this case, since we do want to perform a full backup, and only of the `DatabaseForSQLBackups` database, we can leave this screen exactly as it is (see Figure 8-1).

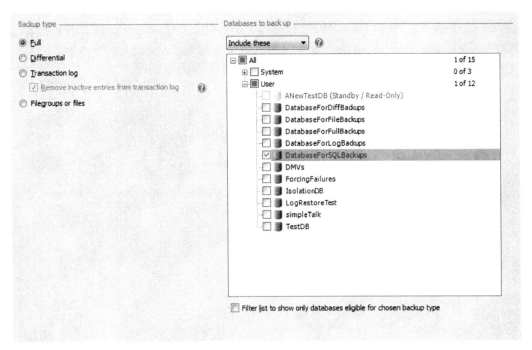

Figure 8-1: SQL Backup Configuration, Step 2.

A few additional features to note on this screen are as follows:

- we can take backups of more than one database at a time; a useful feature when you need one-time backups of multiple databases on a system

- if we wish to backup most, but not all, databases on a server, we can select the databases we *don't* wish to backup, and select **Exclude these** from the top drop-down

- the **Filter list...** check box allows you to screen out any databases that are not available for the current type of backup; for example, this would ensure that you don't attempt to take a log backup of a database that is running under the SIMPLE recovery model.

Step 3 is where we will configure settings to be used during the backup. For this first run through, we're going to focus on just the central **Backup location** portion of this screen, for the moment, and the only two changes we are going to make are to the backup file location and name. Adhering closely to the convention used throughout, we'll place the backup file in the **C:\SQLBackups\Chapter8** folder and call it **DatabaseForSQLBackups_ Full_1.sqb**. Notice the **.sqb** extension that denotes this as a SQL Backup-generated backup file. Once done, the screen will look as shown in Figure 8-2.

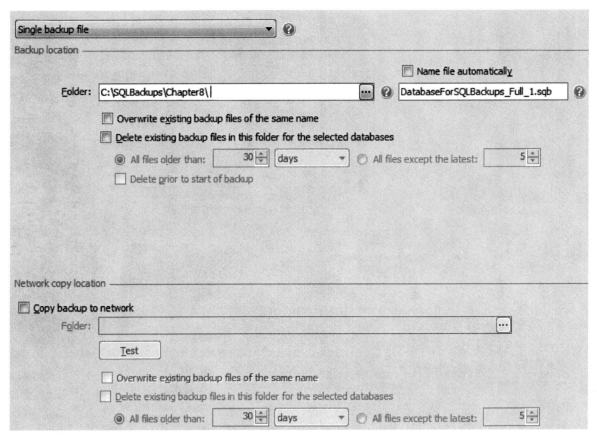

Figure 8-2: SQL Backup Step 3 configuration.

There are two options offered below the path and name settings in the **Backup location** section that allow us to "clean up" our backup files, depending on preferences.

- **Overwrite existing backup files...** Overwrite any backup files in that location that share the same name.

- **Delete existing backup files...** Remove any files that are more than x days old, or remove all but the latest x files. We also have the option of cleaning these files up before we start a new backup. This is helpful if the database backup files are quite large and wouldn't fit on disk if room was not cleared beforehand. However, be sure that any backups targeted for removal have first been safely copied to another location .

The top drop-down box of this screen offers the options to split or mirror a backup file (which we will cover at the end of this chapter). The **Network copy location** section allows us to copy the finished backup to a second network location, after it has completed. This is a good practice, and you also get the same options of cleaning up the files on your network storage. What you choose here doesn't have to match what you chose for your initial backup location; for example, you can store just one day of backups on a local machine, but three days on your network location.

Backup compression and encryption

Step 4 is where we configure some of the most useful features of SQL Backup, including backup compression. We'll compare how SQL Backup compression performs against the native uncompressed and native compressed backups that we investigated in previous chapters.

For the time being, let's focus on the **Backup processing** portion of this screen, where we configure backup compression and backup encryption.

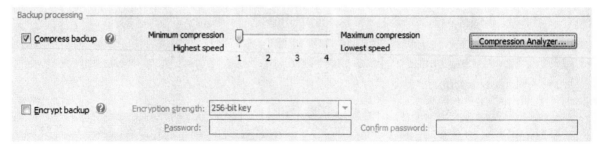

Figure 8-3:   SQL Backup Step 4 configuration.

Backup compression is enabled by default, and there are four levels of compression, offering progressively higher compression and slower backup speeds. Although the compressed data requires lower levels of disk I/O to write to the backup file, the overriding factor is the increased CPU time required in compressing the data in the first place.

As you can probably guess, picking the compression level is a balancing act; the better the compression, the more disk space will be saved, but the longer the backups run, the more likely are issues with the backup operation.

Ultimately, the choice of compression level should be guided by the size of the database and the nature of the data (i.e. its compressibility). For instance, binary data does not compress well, so don't spend CPU time attempting to compress a database full of binary images. In other cases, lower levels of compression may yield higher compression ratios. We can't tell until we test the database, which is where the **Compression Analyzer** comes in. Go ahead and click on the **Compression Analyzer...** button and start a test against the `DatabaseForSQLBackups` database. Your figures will probably vary a bit, but you should see results similar to those displayed in Figure 8-4.

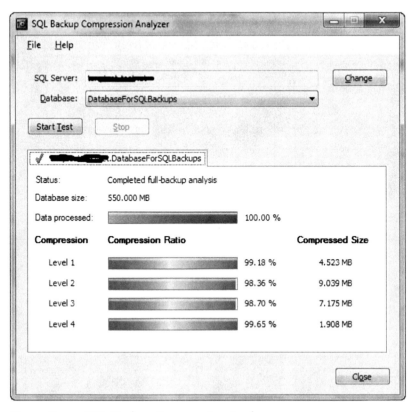

Figure 8-4: SQL Backup Compression Analyzer.

For our database, Levels 1 and 4 offer the best compression ratio, and since a backup size of about 4.5 MB (for database of 550 MB) is pretty good, we'll pick **Level 1 compression**, which should also provide the fastest backup times.

Should I use the compression analyzer for every database?

Using the analyzer for each database in your infrastructure is probably not your best bet. We saw very fast results when testing this database, because is it very small compared to most production databases. The larger the database you are testing, the longer this test will take to run. This tool is recommended for databases that you are having compression issues with, perhaps on a database where you are not getting the compression ratio that you believe you should be.

The next question we need to consider carefully is this: do we want to encrypt all of that data that we are writing to disk? Some companies operate under strict rules and regulations, such as HIPAA and SOX, which *require* database backups to be encrypted. Some organizations just like the added security of encrypted backups, in helping prevent a malicious user getting access to those files.

If encryption is required, simply tick the **Encrypt backup** box, select the level of encryption and provide a secure password. SQL Backup will take care of the rest, but at a cost. Encryption will also add CPU and I/O overhead to your backups and restores. Each of these operations now must go through the "compress | encrypt | store on disk" process to back up, as well as the "retrieve from disk| decrypt | decompress" routines, adding an extra step to the both backup and restore processes.

> *Store your encryption password in a safe and secure location!*
>
> *Not having the password to those backup files will stop you from ever being able to restore those files again, which is just as bad as not having backups at all!*

Our database doesn't contain any sensitive data and we are not going to use encryption on this example.

Backup optimization and verification

We're going to briefly review what options are available in the **Optimization** and **On completion** sections, and some of the considerations in deciding the correct values, but for our demo we'll leave all of them either disabled or at their default settings.

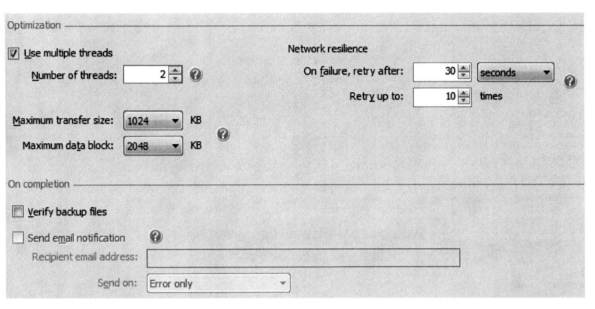

Figure 8-5a: Optimization and **On completion** options.

Depending on the system, some good performance benefits can be had by allowing more threads to be used in the backup process. When using a high-end CPU, or many multi-core CPUs, we can split hefty backup operations across multiple threads, each of which can run in parallel on a separate core. This can dramatically reduce the backup processing time.

The **Maximum transfer size** and **Maximum data block** options can be important parameters in relation to backup performance. The transfer size option dictates the maximum size of each block of memory that SQL Backup will write to the backup file, on disk. The default value is going to be 1,024 KB (*i.e.* 1 MB), but if SQL Server is experiencing memory pressure, it may be wise to lower this value so that SQL Backup can write to smaller memory blocks, and therefore isn't fighting so hard, with other applications, for memory.

If this proves necessary, we can add a DWORD registry key to define a new default value on that specific machine. All values in these keys need to be in multiples of 65,536 (64 KB), up to a maximum of 1,048,576 (1,024 KB, the default).

- `HKEY_LOCAL_MACHINE\SOFTWARE\Red Gate\SQL Backup\
BackupSettingsGlobal\<instance name>\MAXTRANSFERSIZE` (32-bit)

- `HKEY_LOCAL_MACHINE\SOFTWARE\Wow6432Node\Red Gate\SQL Backup\
BackupSettingsGlobal\<instance name>\MAXTRANSFERSIZE` (64-bit)

The **maximum data block** option (by default 2 MB) determines the size of the actual data blocks on disk, when storing backup data. For optimal performance, we want this value to match or fit evenly in the block size of the media to which the files are being written; if the data block sizes overlap the media block boundaries, it may result in performance degradation. Generally speaking, SQL Server will automatically select the correct block size based on the media.

However, if necessary, we can create a registry entry to overwrite the default value:

- `HKEY_LOCAL_MACHINE\SOFTWARE\Red Gate\SQL Backup\
BackupSettingsGlobal\<instance name>\MAXDATABLOCK` (32-bit)

- `HKEY_LOCAL_MACHINE\SOFTWARE\Wow6432Node\Red Gate\SQL Backup\
BackupSettingsGlobal\<instance name>\MAXDATABLOCK` (64-bit)

The **network resilience** options determine how long to wait before retrying a failed backup operation, and how many times to retry; when the retry count has been exhausted, a failure message will be issued. We want to be able to retry a failed backup a few times, but we don't want to retry so many times that a problem in the network or disk subsystem is masked for too long; in other words, rather than extend the backup operation as it retries again and again, it's better to retry only a few times and then fail, therefore highlighting the network issue. This is especially true when performing full backup operations on large databases, where we'll probably want to knock that retry count down from a default of 10 to 2–3 times. Transaction log backups, on the other hand, are typically a short process, so retrying 10 times is not an unreasonable number in this case.

The **On completion** section gives us the option to verify our backup files after completion and send an email once the operations are complete. The verification process is similar to the CHECKSUM operation in native SQL Server backups (see Chapter 2). SQL Backup will make sure that all data blocks have been written correctly and that you have a valid backup file.

Note that, at the time of this book going to print, Red Gate released SQL Backup Pro Version 7, which expands the backup verification capabilities to allow standard backup verification (BACKUP...WITH CHECKSUM) and restore verification (RESTORE VERIFYONLY), as shown in Figure 8-5b. We'll revisit the topic of backup verification with SQL Backup later in the chapter.

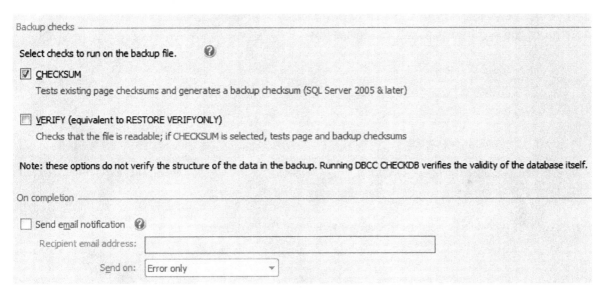

Fig 8-5b: New Backup verification options in SQL Backup 7.

The email notification can be set to alert on any error, warning, or just when the backup has completed in any state including success.

Running the backup

Step 5 of the wizard is simply a summary of the options we selected for our SQL Backup operation. Check this page carefully, making sure each of the selected options looks as it should. At the bottom is a check box that, when enabled, will allow us to save this backup operation configuration as a template, in which case we could then load it on Step 1 of the wizard and then skip straight to Step 5. We are not going to save this example as a template. The **Script** tab of this step allows us to view the T-SQL code that has been generated to perform this backup.

Click on the **Finish** button and the backup will be executed on your server, and a dialog box will report the progress of the operation. Once it completes, the new window will (hopefully) display two green check marks, along with some status details in the lower portion of the window, as seen in Figure 8-6.

```
Database size       : 600.000 MB
Compressed data size: 3.592 MB
Compression rate    : 99.40%

Processed 62696 pages for database 'DatabaseForSQLBackups', file 'DatabaseForSQLBackups' on file 1.
Processed 1 pages for database 'DatabaseForSQLBackups', file 'DatabaseForSQLBackups_log' on file 1.
BACKUP DATABASE successfully processed 62697 pages in 3.100 seconds (158.006 MB/sec).
SQL Backup process ended.
```

Figure 8-6:   Status details from a successful SQL Backup GUI backup operation.

Backup metrics: SQL Backup vs. native vs. native compressed

Figure 8-6 reports an initial database size of 600 MB, a backup file size of 3.6 MB and backup time of about 3 seconds. Remember, these metrics are ballpark figures and won't match exactly the ones you get on your system. Don't necessarily trust SQL Backup on the backup size; double-check it in the backup location folder (in my case it was 3.7 MB; pretty close!). Figure 8-7 compares these metrics to those obtained for identical operations using native backup, compressed native backup, as well as SQL Backup using a higher compression level (3).

Backup Operation	Backup File Size in MB (on disk)	Backup Time (seconds)	% Difference compared to Native Full (+ = bigger / faster)	
			Size	Speed
Native Full	501	19.6		
Native Full with Compression	6.7	4.6	-98.7	+76.5
SQL Backup Full Compression Level 1	3.7	3.1	-99.3	+84.2
SQL Backup Full Compression Level 3	7.3	4.5	-98.5	+77

Figure 8-7: Comparing full backup operations for `DatabaseForSQLBackups` (0.5 GB).

SQL Backup (Compression Level 1) produces a backup file that requires less than 1% of the space required for the native full backup file. To put this into perspective, in the space that we could store 3 days' worth of full native backups using native SQL Server, we could store nearly 400 SQL Backup files. It also increases the backup speed by about 84%. How does that work? Basically, every backup operation reads the data from the disk and writes to a backup-formatted file, on disk. By far the slowest part of the operation is writing the data to disk. When SQL Backup (or native compression) performs its task, it is reading all of the data, passing it through a compression tool and writing much smaller segments of data, so less time is used on the slowest operation.

In this test, SQL Backup with Compression Level 1 outperformed the native compressed backup. However, for SQL Backup with Compression Level 3, their performance was almost identical. It's interesting to note that while Level 3 compression should, in theory, have resulted in a smaller file and a longer backup time, compared to Level 1, we in fact saw a larger file and a longer backup time! This highlights the importance of selecting the compression level carefully.

SQL Backup full backup using T-SQL

We're now going to perform a second full backup our `DatabaseForSQLBackups` database, but this time using a SQL Backup T-SQL script, which will look similar to the one we saw on the **Script** tab of Step 5 of the GUI wizard.

Before we do so, let's populate `MessageTable2` with a million rows of data of the same size and structure as the data in `MessageTable1`, so that our database file should be hovering somewhere around 1 GB in size.

```
USE [DatabaseForSQLBackups]
GO

DECLARE @messageData NVARCHAR(200)

SET @messageData =     'This is a different message we are going to
                        use to fill up the second table.  We want to get
                        this as close to 200 characters as we can to
                        fill up the database as close to our initial
                        size as we can.'

INSERT  INTO dbo.MessageTable2
VALUES  ( @messageData, GETDATE() )
GO 1000000
```

Listing 8-3: Populating the `MessageTable2` table.

Take a look in the **SQLData** folder, and you'll now see that the data file is now about 1GB in size and the log file is still around 100 MB. Now that we have some more data to work with, Listing 8-4 shows the SQL Backup T-SQL script to perform a second full backup of our `DatabaseForSQLBackups` database.

```
EXECUTE master..sqlbackup '-SQL "BACKUP DATABASE [DatabaseForSQLBackups]
TO DISK = ''C:\SQLBackups\Chapter8\DatabaseForSQLBackups_Full_2.sqb''
WITH DISKRETRYINTERVAL = 30, DISKRETRYCOUNT = 10, THREADCOUNT = 2, COMPRESSION = 1"'
GO
```

Listing 8-4: Second full backup of `DatabaseForSQLBackups` using SQL Backup T-SQL.

The first thing to notice is that the backup is executed via an extended stored procedure called `sqlbackup`, which resides in the `master` database and utilizes some compiled DLLs that have been installed on the server. We pass to this stored procedure a set of parameters as a single string, which provides the configuration settings that we wish to use for the backup operation. Some of the names of these settings are slightly different from what we saw for native backups but, nevertheless, the script should look fairly familiar. We see the usual **BACKUP DATABASE** command to signify that we are about to backup the `DatabaseForSQLBackups` database. We also see the **TO DISK** portion and the path to where the backup file will be stored.

The latter portion of the script sets values for some of the optimization settings that we saw on Step 4 of the GUI wizard. These are not necessary for taking the backup, but it's useful to know what they do.

- **DISKRETRYINTERVAL** – One of the network resiliency options; amount of time in seconds SQL Backup will wait before retrying the backup operation, in the case of a failure.

- **DISKRETRYCOUNT** – Another network resiliency option; number of times a backup will be attempted in the event of a failure. Bear in mind that the more times we retry, and the longer the retry interval, the more extended will be the backup operation.

- **THREADCOUNT** – Using multiple processors and multiple threads can offer a huge performance boost when taking backups.

The only setting that could make much of a difference is the `threadcount` parameter, since on powerful multi-processor machines it can spread the load of backup compression over multiple processors.

Go ahead and run the script now and the output should look similar to that shown in Figure 8-8.

```
Backing up DatabaseForSQLBackups (full database) to:
  C:\SQLBackups\Chapter8\DatabaseForSQLBackups_Full_2.sqb

Database size       : 1.074 GB
Compressed data size: 6.679 MB
Compression rate    : 99.39%

Processed 125208 pages for database 'DatabaseForSQLBackups', file 'DatabaseForSQLBackups' on file 1.
Processed 1 pages for database 'DatabaseForSQLBackups', file 'DatabaseForSQLBackups_log' on file 1.
BACKUP DATABASE successfully processed 125209 pages in 5.974 seconds (163.742 MB/sec).
SQL Backup process ended.
```

Figure 8-8:   SQL Backup T-SQL script results.

We are now presented with two result sets. The first result set, shown in Figure 8-8, provides our detailed backup metrics, including database size, and the size and compression rate of the resulting backup file. The second result set (not shown) gives us the exit code from SQL Backup, an error code from SQL Server and a list of files used in the command.

We can see from the first result set that the new backup file size is just under 7 MB, and if we take a look in our directory we can confirm this. Compared to our first Red Gate backup, we can see that this is a bit less than double the original file size, but we will take a closer look at the numbers in just a second.

After these metrics, we see the number of pages processed. Referring back to Chapter 3 confirms that this is the same number of pages as for the equivalent native backup, which is as expected. We also see that the backup took just 6 seconds to complete which, again, is roughly double the figure for the first full backup. Figure 8-9 compares these metrics to those obtained for native backups, and compressed native backups.

Backup Operation	Backup File Size in MB (on disk)	Backup Time (seconds)	% Difference compared to Native Full (+ = bigger / faster)	
			Size	Speed
Native Full	1000	41		
Native Full with Compression	12.7	8.3	-98.7	+80.5
SQL Backup Full Compression Level 1	6.8	6.0	-99.3	+85.4
SQL Backup Full Compression Level 3	14.2	7.5	-98.6	+81.7

Figure 8-9: Comparing full backup operations for `DatabaseForSQLBackups` (1 GB).

All the results are broadly consistent with those we achieved for the first full backup. It confirms that for this data, SQL Backup Compression Level 1 is the best-performing backup, both in terms of backup time and backup file size.

Log Backups

In this section, we'll walk through the process of taking log backups of the example `DatabaseForSQLBackups` database, again using either the SQL Backup GUI, or a SQL Backup T-SQL script.

Preparing for log backups

At this point, the database is operating in `SIMPLE` recovery model, and we cannot take log backups. In order to start taking log backups, and prevent the log file from being auto-truncated from this point on, we need to switch the recovery model of the database to `FULL`, and then take another full backup, as shown in Listing 8-5.

```
USE master
GO
ALTER DATABASE [DatabaseForSQLBackups] SET RECOVERY FULL
GO

EXECUTE master..sqlbackup '-SQL "BACKUP DATABASE [DatabaseForSQLBackups]
TO DISK = ''C:\SQLBackups\Chapter8\DatabaseForSQLBackups_Full_BASE.sqb''
WITH DISKRETRYINTERVAL = 30, DISKRETRYCOUNT = 10, THREADCOUNT = 2, COMPRESSION = 1"'
GO
```

Listing 8-5: Switching `DatabaseForSQLBackups` to `FULL` recovery and taking a full backup.

The database is now operating in **FULL** recovery and this backup file, `DatabaseFor SQLBackups_Full_BASE.sqb`, will be the one to restore, prior to restoring any subsequent log backups.

Finally, let's perform a third, much smaller, data load, adding ten new rows to each message table, as shown in Listing 8-6.

```
USE [DatabaseForSQLBackups]
GO
INSERT  INTO dbo.MessageTable1
VALUES  ( '1st set of short messages for MessageTable1', GETDATE() )
GO 50000

-- this is just to help with our point-in-time restore (Chapter 8)
PRINT GETDATE()
GO
--Dec  3 2011  1:33PM

INSERT  INTO dbo.MessageTable2
VALUES  ( '1st set of short messages for MessageTable2', GETDATE() )
GO 50000
```

Listing 8-6: Loading new messages into our message tables.

SQL Backup log backups

In this section, rather than perform two separate backups, one via the GUI and one via a SQL Backup script, we're just going to do one transaction log backup and let you decide whether you want to perform it via the GUI or the script.

If you prefer the GUI approach, open up SQL Backup and start another a backup operation for the `DatabaseForSQLBackups` database.

On Step 2 of the Wizard, select **Transaction Log** as the **Backup type**. You'll see that the option **Remove inactive entries from transaction log** is auto-checked. This means that the transaction log can be truncated upon backup, making the space in the log available for future entries. This is the behavior we want here, so leave it checked. However, if we were to uncheck it, we could take a log backup that leaves the transactions in the file (similar to a `NO_TRUNCATE` native backup or a copy-only log backup in that it won't affect future backups).

The **Databases to back up** section may list several databases that are grayed out; these will be the ones that are ineligible for transaction log backups, usually because they are operating in `SIMPLE` recovery model, rather than `FULL` or `BULK LOGGED`. Checking the **Filter list...** button at the bottom will limit the list to only the eligible databases. Make sure that only the `DatabaseForSQLBackups` database is selected, then click **Next**.

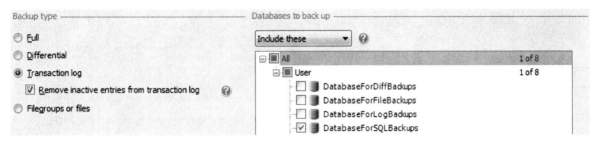

Figure 8-10: Selecting the type of backup and the target database.

On Step 3, we set the name and location for our log backup file. Again, adhering to the convention used throughout the book, we'll place the backup file in the **C:\SQLBackups\ Chapter8** folder and call it **DatabaseForSQLBackups_Log_1.sqb**.

Step 4 of the wizard is where we will configure the compression, optimization and resiliency options of our transaction log backup. The Compression Analyzer only tests full backups and all transaction logs are pretty much the same in terms of compressibility. We'll choose Compression Level 1, again, but since our transaction log backup will, in this case, process only a small amount of data, we could select maximum compression (Level 4) without affecting the processing time significantly.

We're not going to change any of the remaining options on this screen, and we have discussed them all already, so go ahead and click on **Next**. If everything looks as expected on the **Summary** screen, click on **Finish** to start the backup. If all goes well, within a few seconds the appearance of two green checkmarks will signal that all pieces of the operation have been completed, and some backup metrics will be displayed.

If you prefer the script-based approach, Listing 8-7 shows the SQL Backup T-SQL script that does directly what our SQL Backup GUI did under the covers.

```
USE [master]
GO

EXECUTE master..sqlbackup '-SQL "BACKUP LOG [DatabaseForSQLBackups]
TO DISK = ''C:\SQLBackups\Chapter8\DatabaseForSQLBackups_Log_1.sqb''
WITH DISKRETRYINTERVAL = 30, DISKRETRYCOUNT = 10,
COMPRESSION = 1,  THREADCOUNT = 2"'
```

Listing 8-7: A transction log backup, using SQL Backup T-SQL.

Whichever way you decide to execute the log backup, you should see backup metrics similar to those shown in Figure 8-11.

```
Backing up DatabaseForSQLBackups (transaction log) to:
  C:\SQLBackups\Chapter8\DatabaseForSQLBackups_Log_1.sqb

Backup data size    : 50.625 MB
Compressed data size: 7.020 MB
Compression rate    : 86.13%

Processed 6261 pages for database 'DatabaseForSQLBackups', file 'DatabaseForSQLBackups_log'
on file 1.
BACKUP LOG successfully processed 6261 pages in 0.662 seconds (73.877 MB/sec).
SQL Backup process ended.
```

Figure 8-11: Backup metrics for transaction log backup on `DatabaseForSQLBackups`.

The backup metrics report a compressed backup size of 7 MB, which we can verify by checking the actual size of the file in the **C:\SQLBackups\Chapter8** folder, and a processing time of about 0.7 seconds. Once again, Figure 8-12 compares these metrics to those obtained for native backups, compressed native backups and for SQL Backup with a higher compression level.

Backup Operation	Backup File Size in MB (on disk)	Backup Time (seconds)	% Difference compared to Native (+ = bigger / faster)	
			Size	Speed
Native Log	50.2	0.87		
Native Log with Compression	5.6	0.89	-88.8	-2.3
SQL Backup Log Compression Level 1	6.9	0.66	-86.3	+24
SQL Backup Log Compression Level 3	4.5	1.26	-91	-44.8

Figure 8-12: Comparing log backup operations for `DatabaseForSQLBackups`.

In all cases, there is roughly a 90% saving in disk space for compressed backups, over the native log backup. In terms of backup performance, native log backups, native compressed log backups, and SQL Backup Compression Level 1 all run in sub-second times, so it's hard to draw too many conclusions except to say that for smaller log files the time savings are less significant than for full backups, as would be expected. SQL Backup Compression Level 3 does offer the smallest backup file footprint, but the trade-off is backup performance that is significantly slower than for native log backups.

Differential Backups

Finally, let's take a very quick look at how to perform a differential database backup using SQL Backup. For full details on what differential backups are, and when they can be useful, please refer back to Chapter 7.

First, simply adapt and rerun Listing 8-6 to insert a load of 100,000 rows into each of the message tables (also, adapt the message text accordingly).

Then, if you prefer the GUI approach, jump-start SQL Backup and work through in the exactly the same way as described for the full backup. The only differences will be:

- at Step 2, choose **Differential** as the backup type
- at Step 3, call the backup file **DatabaseForSQLBackups_Diff_1.sqb** and locate it in the **C:\SQLBackups\Chapter8** folder
- at Step 4, choose **Compression Level 1**.

If you prefer to run a script, the equivalent SQL Backup script is shown in Listing 8-8.

```
USE [master]
GO
EXECUTE master..sqlbackup '-SQL "BACKUP DATABASE [DatabaseForSQLBackups]
TO DISK = ''C:\SQLBackups\Chapter8\DatabaseForSQLBackups_Diff_1.sqb''
WITH DISKRETRYINTERVAL = 30, DISKRETRYCOUNT = 10,
COMPRESSION = 1, THREADCOUNT = 2, DIFFERENTIAL"'
```

Listing 8-8: SQL Backup differential T-SQL backup code.

Again, there is little new here; the command is more or less identical to the one for full backups, with the addition of the **DIFFERENTIAL** keyword to the **WITH** clause which instructs SQL Server to only backup any data changed since the last full backup was taken.

```
Backing up DatabaseForSQLBackups (differential database) to:
  C:\SQLBackups\Chapter8\DatabaseForSQLBackups_Diff_1.sqb

Backup data size    : 269.063 MB
Compressed data size: 2.575 MB
Compression rate    : 99.04%

Processed 33752 pages for database 'DatabaseForSQLBackups', file 'DatabaseForSQLBackups' on file 1.
Processed 2 pages for database 'DatabaseForSQLBackups', file 'DatabaseForSQLBackups_log' on file 1.
BACKUP DATABASE WITH DIFFERENTIAL successfully processed 33754 pages in 1.695 seconds (155.573 MB/sec).
SQL Backup process ended.
```

Figure 8-13: SQL Backup differential metrics (Compression Level 1).

Let's do a final metrics comparison for a range of differential backups.

Backup Operation	Backup File Size in MB (on disk)	Backup Time (seconds)	% Difference compared to Native (+ = bigger / faster)	
			Size	Speed
Native Log	270.4	4.4		
Native Log with Compression	4.2	2.4	-98.4	+45.5
SQL Backup Log Compression Level 1	2.6	1.7	-99.0	+61.4
SQL Backup Log Compression Level 3	4.7	2.7	-98.3	+38.6

Figure 8-14: Comparing differential backup operations for `DatabaseForSQLBackups`.

Once again, the space and time savings from compressed backup are readily apparent, with SQL Backup Compression Level 1 emerging as the most efficient on both counts, in these tests.

Building a reusable and schedulable backup script

One of the objectives of this book is to provide the reader with a jumping-off point for their SQL Server backup strategy. We'll discuss how to create a SQL Backup script that can be used in a SQL Agent job to take scheduled backups of databases, and allow the DBA to:

- take a backup of selected databases on a SQL Server instance, including relevant system databases
- configure the type of backup required (full, differential, or log)

- store the backup files using the default naming convention set up in
  Red Gate SQL Backup Pro

- capture a report of any error or warning codes during the backup operation.

Take a look at the script in Listing 8-9, and then we'll walk through all the major sections.

```
USE [master]
GO

DECLARE @BackupFileLocation NVARCHAR(200) ,
    @EmailOnFailure NVARCHAR(200) ,
    @SQLBackupCommand NVARCHAR(2000) ,
    @DatabaseList NVARCHAR(2000) ,
    @ExitCode INT ,
    @ErrorCode INT ,
    @BackupType NVARCHAR(4)

-- Conifgure Options Here
SET @BackupFileLocation = N'\\NetworkServer\ShareName\'
                        + @@SERVERNAME + '\'
SET @EmailOnFailure = N'DBATeam@MyCompany.com'
SET @DatabaseList = N'DatabaseForDiffBackups_SB'
SET @BackupType = N'DIFF'

-- Do Not Modify Below
SET @SQLBackupCommand = CASE @BackupType
                    WHEN N'FULL'
                    THEN N'-SQL "BACKUP DATABASES [' + @DatabaseList
                      + N'] TO DISK = ''' + @BackupFileLocation
                      + N'<AUTO>.sqb'' WITH MAILTO_ONERRORONLY = '''
                        + @EmailOnFailure
                        + N''', DISKRETRYINTERVAL = 30,
                            DISKRETRYCOUNT = 10, COMPRESSION = 3,
                            THREADCOUNT = 2"'
                    WHEN N'LOG'
                    THEN N'-SQL "BACKUP LOGS [' + @DatabaseList
                      + N'] TO DISK = ''' + @BackupFileLocation
                      + N'<AUTO>.sqb'' WITH MAILTO_ONERRORONLY = '''
                      + @EmailOnFailure
                      + N''', DISKRETRYINTERVAL = 30,
                            DISKRETRYCOUNT = 10, COMPRESSION = 3,
```

```
                                     THREADCOUNT = 2"'
                      WHEN N'DIFF'
                      THEN N'-SQL "BACKUP DATABASES [' + @DatabaseList
                          + N'] TO DISK = ''' + @BackupFileLocation
                          + N'<AUTO>.sqb'' WITH MAILTO_ONERRORONLY = '''
                          + @EmailOnFailure
                          + N''', DISKRETRYINTERVAL = 30,
                                 DISKRETRYCOUNT = 10, COMPRESSION = 3,
                                 THREADCOUNT = 2, DIFFERENTIAL"'
                 END

EXECUTE master..sqlbackup @SQLBackupCommand, @ExitCode OUTPUT,
    @ErrorCode OUTPUT


-- If our backup operations return any errors or warnings execute below
IF ( @ExitCode >= 500
    OR @ErrorCode > 0
    )
  BEGIN
  -- Raise an error to fail your backup job
      RAISERROR(N'Backup operation error', 10,1)
  END
```

Listing 8-9: Reusable database backup code.

The script starts by declaring the required variables, and the sets the values of the four confugurable variables, as below.

- **@BackupFileLocation** – The backup path for our database backup files. This should be pointed at the centralized storage location. Also notice that the servername variable is used as a subdirectory. It is common practice to separate backup files by server, so this will use each server name as a subdirectory to store that set of backup files.

- **@EmailOnFailure** – We always want to know when backups fail. In some environments, manually checking all database backup operations is just not feasible. Having alerts sent to the DBA team on failure is a good measure to have in place. Be sure to test the email setting on each server occasionally, to guarantee that any failure alerts are getting through. Details of how to configure the email settings are in Appendix A.

- **@DatabaseList** – A comma delimited text list that contains the names of any databases that we want to back up. SQL Backup allows you to back up any number of databases at one time with a single command. When backing up every database on a server, we can simply omit this parameter from the script and, in the BACKUP command, replace [' + @DatabaseList + '] with [*].

- **@BackupType** – Used to determine what type of database backup will be taken. In this script there are three choices for this variable to take; full, log, and differential.

In the next section of the script, we build the BACKUP commands, using the variables for which we have just configured values. We store the BACKUP command in the @SQLBackupCommand variable, until we are ready to execute it. Notice that a simple CASE statement is used to determine the type of backup operation to be performed, according to the value stored in @BackupType. We don't need to modify anything in this section of the script, unless making changes to the other settings being used in the BACKUP command, such as the compression level. Of course, we could also turn those into configurable parameters.

The next section of the script is where we execute our BACKUP command, storing the ExitCode and ErrorCode output parameters in our defined variables, where:

- **ExitCode** is the output value from the SQL Backup extended stored procedure. Any number above 0 indicates some sort of issue with the backup execution.

  - ExitCode >= 500 indicates a serious problem with at least one of the backup files and will need to investigate further.

  - ExitCode < 500 is just a warning code. The backup operation itself may have run successfully, but there was some issue that was not critical enough to cause the entire operation to fail.

- **ErrorCode** is the SQL Server return value. A value above 0 is returned only when SQL Server itself runs into an issue. Having an error code returned from SQL Server almost always guarantees a critical error for the entire operation.

We test the value of each of these codes and, if a serious problem has occurred, we raise an error to SQL Server so that, if this were run in a SQL Server Agent job, it would guarantee to fail and alert someone, if the job were configured to do so. We do have it set up to send email from SQL Backup on a failure, but also having the SQL Agent job alert on failure is a nice safeguard to have in place. What we do in this section is totally customizable and dictated by our needs.

Restoring Database Backups with SQL Backup

Having performed our range of full, log and differential backups, using SQL Backup, it's time to demonstrate several useful restore examples, namely:

- restoring to the end of a given transaction log

- a complete restore, including restores of the tail log backup

- a restore to a particular point in time within a transaction log file.

Preparing for restore

In order to prepare for our restore operations, we're going to add a few new rows to MessageTable1, perform a log backup, and then add a few new rows to MessageTable2, as shown in Listing 8-10.

```
USE [DatabaseForSQLBackups]
GO
INSERT  INTO dbo.MessageTable1
VALUES  ( 'What is the meaning of life, the Universe and everything?',
        GETDATE() )
GO 21

USE [master]
GO

EXECUTE master..sqlbackup '-SQL "BACKUP LOG [DatabaseForSQLBackups]
TO DISK = ''C:\SQLBackups\Chapter8\DatabaseForSQLBackups_Log_2.sqb''
WITH DISKRETRYINTERVAL = 30, DISKRETRYCOUNT = 10,
COMPRESSION = 1, INIT, THREADCOUNT = 2"'

USE [DatabaseForSQLBackups]
GO

INSERT  INTO dbo.MessageTable2
VALUES  ('What is the meaning of life, the Universe and everything?',
        GETDATE() )
GO 21
```

Listing 8-10: Add 21 rows, take a log backup, add 21 rows.

So, to recap, we have 2 million rows captured in the base full backup. We switched the database from SIMPLE to FULL recovery model, added 100,000 rows to our tables, then did a log backup, so the **TLog1** backup captures the details of inserting those 100,000 rows. We then added another 200,000 rows and took a differential backup. Differentials capture all the data added since the last full backup, so 300,000 rows in this case. We then added 21 rows and took a second log backup, so the **TLog2** backup will capture details of 200,021 inserted rows (*i.e.* all the changes since the last log backup). Finally, we added another 21 rows which are not currently captured in any backup. The backup scheme seems quite hard to swallow when written out like that, so hopefully Figure 8-15 will make it easier to digest.

273

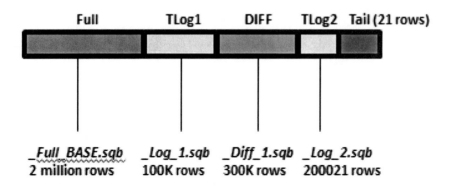

Figure 8-15: Current backup scheme.

SQL Backup GUI restore to the end of a log backup

First, let's see how easy it is to perform a one-off restore via SQL Backup, using the GUI, especially if all the required files are still stored locally, in their original location. We'll then look at the process again, step by step, using scripts. In this first example, we're going to restore the database to the state in which it existed at the time we took the second transaction log backup (`DatabaseForSQLBackups_Log_2.sqb`).

Start up the SQL Backup Restore wizard and, at Step 1, select the required transaction log backup, as shown in Figure 8-16.

In this case, all the required backup files are still stored locally, so they are available from the backup history. As such, we only have to select the last file to be restored and, when we click **Next**, SQL Backup will calculate which other files it needs to restore first, and will load them automatically.

Step 1 of 4: Select backups to restore.

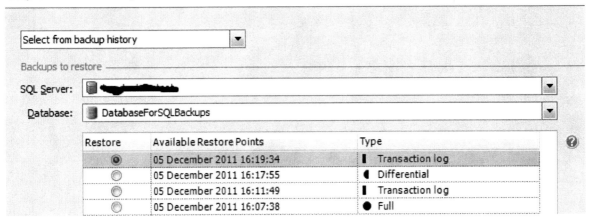

Figure 8-16: Restore the latest transaction log file.

However, if the restore is taking place several days or weeks after the backup, then the files will likely have been moved to a new location, and we'll need to manually locate each of the required files for the restore process before SQL Backup will let us proceed.

To do so, select **Browse for backup files to restore** from the top drop-down box, and then click the **Add Files...** button to locate each of the required files, in turn. We can select multiple files in the same directory by holding down the **Ctrl** button on the keyboard. We can also add a network location into this menu by using the **Add Server** button, or by pasting in a full network path in the file name box.

Whether SQL Backup locates the files for us, or we do it manually, we should end up with a screen that looks similar to that shown in Figure 8-17.

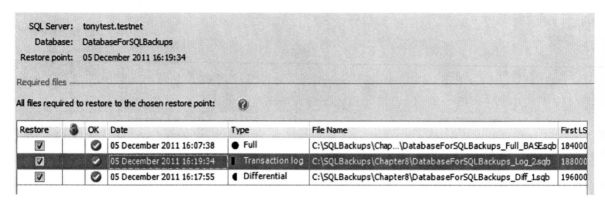

Figure 8-17: Identifying the required files for the restore process.

In this example, we need our base full backup and our differential backup files. Note that the availability of the differential backup means we can bypass our first transaction log backup (`DatabaseForSQLBackups_Log_1.sqb`). However, if for some reason the differential backup was unavailable, then we could still complete the restore process using the full backup followed by both the log files.

We're going to overwrite the existing `DatabaseForSQLBackups` database and leave the data and log files in their original **C:\SQLData** directory. Note that the handy **File locations** drop-down is an innovation in SQL Backup 6.5; if using an older version, you'll need to manually fill in the paths using the ellipsis (**...**) buttons.

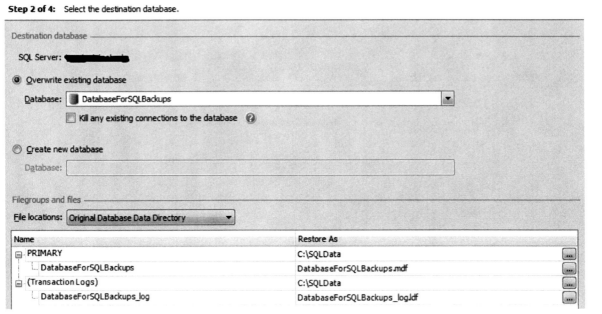

Figure 8-18: Overwrite the existing database.

Click **Next** and, on the following screen, SQL Backup warns us that we've not performed a **tail log backup** and gives us the option to do so, before proceeding. We do not need to restore the tail of the log as part of this restore process as we're deliberately only restoring to the end of our second log backup file. However, remember that the details of our INSERTs into MessageTable2, in Listing 8-10, are not currently backed up, and we don't want to lose details of these transactions, so we're going to go ahead and perform this tail log backup.

Accepting this option catapults us into a log backup operation and we must designate the name and location for the tail log backup, and follow through the process, as was described earlier in the chapter.

Figure 8-19: Backing up the tail of the log.

Once complete, we should receive a message saying that the *backup of the tail of the transaction log was successful* and to click **Next** to proceed with the restore. Having done so, we re-enter Step 3 of our original restore process, offering a number of database restore options.

Step 3 of 4: Destination database restore options.

Recovery completion state

- ● Operational (RESTORE WITH RECOVERY)
- ○ Non-operational (RESTORE WITH NORECOVERY)
- ○ Read only (RESTORE WITH STANDBY)

Undo file: C:\Program Files\Microsoft SQL Server\MSSQL10.MSSQLSERVER\MSSQL\Backup\U

Transaction log

- Restore transaction log to point in time

Transaction log: 05 December 2011 16:19:34

16:17:55   16:19:34   16:19:34

On completion

- ☑ Check for orphaned users and list in log file
- ☐ Send email notification
    Recipient email address:
    Send on: Error only

Figure 8-20: Database restore options.

The first section of the screen defines the **Recovery completion state**, and we're going to stick with the first option, **Operational** (RESTORE WITH RECOVERY). This will leave our database in a normal, usable state once the restore process is completed. The other two options allow us to leave the database in a restoring state, expecting more backup files, or to restore a database in Standby mode. We'll cover each of these later in the chapter.

The **Transaction log** section of the screen is used when performing a restore to a specific point in time within a transaction log backup file, and will also be covered later.

The final section allows us to configure a few special operations, after the restore is complete. The first option will test the database for orphaned users. An orphaned user is created when a database login has permissions set internally to a database, but that user doesn't have a matching login, either as a SQL login or an Active Directory login. Orphaned users often occur when moving a database between environments or servers, and are especially problematic when moving databases between operationally different platforms, such as between development and production, as we discussed in Chapter 3. Be sure to take care of these orphaned users after each restore, by either matching the user with a correct SQL Server login or by removing that user's permission from the database.

The final option is used to send an email to a person or a group of people, when the operation has completed and can be configured such that a mail is sent regardless of outcome, or when an error or warning occurs, or on error only. This is a valuable feature for any DBA. Just as we wrote email notification into our automated backup scripts, so we also need to know if a restore operation fails for some reason, or reports a warning. This may be grayed out unless the mail server options have been correctly configured. Refer to Appendix A if you want to try out this feature here.

Another nice use case for these notifications is when performing time-sensitive restores on VLDBs. We may not want to monitor the restore manually as it may run long into the night. Instead, we can use this feature so that the DBA, and the departments that need the database immediately, get a notification when the restore operation has completed.

Click **Next** to reach the, by now familiar, **Summary** screen. Skip to the **Script** tab to take a sneak preview of the script that SQL Backup has generated for this operation. You'll see that it's a three-step restore process, restoring first the base full backup, then the differential backup, and finally the second log backup (you'll see a similar script again in the next section and we'll go over the full details there).

```
EXECUTE master..sqlbackup '-SQL "RESTORE DATABASE [DatabaseForSQLBackups] FROM DISK =
''C:\SQLBackups\Chapter8\DatabaseForSQLBackups_Full_BASE.sqb'' WITH NORECOVERY, REPLACE"'

EXECUTE master..sqlbackup '-SQL "RESTORE DATABASE [DatabaseForSQLBackups] FROM DISK =
''C:\SQLBackups\Chapter8\DatabaseForSQLBackups_Diff_1.sqb'' WITH NORECOVERY"'

EXECUTE master..sqlbackup '-SQL "RESTORE LOG [DatabaseForSQLBackups] FROM DISK =
''C:\SQLBackups\Chapter8\DatabaseForSQLBackups_Log_2.sqb'' WITH RECOVERY, ORPHAN_CHECK"'
```

Listing 8-11: The SQL Backup script generated by the SQL Backup Wizard.

As a side note, I'm a little surprised to see the **REPLACE** option in the auto-generated script; it's not necessary as we did perform a tail log backup.

If everything is as it should be, click **Finish** and the restore process will start. All steps should show green check marks to let us know that everything finished successfully and some metrics for the restore process should be displayed, a truncated view of which is given in Figure 8-21.

```
…<snip>…
Restoring DatabaseForSQLBackups (database) from:
C:\SQLBackups\Chapter8\DatabaseForSQLBackups_Full_BASE.sqb
Processed 125208 pages for database 'DatabaseForSQLBackups', file 'DatabaseForSQLBackups' on
file 1.
Processed 3 pages for database 'DatabaseForSQLBackups', file 'DatabaseForSQLBackups_log' on
file 1.
RESTORE DATABASE successfully processed 125211 pages in 16.715 seconds (58.522 MB/sec).
SQL Backup process ended.

…<snip>…
```

```
Restoring DatabaseForSQLBackups (database) from:
C:\SQLBackups\Chapter8\DatabaseForSQLBackups_Diff_1.sqb
Processed 33744 pages for database 'DatabaseForSQLBackups', file 'DatabaseForSQLBackups' on
file 1.
Processed 2 pages for database 'DatabaseForSQLBackups', file 'DatabaseForSQLBackups_log' on
file 1.
RESTORE DATABASE successfully processed 33746 pages in 6.437 seconds (40.956 MB/sec).
SQL Backup process ended.

…<snip>…

Restoring DatabaseForSQLBackups (transaction logs) from:
C:\SQLBackups\Chapter8\DatabaseForSQLBackups_Log_2.sqb
Processed 0 pages for database 'DatabaseForSQLBackups', file 'DatabaseForSQLBackups' on file
1.
Processed 12504 pages for database 'DatabaseForSQLBackups', file 'DatabaseForSQLBackups_log'
on file 1.
RESTORE LOG successfully processed 12504 pages in 1.798 seconds (54.330 MB/sec).
No orphaned users detected.
SQL Backup process ended.

…<snip>…
```

Figure 8-21: Metrics for SQL Backup restore to end of the second log backup.

We won't dwell on the metrics here as we'll save that for a later section, where we compare the SQL Backup restore performance with native restores.

Being pessimistic DBAs, we won't believe the protestations of success from the output of the restore process, until we see with our own eyes that the data is as it should be.

```
USE DatabaseForSQLBackups
GO
SELECT MessageData, COUNT(MessageData)
FROM dbo.MessageTable1
GROUP BY MessageData

SELECT MessageData, COUNT(MessageData)
FROM dbo.MessageTable2
GROUP BY MessageData
```

Listing 8-12: Verifying our data.

The result confirms that all the data is there from our full, differential, and second log backups, but that the 21 rows we inserted into `MessageTable2` are currently missing.

	MessageData	(No column name)
1	Second set of short messages for MessageTable1	100000
2	What is the meaning of life, the Universe and everything?	21
3	1st set of short messages for MessageTable1	50000
4	This is the message we are going to use to fill up th...	1000000

	MessageData	(No column name)
1	Second set of short messages for MessageTable2	100000
2	This is a different message we are going to use t...	1000000
3	1st set of short messages for MessageTable2	50000

Figure 8-22: Results of data verification.

Never fear; since we had the foresight to take a tail log backup, we can get those missing 21 rows back.

SQL Backup T-SQL complete restore

We're now going to walk through the restore process again, but this time we'll use a SQL Backup script, as shown in Listing 8-13, and we'll perform a complete restore, including the tail log backup.

```
USE master
go
--step 1: Restore the base full backup
EXECUTE master..sqlbackup '-SQL "RESTORE DATABASE [DatabaseForSQLBackups]
FROM DISK = ''C:\SQLBackups\Chapter8\DatabaseForSQLBackups_Full_BASE.sqb'' WITH
NORECOVERY, DISCONNECT_EXISTING, REPLACE"'
```

```
--step 2: Restore the diff backup
EXECUTE master..sqlbackup '-SQL "RESTORE DATABASE [DatabaseForSQLBackups]
FROM DISK = ''C:\SQLBackups\Chapter8\DatabaseForSQLBackups_Diff_1.sqb'' WITH
NORECOVERY"'

--step 3: Restore the second log backup
EXECUTE master..sqlbackup '-SQL "RESTORE LOG [DatabaseForSQLBackups]
FROM DISK = ''C:\SQLBackups\Chapter8\DatabaseForSQLBackups_Log_2.sqb'' WITH
NORECOVERY"'

--step 4: Restore the tail log backup and recover the database
EXECUTE master..sqlbackup '-SQL "RESTORE LOG [DatabaseForSQLBackups]
FROM DISK = ''C:\SQLBackups\Chapter8\DatabaseForSQLBackups_Log_Tail.sqb'' WITH
RECOVERY, ORPHAN_CHECK"'
```

Listing 8-13: A complete restore operation with SQL Backup T-SQL.

There shouldn't be too much here that is new, but let's go over some of the **WITH** clause options.

- **DISCONNECT_EXISTING** – Used in Step 1, this kills any current connections to the database. Without this option, we would need to use functionality similar to that which we built into our native restore script in Chapter 3 (see Listing 4-2).

- **REPLACE** – This is required here, since we are now working with a new, freshly-restored copy of the database and we aren't performing a tail log backup as the first step of this restore operation. SQL Server will use the logical file names and paths that are stored in the backup file. Remember that this only works if the paths in the backup file exist on the server to which you are restoring.

- **NORECOVERY** – Used in Steps 1–3, this tells SQL Server to leave the database in a restoring state and to expect more backup files to be applied.

- **ORPHAN_CHECK** – Used in Step 4, this is the orphaned user check on the database, after the restore has completed, as described in the previous section.

- **RECOVERY** – Used in Step 4, this instructs SQL Server to recover the database to a normal usable state when the restore is complete.

Execute the script, then, while it is running, we can take a quick look at the SQL Backup monitoring stored procedure, sqbstatus, a feature that lets us monitor any SQL Backup restore operation, while it is in progress. Quickly open a second tab in SSMS and execute Listing 8-14.

```
EXEC master..sqbstatus
GO
```

Listing 8-14: Red Gate SQL Backup Pro monitoring stored procedure.

The stored procedure returns four columns: the name of the database being restored; the identity of the user running the restore; how many bytes of data have been processed; and the number of compressed bytes that have been produced in the backup file. It can be useful to check this output during a long-running restore the first time you perform it, to gauge compression rates, or to get an estimate of completion time for restores and backups on older versions of SQL Server, where Dynamic Management Views are not available to tell you that information.

Once the restore completes, you'll see restore metrics similar to those shown in Figure 8-21, but with an additional section for the tail log restore. If you rerun Listing 8-12 to verify your data, you should find that the "missing" 21 rows in MessageTable2 are back!

SQL Backup point-in-time restore to standby

In our final restore example, we're going to restore a standby copy of the DatabaseFor-SQLBackups database to a specific point in time in order to attempt to retrieve some accidentally deleted data.

Standby servers are commonly used as a High Availability solution; we have a secondary, or standby, server that can be brought online quickly in the event of a failure of the primary server. We can restore a database to the standby server, and then successively ship over and apply transaction logs, using the WITH STANDBY option, to roll forward the standby database and keep it closely in sync with the primary. In between log restores, the standby database remains accessible but in a read-only state. This makes it a good choice for near real-time reporting solutions where some degree of time lag in the reporting data is acceptable.

However, this option is occasionally useful when in the unfortunate position of needing to roll forward through a set of transaction logs to locate exactly where a data mishap occurred. It's a laborious process (roll forward a bit, query the standby database, roll forward a bit further, query again, and so on) but, in the absence of any other means to restore a particular object or set of data, such as a tool that supports object-level restore (more on this a little later) it could be a necessity.

In order to simplify our point-in-time restore, let's run another full backup, as shown in Listing 8-15.

```
EXECUTE master..sqlbackup '-SQL "BACKUP DATABASE [DatabaseForSQLBackups]
TO DISK = ''C:\SQLBackups\Chapter8\DatabaseForSQLBackups_Full_BASE2.sqb''
WITH DISKRETRYINTERVAL = 30, DISKRETRYCOUNT = 10, THREADCOUNT = 2, COMPRESSION =
1"'
GO
```

Listing 8-15: A new base full backup of DatabaseForSQLBackups.

We'll then add some more data to each of our message tables, before simulating a disaster, in the form of someone accidentally dropping MessageTable2.

```
USE [DatabaseForSQLBackups]
GO
INSERT  INTO dbo.MessageTable1
VALUES  ( 'MessageTable1, I think the answer might be 41. No, wait...',
          GETDATE() )
GO 41
```

```
/* Find date of final INSERT from previous statement
   This is to help us with the RESTORE process

USE DatabaseForSQLBackups
GO
SELECT  TOP(1) MessageData,MessageDate
FROM dbo.MessageTable1
WHERE MessageData LIKE 'MessageTable1%'
ORDER BY MessageDate DESC

-- Output: 2011-12-06 10:41:36.540

*/
INSERT  INTO dbo.MessageTable2
VALUES  ( 'MessageTable2, the true answer is 42!', GETDATE() )
GO 42
-- final insert time: 2011-12-06 10:42:45.897

--Disaster strikes!
DROP TABLE dbo.MessageTable2
GO
```

Listing 8-16: Disaster strikes MessageTable2.

In this simple example, we have the luxury of knowing exactly when each event occurred. However, imagine this is a busy production database, and we only find out about the accidental table loss many hours later. Listing 8-17 simulates one of our regular, scheduled log backups, which runs after the data loss has occurred.

```
USE [master]
GO
EXECUTE master..sqlbackup '-SQL "BACKUP LOG [DatabaseForSQLBackups]
TO DISK = ''C:\SQLBackups\Chapter8\DatabaseForSQLBackups_Log_3.sqb''
WITH DISKRETRYINTERVAL = 30, DISKRETRYCOUNT = 10,
COMPRESSION = 1, THREADCOUNT = 2"'
```

Listing 8-17: A post-disaster log backup.

Restore to standby using the SQL Backup GUI

Having contrived the data loss, we can now start the restore process. Right-click on
`DatabaseForSQLBackups`, pick the latest transaction log backup (`DatabaseForSQL-`
`Backups_Log_3.sqb`) and click **Next**. Again, since the files are still in their original
location, SQL Backup will locate any other files it needs from further back down the
chain, in this case, just the latest full backup. If you've moved the full backup file, locate it
manually, as described before.

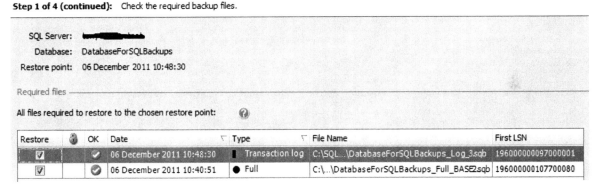

Figure 8-23: Identifying the backup files for our PIT restore.

Our intention here, as discussed, is to restore a copy of the `DatabaseForSQLBackups`
database in Standby mode. This will give us read access to the standby copy as we attempt
to roll forward to just before the point where we lost `Messagetable2`. So, this time, we'll
restore to a new database, called `DatabaseForSQLBackups_Standby`, as shown in
Figure 8-24.

Figure 8-24: Restoring to a new, standby copy of the `DatabaseForSQLBackups` database.

At Step 3, we're going to choose a new option for the completion state of our restored database, which is **Read-only** (`RESTORE WITH STANDBY`). In doing so, we must create an undo file for the standby database. As we subsequently apply transaction log backups to our standby database, to roll forward in time, SQL Server needs to be able to roll back the effects of any transactions that were uncommitted at the point in time to which we are restoring. However, the effects of these uncommitted transactions must be preserved. As we roll further forward in time, SQL Server may need to reapply the effects of a transaction it previously rolled back. If SQL Server doesn't keep a record of that activity, we wouldn't be able to keep our database relationally sound. All of this information regarding the rolled back transactions is managed through the undo file.

We'll place the undo file in our usual **SQLBackups** directory. In the central portion of the screen, we have the option to restore the transaction log to a specific point in time; we're going to roll forward in stages, first to a point as close as we can after 10:41:36.540, which should be the time we completed the batch of 41 INSERTs into `MessageTable1`. Again, remember that in a real restore scenario, you will probably not know which statements were run when.

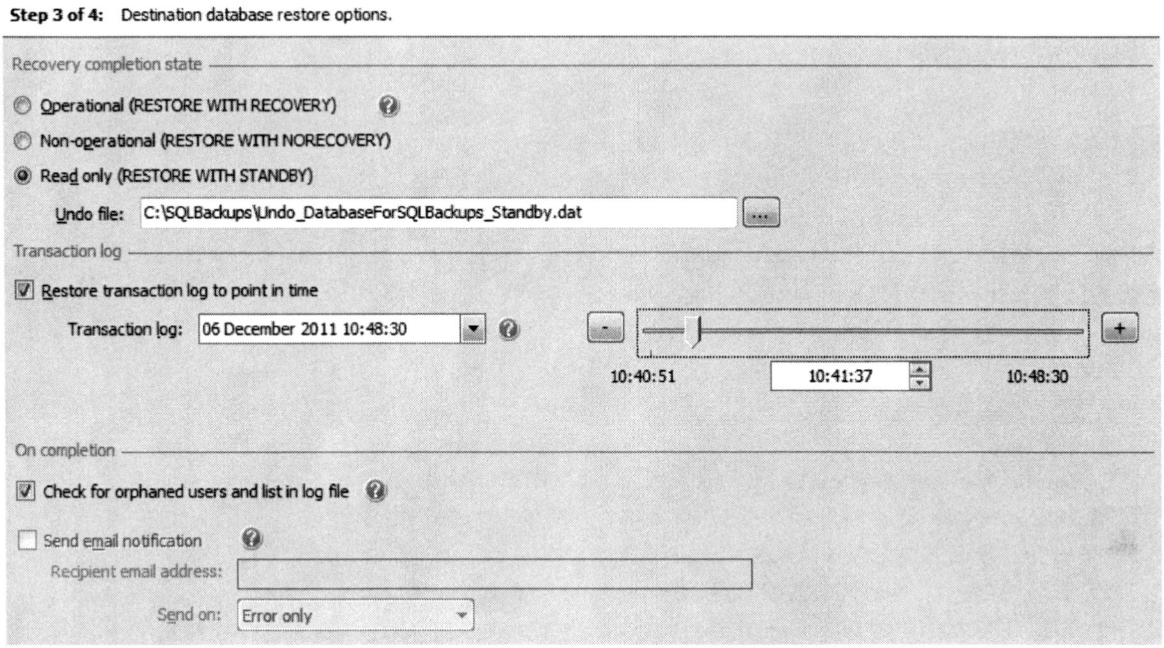

Step 3 of 4: Destination database restore options.

Recovery completion state

○ Operational (RESTORE WITH RECOVERY)

○ Non-operational (RESTORE WITH NORECOVERY)

● Read only (RESTORE WITH STANDBY)

Undo file: C:\SQLBackups\Undo_DatabaseForSQLBackups_Standby.dat

Transaction log

☑ Restore transaction log to point in time

Transaction log: 06 December 2011 10:48:30

10:40:51   10:41:37   10:48:30

On completion

☑ Check for orphaned users and list in log file

☐ Send email notification

Recipient email address:

Send on: Error only

Figure 8-25: Restoring `WITH STANDBY` to a specific point in a transaction log.

Click **Next** to reach the **Summary** screen, where we can also take a quick preview of the script that's been generated (we'll discuss this in more detail shortly). Click **Finish** to execute the restore operation and it should complete quickly and successfully, with the usual metrics output. Refresh the SSMS Object Explorer to reveal a database called `DatabaseForSQLBackups_Standby`, which is designated as being in a Standby/Read-Only state. We can query it to see if we restored to the point we intended.

```
USE DatabaseForSQLBackups_Standby
GO
SELECT  MessageData ,
        COUNT(MessageData)
FROM    dbo.MessageTable1
GROUP BY MessageData
```

```
SELECT   MessageData ,
         COUNT(MessageData)
FROM     dbo.MessageTable2
GROUP BY MessageData
GO
```

Listing 8-18: Querying the standby database.

As we hoped, we've got both tables back, and we've restored the 41 rows in `Message-eTable1`, but not the 42 in `MessageTable2`.

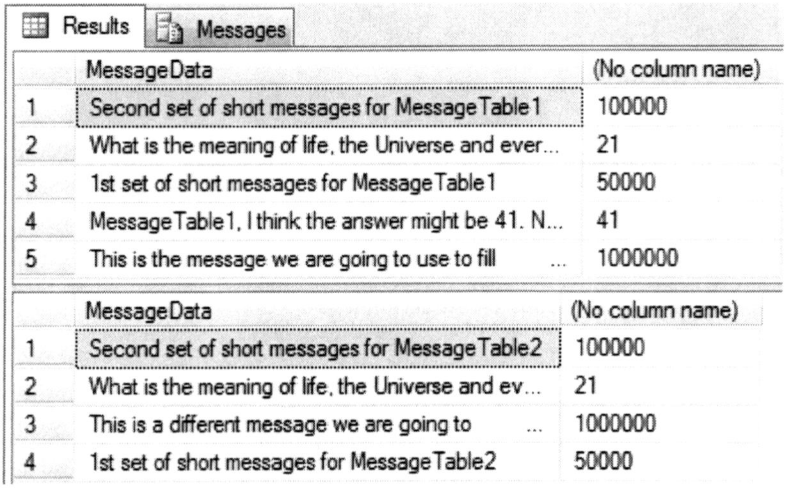

	MessageData	(No column name)
1	Second set of short messages for MessageTable1	100000
2	What is the meaning of life, the Universe and ever...	21
3	1st set of short messages for MessageTable1	50000
4	MessageTable1, I think the answer might be 41. N...	41
5	This is the message we are going to use to fill ...	1000000

	MessageData	(No column name)
1	Second set of short messages for MessageTable2	100000
2	What is the meaning of life, the Universe and ev...	21
3	This is a different message we are going to ...	1000000
4	1st set of short messages for MessageTable2	50000

Figure 8-26: Verifying our data, Part 1.

To get these 42 rows back, so the table is back to the state it was when dropped, we'll need to roll forward a little further, but stop just before the `DROP TABLE` command was issued. Start another restore operation on `DatabaseForSQLBackups`, and proceed as before to Step 2. This time, we want to overwrite the current `DatabaseForSQLBackups_Standby` database, so select it from the drop-down box.

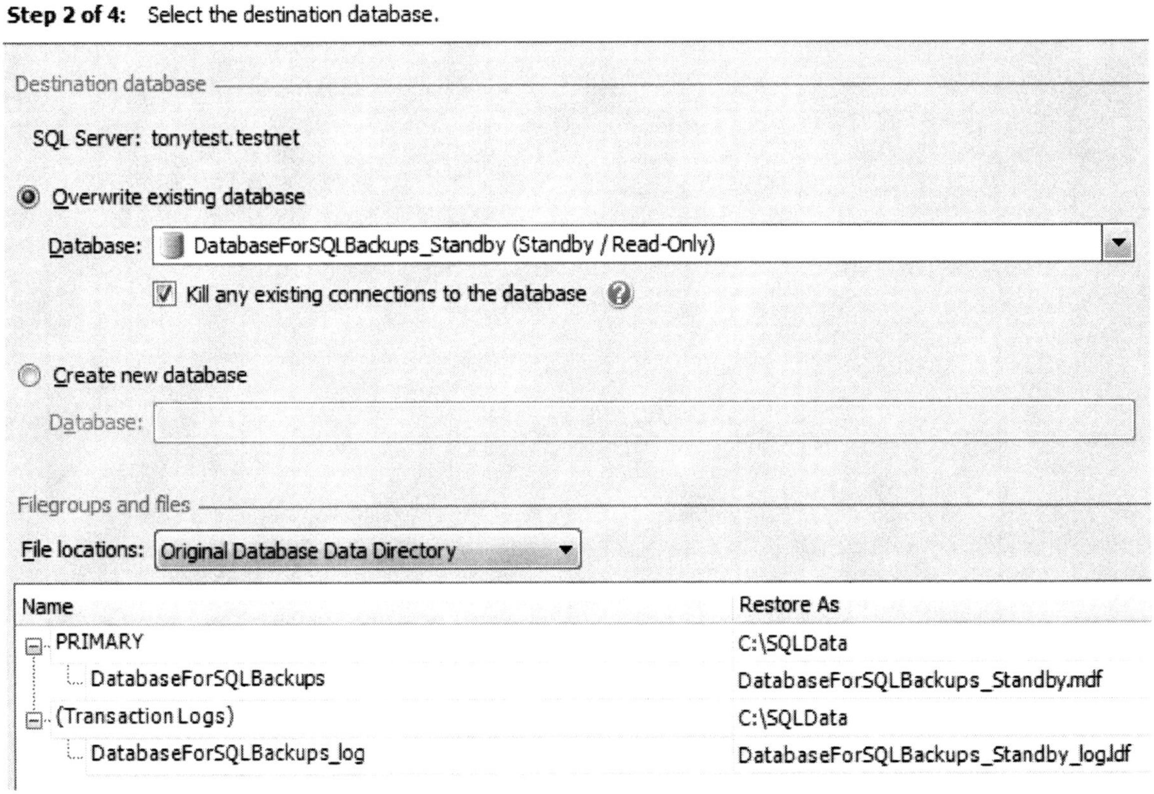

Step 2 of 4: Select the destination database.

Destination database

SQL Server: tonytest.testnet

◉ Overwrite existing database

Database: ▊ DatabaseForSQLBackups_Standby (Standby / Read-Only) ▼

☑ Kill any existing connections to the database ❓

○ Create new database

Database:

Filegroups and files

File locations: Original Database Data Directory ▼

Name	Restore As
⊟ PRIMARY	C:\SQLData
⌐ DatabaseForSQLBackups	DatabaseForSQLBackups_Standby.mdf
⊟ (Transaction Logs)	C:\SQLData
⌐ DatabaseForSQLBackups_log	DatabaseForSQLBackups_Standby_log.ldf

Figure 8-27: Overwriting the current standby database.

At Step 3, we'll specify another standby restore, using the same undo file, and this time we'll roll forward to just after we completed the load of 42 rows into Messagetable2, but just before that table got dropped (*i.e.* as close as we can to 10:42:45.897).

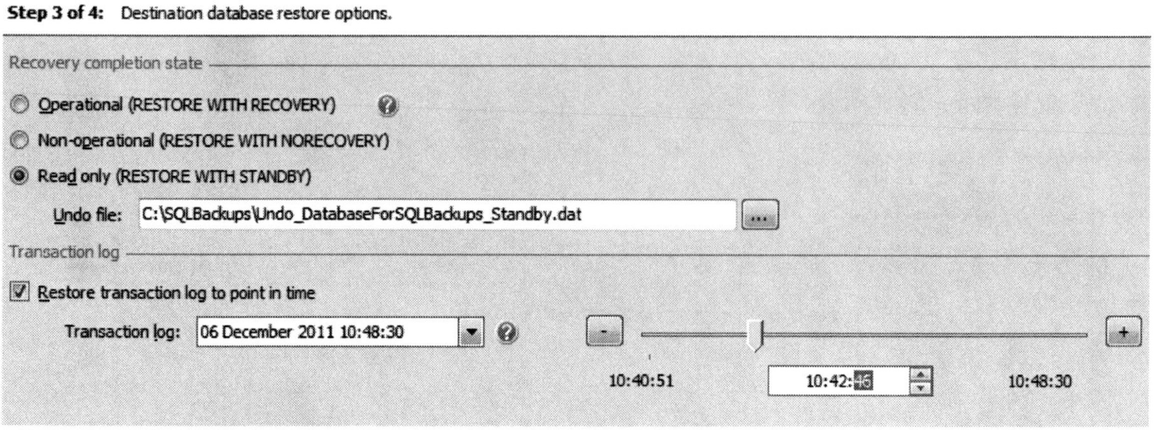

Step 3 of 4: Destination database restore options.

Recovery completion state

○ Operational (RESTORE WITH RECOVERY) ❓

○ Non-operational (RESTORE WITH NORECOVERY)

◉ Read only (RESTORE WITH STANDBY)

Undo file: C:\SQLBackups\Undo_DatabaseForSQLBackups_Standby.dat   [...]

Transaction log

☑ Restore transaction log to point in time

Transaction log: 06 December 2011 10:48:30 ▼ ❓   [-] ————————●———————— [+]

10:40:51   10:42:[ ] ▲▼   10:48:30

Figure 8-28: Rolling further forward.

Once again, the operation should complete successfully, with metrics similar to those shown in Figure 8-29.

```
Restoring DatabaseForSQLBackups_Standby (database) from:
C:\SQLBackups\Chapter8\DatabaseForSQLBackups_Full_BASE2.sqb
Processed 125208 pages for database 'DatabaseForSQLBackups_Standby', file
'DatabaseForSQLBackups' on file 1.
Processed 3 pages for database 'DatabaseForSQLBackups_Standby', file 'DatabaseForSQLBackups_
log' on file 1.
RESTORE DATABASE successfully processed 125211 pages in 16.512 seconds (59.241 MB/sec).
SQL Backup process ended.

Restoring DatabaseForSQLBackups_Standby (transaction logs) from:
C:\SQLBackups\Chapter8\DatabaseForSQLBackups_Log_3.sqb
Processed 0 pages for database 'DatabaseForSQLBackups_Standby', file 'DatabaseForSQLBackups'
on file 1.
Processed 244 pages for database 'DatabaseForSQLBackups_Standby', file 'DatabaseForSQLBackups_
log' on file 1.
RESTORE LOG successfully processed 244 pages in 0.032 seconds (59.555 MB/sec).
No orphaned users detected.
SQL Backup process ended.
```

Figure 8-29: Output metrics for the PIT restore.

Rerun our data verification query, from Listing 8-18 and you should see that we now have the 42 rows restored to `MessageTable2`.

Restore to standby using a SQL Backup script

Before we move on, it's worth taking a more detailed look at the SQL Backup T-SQL script that we'd use to perform the same point-in-time restore operation.

```
EXECUTE master..sqlbackup '-SQL "RESTORE DATABASE [DatabaseForSQLBackups_Standby]
FROM DISK = ''C:\SQLBackups\Chapter8\DatabaseForSQLBackups_Full_BASE2.sqb''
WITH NORECOVERY, MOVE ''DatabaseForSQLBackups''
TO ''C:\SQLData\DatabaseForSQLBackups_Standby.mdf'',
MOVE ''DatabaseForSQLBackups_log'' TO
''C:\SQLData\DatabaseForSQLBackups_Standby_log.ldf''"'

EXECUTE master..sqlbackup '-SQL "RESTORE LOG [DatabaseForSQLBackups_Standby]
FROM DISK = ''C:\SQLBackups\Chapter8\DatabaseForSQLBackups_Log_3.sqb''
WITH STANDBY = ''C:\SQLBackups\Undo_DatabaseForSQLBackups_Standby.dat'',
STOPAT = ''2011-12-06T10:42:46'', ORPHAN_CHECK"'
```

Listing 8-19: Restore to standby SQL Backup script.

The first command restores the base backup file to a new database, using the MOVE argument to copy the existing data and log files to the newly designated files. We specify NORECOVERY so that the database remains in a restoring state, to receive further backup files.

The second command applies the log backup file to this new database. Notice the use of the WITH STANDBY clause, which indicates the restored state of the new database, and associates it with the correct undo file. Also, we use the STOPAT clause, with which you should be familiar from Chapter 4, to specify the exact point in time to which we wish to roll forward. Any transactions that were uncommitted at the time will be rolled back during the restore.

This is the first of our restore operations that didn't end with the RECOVERY keyword. The STANDBY is one of three ways (RECOVERY, NORECOVERY, STANDBY) to finalize a restore, and one of the two ways to finalize a restore and leave the data in an accessible state. It's important to know which finalization technique to use in which situations, and to remember they don't all do the same thing.

Alternatives to restore with standby

In a real-world restore, our next step, which we have not yet tackled here, would be to transfer the lost table back into the production database (DatabaseForSQLBackups). This, however, is not always an easy thing to do. If we do have to bring back data this way, we may run into referential integrity issues with data in related tables. If the data in other tables contains references to the lost table, but the database doesn't have the proper constraints in place, then we could have a bit of a mess to clean up when we import that data back into the production database.

Also, one of the problems with this restore to standby approach is that you might also find yourself in a position where you have a VLDB that would require a great deal of time and space to restore just to get back one table, as in our example. In this type of situation, if your VLDB wasn't designed with multiple data files and filegroups, you might be able turn to an object-level restore solution. These tools will restore, from a database backup, just a single table or other object without having to restore the entire database.

Restore metrics: native vs. SQL Backup

In order to get some comparison between the performances of native restores versus restores from compressed backups, via SQL Backup, we'll first simply gather metrics for a SQL backup restore of our latest base backup of DatabaseForSQBackups (_Full_ BASE2.sqb), shown in Listing 8-20.

```
USE master
go
--Restore the base full backup
EXECUTE master..sqlbackup '-SQL "RESTORE DATABASE [DatabaseForSQLBackups]
FROM DISK = ''C:\SQLBackups\Chapter8\DatabaseForSQLBackups_Full_BASE2.sqb''
WITH RECOVERY, DISCONNECT_EXISTING, REPLACE"'
```

```
...
Restoring DatabaseForSQLBackups (database) from:
C:\SQLBackups\Chapter8\DatabaseForSQLBackups_Full_BASE2.sqb
Processed 125208 pages for database 'DatabaseForSQLBackups', file 'DatabaseForSQLBackups' on file 1.
Processed 3 pages for database 'DatabaseForSQLBackups', file 'DatabaseForSQLBackups_log' on file 1.
RESTORE DATABASE successfully processed 125211 pages in 15.901 seconds (82.195 MB/sec).
```

Listing 8-20: Metrics for SQL restore of full database backup.

Then, we'll take a native, compressed full backup of the newly restored database, and then a native restore from that backup.

```
USE [master]
GO
BACKUP DATABASE DatabaseForSQLBackups TO
DISK = N'C:\SQLBackups\Chapter8\DatabaseForSQLBackups_Full_Native.bak'
WITH COMPRESSION, INIT,  NAME = N'DatabaseForSQLBackups-Full Database Backup'
GO

RESTORE DATABASE [DatabaseForSQLBackups] FROM
DISK = N'C:\SQLBackups\Chapter8\DatabaseForSQLBackups_Full_Native.bak'
WITH FILE = 1, STATS = 25, REPLACE
GO
```

```
...
25 percent processed.
50 percent processed.
75 percent processed.
100 percent processed.
Processed 125208 pages for database 'DatabaseForSQLBackups', file 'DatabaseForSQLBackups' on file 1.
Processed 2 pages for database 'DatabaseForSQLBackups', file 'DatabaseForSQLBackups_log' on file 1.
RESTORE DATABASE successfully processed 125210 pages in 13.441 seconds (53.044 MB/sec).
```

Listing 8-21: Code and metrics for native restore of full database backup.

As a final test, we can rerun Listing 8-21, but performing a native, non-compressed backup, and then restoring from that. In my tests, the restore times for native compressed and SQL Backup compressed backups were roughly comparable, with the native compressed restores performing slightly faster. Native non-compressed restores were somewhat slower, running in around 21 seconds in my tests.

Verifying Backups

As discussed in Chapter 2, the only truly reliable way of ensuring that your various backup files really can be used to restore a database is to perform regular test restores. However, there are a few other things you can do to minimize the risk that, for some reason, one of your backups will be unusable.

SQL Backup backups, like native backups can, to some extent, be checked for validity using both BACKUP...WITH CHECKSUM and RESTORE VERIFYONLY. If both options are configured for the backup process (see Figure 8-5b) then SQL Backup will verify that the backup is complete and readable and then recalculate the checksum on the data pages contained in the backup file and compare it against the checksum values generated during the backup. Listing 8-22 shows the script.

```
EXECUTE master..sqlbackup '-SQL "BACKUP DATABASE [DatabaseForSQLBackups]
TO DISK = ''D:\SQLBackups\Chapter8\DatabaseForSQLBackups_FULL.sqb''
WITH CHECKSUM, DISKRETRYINTERVAL = 30, DISKRETRYCOUNT = 10, THREADCOUNT = 2,
VERIFY"'
```

Listing 8-22: BACKUP...WITH CHECKSUM and RESTORE VERIFYONLY with SQL Backup.

Alternatively, we can run either of the validity checks separately. As discussed in Chapter 2, BACKUP...WITH CHECKSUM verifies only that each page of data written to the backup file is error free in relation to how it was read from disk. It does not validate that the backup data is valid, only that what was being written, was written correctly. It can cause a lot of overhead and slow down backup operations significantly, so evaluate its use carefully, based on available CPU capacity.

Nevertheless, these validity checks do provide some degree of reassurance, without the need to perform full test restores. Remember that we also need to be performing DBCC CHECKDB routines on our databases at least weekly, to make sure they are in good health and that our backups will be restorable.

There are two ways to do this: we can run DBCC CHECKDB before the backup, as a T-SQL statement, in front of the extended stored procedure that calls SQL Backup Pro or, with version 7 of the tool, we can also enable the integrity check via the Schedule Restore Jobs... wizard, as shown in Figure 8-30.

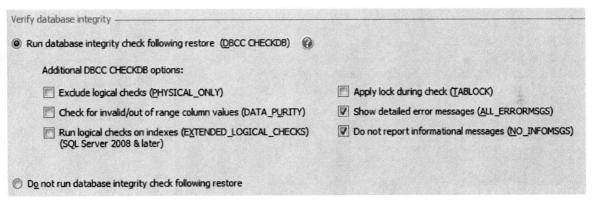

Figure 8-30: Configuring DBCC CHECKDB options as part of a restore job.

Backup Optimization

We discussed many ways to optimize backup storage and scheduling back in Chapter 2, so here, we'll focus just on a few optimization features that are supported by SQL Backup. The first is the ability to back up to multiple backup files on multiple devices. This is one of the best ways to increase throughput in backup operations, since we can write to several backup files simultaneously. This only applies when each disk is physically separate hardware; if we have one physical disk that is partitioned into two or more logical drives, we will not see a performance increase since the backup data can only be written to one of those logical drives at a time.

Listing 8-23 shows the SQL Backup command to back up a database to multiple backup files, on separate disks. The listing will also show how to restore from these multiple files, which requires the addition of extra file locations.

```
EXECUTE master..sqlbackup '-SQL "BACKUP DATABASE [DatabaseForSQLBackups]
TO DISK = ''C:\SQLBackups\Chapter8\DatabaseForSQLBackups_FULL_1.sqb'',
DISK = ''D\SQLBackups\Chapter8\DatabaseForSQLBackups_FULL_2.sqb'',
WITH DISKRETRYINTERVAL = 30, DISKRETRYCOUNT = 10, COMPRESSION = 3"'

EXECUTE master..sqlbackup '-SQL "RESTORE DATABASE [DatabaseForSQLBackups]
FROM DISK = ''C:\SQLBackups\Chapter8\DatabaseForSQLBackups_FULL_1.sqb'',
DISK = ''D:\SQLBackups\Chapter8\DatabaseForSQLBackups_FULL_2.sqb'',
WITH RECOVERY"'
```

Listing 8-23: Backing up a database to multiple files with SQL Backup.

This is useful not only for backup throughput/performance; it is also a useful way to cut down on the size of a single backup, for transfer to other systems. Nothing is more infuriating than trying to copy a huge file to another system only to see it fail after 90% of the copy is complete. With this technique, we can break down that large file and copy the pieces separately.

Note that backup to multiple files is also supported in native T-SQL and for native backups, as shown in Listing 8-24.

```
BACKUP DATABASE [DatabaseForSQLBackups]
TO DISK = 'C:\SQLBackups\Chapter8\DatabaseForSQLBackups_FULL_Native_1.bak',
 DISK = 'C:\SQLBackups\Chapter8\DatabaseForSQLBackups_FULL_Native_2.bak'
```

Listing 8-24: Native backup to multiple files.

Having covered how to split backups to multiple locations, let's now see how to back up a single file, but have it stored in multiple locations, as shown in Listing 8-25. This is useful when we want to back up to a separate location, such as a network share, when taking the original backup. This is only an integrated option when using the SQL Backup tool.

```
EXECUTE master..sqlbackup '-SQL "BACKUP DATABASE [DatabaseForSQLBackups]
TO DISK = ''C:\SQLBackups\Chatper8\DatabaseForSQLBackups_FULL.sqb''
WITH COMPRESSION = 3, COPYTO = ''\\NETWORKMACHINE\SHARENAME\'', THREADCOUNT = 2"'
```

Listing 8-25: Back up a database with a copy to a separate location.

This will cause the backup process to run a bit longer, since it has to back up the database as well as copy it to another location. Just remember that network latency can be a major time factor in the completion of the backups, when using this option.

Ultimately, to get the most performance out of a backup, we will need to tune each backup routine to match the specific environment. This requires testing the disk subsystem, the throughput of SQL Server, and making adjustments in the backup process to get the best backup performance. There is a useful listing on the Red Gate support site that offers some tips on how to do this using just a few extra parameters in the SQL Backup stored procedure: WWW.RED-GATE.COM/SUPPORTCENTER/CONTENT/SQL_BACKUP/HELP/6.5/ SBU_OPTIMIZINGBACKUP.

Summary

All of the same principles that we have discussed when using native SQL Server backup procedures apply when using Red Gate SQL Backup Pro. We want to follow the same best practices, and we can implement the same type of backup strategies if we are using SQL Backup in our environment. Red Gate SQL Backup Pro is not a requirement for our backup strategies, but it is a great tool that can save substantial amounts of time and disk space. Always remember to use the right tool for the right job.

Chapter 9: File and Filegroup Backup and Restore

So far in this book, all of the full and differential backups we've taken have been database backups; in other words our full and differential backups have been capturing the contents of all data files in all filegroups. However, it's also possible to perform these types of backups on individual files or filegroups. Likewise, it's also possible in some cases, and assuming you have a complete set of accompanying transaction log backups, to restore just a subset of a database, such as an individual file or filegroup, rather than the entire database.

I'll state upfront that, in my experience, it is relatively rare for a DBA to have too many databases that are subject to either file backups or filed-based restores. Even databases straying into the hundreds of gigabytes range, which may take a few hours to back up, will be managed, generally, using the usual mix of full database backups, supplemented by differential database backups (and, of course, log backups). Likewise, these databases will be restored, as necessary, using the normal database restore techniques we've discussed in previous chapters.

However, it's when we start managing databases that run into the terabyte range that we start getting into trouble using these standard database backup and restore techniques, since it may no longer be possible to either back up the database in the required time, or restore the whole database within the limits of acceptable down-time. In such cases, file-based backup and restore becomes a necessity, and in this chapter, we'll discuss:

- potential advantages of file-based backup and restore

- common file architectures to support file-based backup and restore

- performing full and differential file backups using native SSMS and T-SQL, as well as SQL Backup

- performing several different types of file-based restore, namely:

  - **complete restores** – restore right to the point of failure

  - **point-in-time restores** – restore to a specific point in a transaction log backup using the **STOPAT** parameter

  - **restoring just a single data file** – recovering the database as a whole, by restoring just a single "failed" secondary data file

  - **online piecemeal restore**, with partial database recovery – bringing a database back online quickly after a failure, by restoring just the primary data file, followed later by the other data files. This operation requires SQL Server Enterprise (or Developer) Edition.

Advantages of File Backup and Restore

In order to exploit the potential benefits of file-based backup and restore, we need to have a database where the filegroup architecture is such that data is split down intelligently across multiple filegroups. We'll discuss some ways to achieve this in the next section but, assuming for now that this is the case, the benefits below can be gained.

- **Easier VLDB backup administration** – For very large databases (*i.e.* in the terabyte range) it is often not possible to run a nightly database backup, simply due to time constraints and the fact that such backups have a higher risk of failure because of the very long processing times. In such cases, file backups become a necessity.

- **Restoring a subset of the data files** – Regardless of whether we take database or file backups, it's possible in some cases to recover a database by restoring only a subset of that database, say, a single filegroup (though it's also possible to restore just a single page), rather than the whole database.

- **Online piecemeal restores** – In the Enterprise Edition of SQL Server 2005, and later, we can make a database "partially available" by restoring only the **PRIMARY** filegroup and bringing the database back online, then later restoring other secondary filegroups.

- **Improved disk I/O performance** – Achieved by separating different files and filegroups onto separate disk drives. This assumes that the SAN, DAS, or local storage is set up to take advantage of the files being on separate *physical* spindles, or SSDs, as opposed to separate *logical* disks.

Piecemeal restores can be a massive advantage for any database, and may be a necessity for VLDBs, where the time taken for a full database restore would fall outside the down-time stipulated in the SLA.

In terms of disk I/O performance, it's possible to gain performance advantages by creating multiple data files within a filegroup, and placing each file on a separate drive and, in some case, by separating specific tables and indexes into a filegroup, again on a dedicated drive. It's even possible to partition a single object across multiple filegroups (a topic we won't delve into further in this book, but see HTTP://MSDN.MICROSOFT.COM/EN-US/LIBRARY/MS162136.ASPX for a general introduction).

In general, I would caution against going overboard with the idea of trying to optimize disk I/O by manual placement of files and filegroups on different disk spindles, unless it is a proven necessity from a performance or storage perspective. It's a complex process that requires a lot of prior planning and ongoing maintenance, as data grows. Instead, I think there is much to be said for keeping file architecture as simple as is appropriate for a given database, and then letting your SAN or direct-attached RAID array take care of the disk I/O optimization. If a specific database requires it, then by all means work with the SAN administrators to optimize file and disk placement, but don't feel the need to do this on every database in your environment. As always, it is best to test and see what overhead this would place on the maintenance and administration of the server as opposed to the potential benefits which it provides.

With that in mind, let's take a closer, albeit still relatively brief, look at possible filegroup architectures.

Common Filegroup Architectures

A filegroup is simply a logical collection of one or more database files. So far in this book, our database creation statements have been very straightforward, and similar in layout to the one shown in Listing 9-1.

```
CREATE DATABASE [FileBackupsTest] ON PRIMARY
(    NAME = N'FileBackupsTest'
  , FILENAME = N'C:\SQLData\FileBackupsTest.mdf'
) LOG ON
(    NAME = N'FileBackupsTest_log'
  , FILENAME = N'C:\SQLData\FileBackupsTest_log.ldf'
)
GO
```

Listing 9-1:   A simple database file architecture.

In other words, a single data file in the **PRIMARY** filegroup, plus a log file (remember that log files are entirely separate from data files; log files are never members of a filegroup). However, as discussed in Chapter 1, it's common to create more than one data file per filegroup, as shown in Listing 9-2.

```
CREATE DATABASE [FileBackupsTest] ON PRIMARY
(    NAME = N'FileBackupsTest',
      FILENAME = N'C:\SQLData\FileBackupsTest.mdf'),
(    NAME = N'FileBackupsTest2',
      FILENAME = N'D:\SQLData\FileBackupsTest2.ndf')
 LOG ON
(    NAME = N'FileBackupsTest_log',
      FILENAME = N'E:\SQLData\FileBackupsTest_log.ldf'
)
GO
```

Listing 9-2:   Two data files in the **PRIMARY** filegroup.

Now we have two data files in the PRIMARY filegroup, plus the log file. SQL Server will utilize all the data files in a given database on a "proportionate fill" basis, making sure that each data file is used equally, in a round-robin fashion. We can also back up each of those files separately, if we wish.

We can place each data file on a separate spindle to increase disk I/O performance. However, we have no control over exactly which data gets placed where, so we may end up with most of the data that is very regularly updated written to one file and most of the data that is rarely touched in the second. We'd have one disk working to peak capacity while the other sat largely idle, and we wouldn't achieve the desired performance benefit.

The next step is to exert some control over exactly what data gets stored where, and this means creating some secondary filegroups, and dictating which objects store their data where. Take a look at Listing 9-3; in it we create the usual PRIMARY filegroup, holding our mdf file, but also a user-defined filegroup called SECONDARY, in which we create three secondary data files.

```
CREATE DATABASE [FileBackupsTest] ON PRIMARY
( NAME = N'FileBackupsTest',
        FILENAME = N'E:\SQLData\FileBackupsTest.mdf' ,
            SIZE = 51200KB , FILEGROWTH = 10240KB ),
    FILEGROUP [Secondary]
( NAME = N'FileBackupsTestUserData1',
        FILENAME = N'G:\SQLData\FileBackupsTestUserData1.ndf' ,
            SIZE = 5120000KB , FILEGROWTH = 1024000KB ),
( NAME = N'FileBackupsTestUserData2',
        FILENAME = N'H:\SQLData\FileBackupsTestUserData2.ndf' ,
            SIZE = 5120000KB , FILEGROWTH = 1024000KB ),
( NAME = N'FileBackupsTestUserData3',
        FILENAME = N'I:\SQLData\FileBackupsTestUserData3.ndf' ,
            SIZE = 5120000KB , FILEGROWTH = 1024000KB )
    LOG ON
( NAME = N'FileBackupsTest_log',
        FILENAME = N'F:\SQLData\FileBackupsTest_log.ldf' ,
            SIZE = 1024000KB , FILEGROWTH = 512000KB )
GO
USE [FileBackupsTest]
GO
```

```
IF NOT EXISTS ( SELECT   name
                FROM     sys.filegroups
                WHERE    is_default = 1
                         AND name = N'Secondary' )
    ALTER DATABASE [FileBackupsTest] MODIFY FILEGROUP [Secondary] DEFAULT
GO
```

Listing 9-3:   A template for creating a multi-filegroup database.

Crucially, we can now dictate, to a greater or less degree, what data gets put in which filegroup. In this example, immediately after creating the database, we have stipulated the SECONDARY filegroup, rather than the PRIMARY filegroup, as the default filegroup for this database. This means that our PRIMARY filegroup will hold only our system objects and data (plus pointers to the secondary data files). By default, any user objects and data will now be inserted into one of the data files in the SECONDARY filegroup, unless this was overridden by specifying a different target filegroup when the object was created. Again, the fact that we have multiple data files means that we can back each file up separately, if the entire database can't be backed up in the allotted nightly window.

There are many different ways in which filegroups can be used to dictate, at the file level, where certain objects and data are stored. In this example, we've simply decided that the PRIMARY is for system data, and SECONDARY is for user data, but we can take this further. We might decide to store system data in PRIMARY, plus any other data necessary for the functioning of a customer-facing sales website. The actual sales and order data might be in a separate, dedicated filegroup. This architecture might be especially beneficial when running an Enterprise Edition SQL Server, where we can perform online piecemeal restores. In this case, we could restore the PRIMARY first, and get the database back online and the website back up. Meanwhile we can get to work restoring the other, secondary filegroups.

We might also split tables logically into different filegroups, for example:

*   separating rarely-used archive data from current data (e.g. current year's sales data in one filegroup, archive data in others)

- separating out read-only data from read-write data

- separating out critical reporting data.

Another scheme that you may encounter is use of filegroups to separate the non-clustered indexes from the indexed data, although this seems to be a declining practice in cases where online index maintenance is available, with Enterprise Editions of SQL Server, and due to SAN disk systems becoming faster. Remember that the clustered index data is always in the same filegroup as the base table.

We can also target specific filegroups at specific types of storage, putting the most frequently used and/or most critical data on faster media, while avoiding eating up high-speed disk space with data that is rarely used. For example, we might use SSDs for critical report data, a slower SAN-attached drive for archive data, and so on.

All of these schemes may or may not represent valid uses of filegroups in your environment, but almost all of them will add complexity to your architecture, and to your backup and restore process, assuming you employ file-based backup and restore. As discussed earlier, I only recommend you go down this route if the need is proven, for example for VLDBs where the need is dictated by backup and or restore requirements. For databases of a manageable size, we can continue to use database backups and so gain the benefit of using multiple files/filegroups without the backup and restore complexity.

Of course, one possibility is that a database, originally designed with very simple file architecture, grows to the point that it is no longer manageable in this configuration. What is to be done then? Changing the file architecture for a database requires very careful planning, both with regard to immediate changes to the file structure and how this will evolve to accommodate future growth. For the initial redesign, we'll need to consider questions such as the number of filegroups required, how the data is going to be separated out across those filegroups, how many data files are required, where they are going to be stored on disk, and so on. Having done this, we're then faced with the task of planning how to move all the data, and how much time is available each night to get the job done.

These are all questions we need to take seriously and plan carefully, with the help of our most experienced DBAs; getting this right the first time will save some huge headaches later.

Let's consider a simple example, where we need to re-architect the file structure for a database which currently stores all data in a single data file in PRIMARY. We have decided to create an additional secondary filegroup, named UserDataFilegroup, which contains three physical data files, each of which will be backed up during the nightly backup window. This secondary filegroup will become the default filegroup for the database, and the plan is that from now on only system objects and data will be stored in the PRIMARY data file.

How are we going to get the data stored in the primary file into this new filegroup? It depends on the table index design, but ideally each table in the database will have a clustered index, in which case the easiest way to move the data is to re-create the clustered index while moving the data currently in the leaf level of that index over to the new filegroup. The code would look something like that shown in Listing 9-4. In Enterprise editions of SQL Server, we can set the ONLINE parameter to ON, so that the index will be moved but still be available. When using Standard edition go ahead and switch this to OFF.

```
CREATE CLUSTERED INDEX [IndexName]
ON [dbo].[TableName] ([ColumnName] ASC)
WITH (DROP_EXISTING = ON, ONLINE = ON) ON [UserDataFileGroup]
```

Listing 9-4: Rebuilding an index in a new filegroup.

If the database doesn't have any clustered indexes, then this was a poor design choice; it should! We can create one for each table, on the most appropriate column or columns, using code similar to Listing 9-4 (omitting the DROP_EXISTING clause, though it won't hurt to include it). Once the clustered index is built, the table will be moved, along with the new filegroup.

If this new index is not actually required, we can go ahead and drop it, as shown in Listing 9-5, but ideally we'd work hard to create a useful index instead that we want to keep.

```
DROP INDEX [IndexName] ON [dbo].[TableName] WITH ( ONLINE = ON )
GO
```

Listing 9-5: Dropping the newly created index.

Keep in mind that these processes will move the data and clustered indexes over to the new filegroup, but not the non-clustered, or other, indexes. We will still need to move these over manually. Many scripts can be found online that will interrogate the system tables, find all of the non-clustered indexes and move them.

Remember, also, that the process of moving indexes and data to a different physical file or set of files can be long, and disk I/O intensive. Plan out time each night, over a certain period, to get everything moved with as little impact to production as possible. This is also not a task to be taken lightly, and it should be planned out with the senior database administration team.

File Backup

When a database creeps up in size towards the high hundreds of gigabytes, or into the terabyte realm, then database backups start to become problematic. A full database backup of a database of this size could take over half of a day, or even longer, and still be running long into the business day, putting undue strain on the disk and CPU and causing performance issues for end-users. Also, most DBAs have experienced the anguish of seeing such a backup fail at about 80% completion, knowing that starting it over will eat up another 12 hours.

Hopefully, as discussed in the previous sections, this database has been architected such that the data is spread across multiple data files, in several filegroups, so that we can still back up the whole database bit by bit, by taking a series of file backups, scheduled on separate days. While this is the most common reason for file backups, there are other valid reasons too, as we have discussed; for example if one filegroup is read-only, or modified very rarely, while another holds big tables, subject to frequent modifications, then the latter may be on a different and more frequent backup schedule.

A file backup is simply a backup of a single data file, subset of data files or an entire filegroup. Each of the file backups contains only the data from the files or filegroups that we have chosen to be included in that particular backup file. The combination of all of the file backups, along with all log backups taken over the same period of time, is the equivalent of a full database backup. Depending on the size of the database, the number of files, and the backup schedule, this can constitute quite a large number of backups.

We can capture both **full file backups**, capturing the entire contents of the designated file or filegroup, and **differential file backups**, capturing only the pages in that file or filegroup that have been modified since the last full file backup (there are also partial and partial differential file backups, but we'll get to those in Chapter 10).

Is there a difference between file and filegroup backups?

The short answer is no. When we take a filegroup backup we are simply specifying that the backup file should contain all of the data files in that filegroup. It is no different than if we took a file backup and explicitly referenced each data file in that group. They are the exact same backup and have no differences. This is why you may hear the term file backup used instead of filegroup backup. We will use the term file backup for the rest of this chapter.

Of course, the effectiveness of file backups depends on these large databases being designed so that there is, as best as can be achieved, a distribution of data across the data files and filegroups such that the file backups are manageable and can complete in the required time frame. For example, if we have a database of 900 GB, split across three file groups, then ideally each filegroup will be a more manageable portion of the total size. Depending on which tables are stored where, this ideal data distribution may not be possible, but if one of those groups is 800 GB, then we might as well just take full database backups.

For reasons that we'll discuss in more detail in relation to file restores, it's essential, when adopting a backup strategy based on file backups, to also take transaction log backups. It's not possible to perform file-based restores unless SQL Server has access to the full set of accompanying transaction logs. The file backups can and will be taken at different times, and SQL Server needs the subsequent transaction log backups in order to guarantee its ability to roll forward each individual file backup to the required point, and so restore the database, as a whole, to a consistent state.

> ### File backups and read-only filegroups
>
> *The only time we don't have to apply a subsequent transaction log backup when restoring a file backup, is when SQL Server knows for a fact that the data file could not have been modified since the backup was taken, because the backup was of a filegroup explicitly designated as* READ_ONLY). *We'll cover this in more detail in Chapter 10, Partial Backup and Restore.*

So, for example, if we take a weekly full file backup of a particular file or filegroup, then in the event of a failure of that file, we'd potentially need to restore the file backup plus a week's worth of log files, to get our database back online in a consistent state. As such, it often makes sense to supplement occasional full file backups with more frequent differential file backups. In the same way as differential database backups, these differential file backups can dramatically reduce the number of log files that need processing in a recovery situation.

In coming sections, we'll first demonstrate how to take file backups using both the SSMS GUI and native T-SQL scripts. We'll take **full file backups** via the SSMS GUI, and then **differential file backups** using T-SQL scripts. We'll then demonstrate how to perform the same actions using the Red Gate SQL Backup tool.

Note that it is recommended, where possible, to take a full database backup and start the log backups, *before* taking the first file backup (see: HTTP://MSDN.MICROSOFT.COM/EN-US/LIBRARY/MS189860.ASPX). We'll discuss this in more detail shortly, but note that, in order to focus purely on the logistics of file backups, we don't follow this advice in our examples.

Preparing for file backups

Before we get started taking file backups, we need to do the usual preparatory work, namely choosing an appropriate recovery model for our database, and then creating that database along with some populated sample tables. Since we've been through this process many times now, I'll only comment on those parts of the scripts that are substantially different from what has gone before. Please refer back to Chapters 3 and 5 if you need further explanation of any other aspects of these scripts.

Recovery model

Since we've established the need to take log backups, we will need to operate the database in FULL recovery model. We can also take log backups in the BULK_LOGGED model but, as discussed in Chapter 1, this model is only suitable for short-term use during bulk operations. For the long-term operation of databases requiring file backups, we should be using the FULL recovery model.

Sample database and tables plus initial data load

Listing 9-6 shows the script to create a database with both a PRIMARY and a SECONDARY filegroup, and one data file in each filegroup. Again, note that I've used the same drive for each filegroup and the log file, purely as a convenience for this demo; in reality, they would be on three different drives, as demonstrated previously in Listing 9-3.

```
USE [master]
GO

CREATE DATABASE [DatabaseForFileBackups] ON PRIMARY
(      NAME = N'DatabaseForFileBackups'
  , FILENAME = N'C:\SQLData\DatabaseForFileBackups.mdf'
  , SIZE = 10240KB , FILEGROWTH = 10240KB ), FILEGROUP [SECONDARY]
(      NAME = N'DatabaseForFileBackups_Data2'
  , FILENAME = N'C:\SQLData\DatabaseForFileBackups_Data2.ndf'
  , SIZE = 10240KB , FILEGROWTH = 10240KB ) LOG ON
(      NAME = N'DatabaseForFileBackups_log'
  , FILENAME = N'C:\SQLData\DatabaseForFileBackups_log.ldf'
  , SIZE = 10240KB , FILEGROWTH = 10240KB )
GO

ALTER DATABASE [DatabaseForFileBackups] SET RECOVERY FULL
GO
```

Listing 9-6: Multiple data file database creation script.

The big difference between this database creation script, and any that have gone before, is that we're creating two data files: a primary (mdf) data file called DatabaseForFile-Backups, in the PRIMARY filegroup, and a secondary (ndf) data file called Database-ForFileBackups_Data2 in a user-defined filegroup called SECONDARY. This name is OK here, since we will be storing generic data in the second filegroup, but if the filegroup was designed to store a particular type of data then it should be named appropriately to reflect that. For example, if creating a secondary filegroup that will group together files used to store configuration information for an application, we could name it CONFIGURATION.

Listing 9-7 creates two sample tables in our DatabaseForFileBackups database, with Table_DF1 stored in the PRIMARY filegroup and Table_DF2 stored in the SECONDARY filegroup. We then load a single initial row into each table.

```
USE [DatabaseForFileBackups]
GO

CREATE TABLE dbo.Table_DF1
    (
        Message NVARCHAR(50) NOT NULL
    )
ON  [PRIMARY]
GO

CREATE TABLE dbo.Table_DF2
    (
        Message NVARCHAR(50) NOT NULL
    )
ON  [SECONDARY]
GO

INSERT  INTO Table_DF1
VALUES  ( 'This is the initial data load for the table' )

INSERT  INTO Table_DF2
VALUES  ( 'This is the initial data load for the table' )
GO
```

Listing 9-7: Table creation script and initial data load for file backup configuration.

Notice that we specify the filegroup for each table as part of the table creation statement, via the ON keyword. SQL Server will create a table on whichever of the available filegroups is marked as the default group. Unless specified otherwise, the default group will be the PRIMARY filegroup. Therefore, the ON PRIMARY clause, for the first table, is optional, but the ON SECONDARY clause is required.

In previous chapters, we've used substantial data loads in order to capture meaningful metrics for backup time and file size. Here, we'll not be gathering these metrics, but rather focusing on the complexities of the backup (and restore) processes, so we're keeping row counts very low.

SSMS native full file backups

We're going to perform full file backups of each of our data files for the `Database-ForFileBackups` database, via the SSMS GUI. So, open up SSMS, connect to your test server, and bring up the **Back Up Database** configuration screen.

In the **Backup component** section of the screen, select the **Files and filegroups** radio button and it will instantly bring up a **Select Files and Filegroups** window. We want to back up all the files (in this case only one file) in the `PRIMARY` filegroup, so tick the `PRIMARY` box, so the screen looks as shown in Figure 9-1, and click **OK**.

Figure 9-1: Selecting the files to include in our file backup operation.

Following the convention used throughout the book, we're going to store the backup files in **C:\SQLBackups\Chapter9**, so go ahead and create that subfolder on your database server, and then, in the Backup wizard, **Remove** the default backup destination, click **Add...**, locate the **Chapter9** folder and call the backup file `DatabaseForFileBackups_ FG1_Full.bak`.

Once back on the main configuration page, double-check that everything on the screen looks as expected and if so, we have no further work to do, so we can click **OK** to start the file backup operation. It should complete in the blink of an eye, and our first file/filegroup backup is complete!

We aren't done yet, however. Repeat the whole file backup process exactly as described previously but, this time, pick the SECONDARY filegroup in the **Select Files and Filegroups** window and, when setting the backup file destination, call the backup file `Database-ForFileBackups_FG2_Full.bak`. Having done this, check the **Chapter9** folder and you should find your two backup files, ready for use later in the chapter.

We've completed our file backups, but we're *still* not quite done here. In order to be able to restore a database from its component file backups, we need to be able to apply transaction log backups so that SQL Server can confirm that it is restoring the database to a consistent state. So, we are going to take one quick log backup file. Go back into the **Back Up Database** screen a third time, select **Transaction Log** as the **Backup type**, and set the backup file destination as **C:\SQLBackups\Chapter9\DatabaseForFileBackups_ TLOG.trn**.

Native T-SQL file differential backup

We're now going to perform differential file backups of each of our data files for the `DatabaseForFileBackups` database, using T-SQL scripts. First, let's load another row of sample data into each of our tables, as shown in Listing 9-8.

```
USE [DatabaseForFileBackups]
GO

INSERT  INTO Table_DF1
VALUES  ( 'This is the second data load for the table' )

INSERT  INTO Table_DF2
VALUES  ( 'This is the second data load for the table' )
GO
```

Listing 9-8: Second data load for `DatabaseForFileBackups`.

Without further ado, the script to perform a differential file backup of our primary data file is shown in Listing 9-9.

```
USE [master]
GO

BACKUP DATABASE [DatabaseForFileBackups] FILE = N'DatabaseForFileBackups'
TO DISK = N'C:\SQLBackups\Chapter9\DatabaseForFileBackups_FG1_Diff.bak'
WITH DIFFERENTIAL,  STATS = 10
GO
```

Listing 9-9: Differential file backup of the primary data file for `DatabaseForFileBackups`.

The only new part of this script is the use of the **FILE** argument to specify which of the data files to include in the backup. In this case, we've referenced by name our primary data file, which lives in the **PRIMARY** filegroup. We've also used the **DIFFERENTIAL** argument to specify a differential backup, as described in Chapter 7.

Go ahead and run the script now and you should see output similar that shown in Figure 9-2.

```
Messages
57 percent processed.
71 percent processed.
85 percent processed.
100 percent processed.
Processed 56 pages for database 'DatabaseForFileBackups', file 'DatabaseForFileBackups' on file 1.
Processed 1 pages for database 'DatabaseForFileBackups', file 'DatabaseForFileBackups_log' on file 1.
BACKUP DATABASE...FILE=<name> WITH DIFFERENTIAL successfully processed 57 pages in 0.079 seconds (5.550 MB/sec).
```

Figure 9-2: File differential backup command results.

What we're interested in here are the files that were processed during the execution of this command. You can see that we only get pages processed on the primary data file and the log file. This is exactly what we were expecting, since this is a differential file backup, capturing the changed data in the primary data file, and not a differential database backup.

If we had performed a differential (or full) database backup on a database that has multiple data files, then all those files will be processed as part of the **BACKUP** command and we'd capture all data changed in all of the data files. So, in this case, it would have processed both the data files and the log file.

Let's now perform a differential file backup of our secondary data file, as shown in Listing 9-10.

```
USE [master]
GO

BACKUP DATABASE [DatabaseForFileBackups] FILEGROUP = N'SECONDARY'
TO DISK = N'C:\SQLBackups\Chapter9\DatabaseForFileBackups_FG2_Diff.bak'
WITH DIFFERENTIAL,  STATS = 10
GO
```

Listing 9-10: Differential filegroup backup for DatabaseForFileBackups.

This time, the script demonstrates the use of the **FILEGROUP** argument to take a backup of the **SECONDARY** filegroup as a whole. Of course, in this case there is only a single data file in this filegroup and so the outcome of this command will be exactly the same as if we had specified `FILE = N'DatabaseForFileBackups_Data2'` instead. However, if the **SECONDARY** filegroup had contained more than one data file, then all of these files would have been subject to a differential backup. If you look at the message output, after running the command, you'll see that only the `N'DatabaseForFileBackups_Data2` data file and the log file are processed.

Now we have a complete set of differential file backups that we will use to restore the database a little later. However, we are not quite done. Since we took the differential backups at different times, there is a possible issue with the consistency of the database, so we still need to take another transaction log backup. In Listing 9-11, we first add one more row each to the two tables and capture a date output (we'll need this later in a point-in-time restore demo) and then take another log backup.

```
USE [master]
GO

INSERT  INTO DatabaseForFileBackups.dbo.Table_DF1
VALUES  ( 'Point-in-time data load for  Table_DF1' )

INSERT  INTO DatabaseForFileBackups.dbo.Table_DF2
VALUES  ( 'Point-in-time data load for Table_DF2' )
GO

SELECT  GETDATE() -- note the date value. We will need it later.

BACKUP LOG [DatabaseForFileBackups]
TO DISK = N'C:\SQLBackups\Chapter9\DatabaseForFileBackups_TLOG2.trn'
GO
```

Listing 9-11: Taking our second native transaction log backup.

SQL Backup file backups

Let's take a quick look at how to capture both types of file backup, full and differential, via the Red Gate SQL Backup tool. I assume basic familiarity with the tool, based on the coverage provided in the previous chapter, and so focus only on aspects of the process that are different from what has gone before, with database backups. We're going to take a look at file backups using SQL Backup scripts only, and not via the SQL Backup GUI. There are a couple of reasons for this:

- the version of SQL Backup (6.4) that was used in this book did not support differential file backups via the GUI

- assuming that, if you worked through Chapter 8, you are now comfortable using the basic SQL Backup functionality, so you don't need to see both methods.

To get started, we'll need a new sample database on which to work. We can simply adapt the database creation script in Listing 9-6 to create a new, identically-structured database, called `DatabaseForFileBackup_SB` and then use Listing 9-7 to create the tables and insert the initial row. Alternatively, the script to create the database and tables, and insert the initial data, is provided ready-made (**DatabaseForFileBackup_SB.sql**) in code download for this book, at HTTP://WWW.SIMPLE-TALK.COM/REDGATEBOOKS/ SHAWNMCGEHEE/SQLSERVERBACKUPANDRESTORE_CODE.ZIP.

SQL Backup full file backups

Having created the sample database and tables, and loaded some initial data, let's jump straight in and take a look at the script to perform full file backups of both the PRIMARY and SECONDARY data files, as shown in Listing 9-12.

```
USE [master]
GO
--SQL Backup Full file backup of PRIMARY filegroup
EXECUTE master..sqlbackup '-SQL "BACKUP DATABASE [DatabaseForFileBackups_SB]
FILEGROUP = ''PRIMARY'' TO DISK =
''C:\SQLBackups\Chapter9\DatabaseForFileBackups_SB.sqb''
WITH DISKRETRYINTERVAL = 30, DISKRETRYCOUNT = 10, COMPRESSION = 3, THREADCOUNT = 2"'

--SQL Backup Full file backup of secondary data file
EXECUTE master..sqlbackup '-SQL "BACKUP DATABASE [DatabaseForFileBackups_SB]
FILE = ''DatabaseForFileBackups_SB_Data2''
TO DISK = ''C:\SQLBackups\Chapter9\DatabaseForFileBackups_SB_Data2.sqb''
WITH DISKRETRYINTERVAL = 30, DISKRETRYCOUNT = 10, COMPRESSION = 3, THREADCOUNT = 2"'
```

Listing 9-12: SQL Backup full file backup of primary and secondary data files.

Most of the details of this script, with regard to the SQL Backup parameters that control the compression and resiliency options, have been covered in detail in Chapter 8, so I won't repeat them here. We can see that we are using the **FILEGROUP** parameter here to perform the backup against all files in our **PRIMARY** filegroup. Since this filegroup includes just our single primary data file, we could just as well have specified the file explicitly, which is the approach we take when backing up the secondary data file.

Having completed the full file backups, we are going to need to take a quick log backup of this database, just as we did with the native backups, in order to ensure we can restore the database to a consistent state, from the component file backups. Go ahead and run Listing 9-13 in a new query window to get a log backup of our **DatabaseForFile-Backups_SB** test database.

```
USE [master]
GO

EXECUTE master..sqlbackup '-SQL "BACKUP LOG [DatabaseForFileBackups_SB]
TO DISK = ''C:\SQLBackups\Chapter9\DatabaseForFileBackups_SB_TLOG.sqb''"'
```

Listing 9-13: Taking our log backup via SQL Backup script.

SQL Backup differential file backups

The SQL Backup commands for differential file backups are very similar to those for the full file backups, so we'll not dwell long here. First, we need to insert a new row into each of our sample tables, as shown in Listing 9-14.

```
USE [DatabaseForFileBackups_SB]
GO

INSERT  INTO Table_DF1
VALUES  ( 'This is the second data load for the table' )

INSERT  INTO Table_DF2
VALUES  ( 'This is the second data load for the table' )
GO
```

Listing 9-14: Second data load for `DatabaseForFileBackups_SB`.

Next, Listing 9-15 shows the script to perform the differential file backups for both the primary and secondary data files.

```
USE [master]
GO
EXECUTE master..sqlbackup '-SQL "BACKUP DATABASE [DatabaseForFileBackups_SB]
FILEGROUP = ''PRIMARY'' TO DISK =
''C:\SQLBackups\Chapter9\DatabaseForFileBackups_SB_Diff.sqb''
WITH DIFFERENTIAL, DISKRETRYINTERVAL = 30, DISKRETRYCOUNT = 10, COMPRESSION = 3,
THREADCOUNT = 2"'

EXECUTE master..sqlbackup '-SQL "BACKUP DATABASE [DatabaseForFileBackups_SB]
FILE = ''DatabaseForFileBackups_SB_Data2''
TO DISK = ''C:\SQLBackups\Chapter9\DatabaseForFileBackups_SB_Data2_Diff.sqb''
WITH DIFFERENTIAL, DISKRETRYINTERVAL = 30, DISKRETRYCOUNT = 10, COMPRESSION = 3,
THREADCOUNT = 2"'
```

Listing 9-15: SQL Backup differential file backup of primary and secondary data files.

The only significant difference in this script compared to the one for the full file backups, apart from the different backup file names, is use of the **DIFFERENTIAL** argument to denote that the backups should only take into account the changes made to each file since the last full file backup was taken.

Take a look at the output for this script, shown in truncated form in Figure 9-3; the first of the two SQL Backup operations processes the primary data file (**DatabaseForFile-Backups**), and the transaction log, and the second processes the secondary data file (**DatabaseForFileBackups_Data2**) plus the transaction log.

```
Backing up DatabaseForFileBackups_SB (files/filegroups differential) to:
  C:\SQLBackups\Chapter9\DatabaseForFileBackups_SB_Diff.sqb

Backup data size    : 3.250 MB
Compressed data size: 55.500 KB
Compression rate    : 98.33%

Processed 56 pages for database 'DatabaseForFileBackups_SB', file
'DatabaseForFileBackups_SB' on file 1.
Processed 2 pages for database 'DatabaseForFileBackups_SB', file
'DatabaseForFileBackups_SB_log' on file 1.
BACKUP DATABASE...FILE=<name> WITH DIFFERENTIAL successfully processed 58 pages in 0.036
seconds (12.396 MB/sec).
SQL Backup process ended.
```

Figure 9-3: SQL Backup differential file backup results.

Having completed the differential file backups, we do need to take one more backup and I think you can guess what it is. Listing 9-16 takes our final transaction log backup of the chapter.

```
USE [master]
GO


EXECUTE master..sqlbackup '-SQL "BACKUP LOG [DatabaseForFileBackups_SB]
TO DISK = ''C:\SQLBackups\Chapter9\DatabaseForFileBackups_SB_TLOG2.sqb''"'
```

Listing 9-16: Second SQL Backup transaction log backup.

File Restore

In all previous chapters, when we performed a restore operation, we restored the database as a whole, including all the data in all the files and filegroups, from the full database backup, plus any subsequent differential database backups. If we then wished to roll forward the database, we could do so by applying the full chain of transaction log backups.

However, it is also possible to restore a database from a set individual file backups; the big difference is that that we can't restore a database just from the latest set of full (plus differential) file backups. We must also apply the full set of accompanying transaction log backups, up to and including the log backup taken after the final file backup in the set. This is the only way SQL Server can guarantee that it can restore the database to a consistent state.

Consider, for example, a simple case of a database comprising three data files, each in a separate filegroup and where **FG1_1**, **FG2_1**, **FG3_1** are full files backups of each separate filegroup, as shown in Figure 9-4.

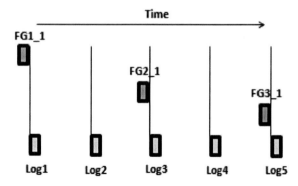

Figure 9-4: A series of full file and transaction log backups.

Notice that the three file backups are taken at different times. In order to restore this database, using backups shown, we have to restore the **FG1_1**, **FG2_1** and **FG3_1** file backups, and then the chain of log backups 1–5. Generally speaking, we need the chain of log files starting directly after the oldest full file backup in the set, and finishing with the one taken directly after the most recent full file backup. Note that even if we are absolutely certain that in **Log5** no further transactions were recorded against any of the three filegroups, SQL Server will not trust us on this and requires this log backup file to be processed in order to guarantee that any changes recorded in **Log5** that were made to any of the data files, up to the point the **FG3_1** backup completed, are represented in the restore, and so the database has transactional consistency.

We can also perform point-in-time restores, to a point within the log file taken after all of the current set of file backups; in Figure 9-4, this would be to some point in time within the **Log5** backup. If we wished to restore to a point in time within, say, **Log4**, we'd need to restore the backup for filegroup 3 taken before the one shown in Figure 9-4 (let's call it **FG3_0**), followed by **FG1_1** and **FG2_1**, and then the chain of logs, starting with the one taken straight after **FG3_0** and ending with **Log4**.

This also explains why Microsoft recommends taking an initial full database backup and starting the log backup chain before taking the first full file backup. If we imagine that **FG1_1**, **FG2_1** and **FG3_1** file backups were the first-ever full file backups for this database, and that they were taken on Monday, Wednesday and Friday, then we'd have no restore capability in that first week, till the **FG3_1** and **Log5** backups were completed.

It's possible, in some circumstances, to restore a database by restoring only a single file backup (plus required log backups), rather than the whole set of files that comprise the database. This sort of restore is possible as long as you've got a database composed of several data files or filegroups, regardless of whether you're taking database or file backups; as long as you've also got the required set of log backups, it's possible to restore a single file from a database backup.

The ability to recover a database by restoring only a subset of the database files can be very beneficial. For example, if a single data file for a VLDB goes offline for some reason, we have the ability to restore from file backup just the damaged file, rather than restoring the entire database. With a combination of the file backup, plus the necessary transaction log backups, we can get that missing data file back to the state it was in as close as possible to the time of failure, and much quicker than might be possible if we needed to restore the whole database from scratch!

With Enterprise Edition SQL Server, as discussed earlier, we also have the ability to perform online piecemeal restores, where again we start by restoring just a subset of the data files, in this case the primary filegroup, and then immediately bringing the database online having recovered only this subset of the data.

As you've probably gathered, restoring a database from file backups, while potentially very beneficial in reducing down-time, can be quite complex and can involve managing and processing a large number of backup files. The easiest way to get a grasp of how the various types of file restore work is by example. Therefore, over the following sections, we'll walk though some examples of how to perform, with file backups, the same restore processes that we've seem previously in the book, namely a complete restore and a point-in-time restore. We'll then take a look at an example each of recovering from a "single data file failure," as well as online piecemeal restore.

We're not going to attempt to run through each type of restore in four different ways (SSMS, T-SQL, SQL Backup GUI, SQL Backup T-SQL), as this would simply get tedious. We'll focus on scripted restores using either native T-SQL or SQL Backup T-SQL, and leave the equivalent restores, via GUI methods, as an exercise for the reader. It's worth noting, though, that whereas for database backups the SQL Backup GUI will automatically detect all required backup files (assuming they are still in their original locations), it will not do so for file backups; each required backup file will need to be located manually.

Performing a complete restore (native T-SQL)

We're going to take a look at an example of performing a complete restore of our `DatabaseForFileBackups` database. Before we start, let's insert a third data load, as shown in Listing 9-17, just so we have one row in each of the tables in the database that isn't yet captured in any of our backup files.

```
USE [DatabaseForFileBackups]
GO


INSERT  INTO Table_DF1
VALUES  ( 'This is the third data load for the table' )

INSERT  INTO Table_DF2
VALUES  ( 'This is the third data load for the table' )
GO
```

Listing 9-17: Third data load for `DatabaseForFileBackups`.

Figure 9-5 depicts the current backups we have in place. We have the first data load captured in full file backups, the second data load captured in the differential file backups, and a third data load that is not in any current backup file, but we'll need to capture it in a tail log backup in order to restore the database to its current state. In a case where we were unable to take a final tail log backup we'd only be able to roll forward to the end of the `TLOG2` backup. In this example, we are going to take one last backup, just to get our complete database back intact.

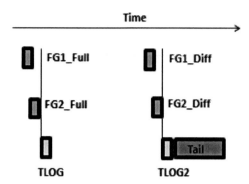

Figure 9-5: Required backups for our complete restore of `DatabaseForFileBackups`.

The first step is to capture that tail log backup, and prepare for the restore process, as shown in Listing 9-18.

```
USE master
GO
--backup the tail
BACKUP LOG [DatabaseForFileBackups]
TO DISK = N'C:\SQLBackups\Chapter9\DatabaseForFileBackups_TLOG_TAIL.trn'
WITH NORECOVERY
GO
```

Listing 9-18: Tail log backup.

Notice the use of the **NORECOVERY** option in a backup; this lets SQL Server know that we want to back up the transactions in the log file and immediately place the database into a restoring state. This way, no further transactions can slip past us into the log while we are preparing the **RESTORE** command.

We're now ready to start the restore process. The first step is to restore the two full file backups. We're going to restore over the top of the existing database, as shown in Listing 9-19.

```
USE master
GO
RESTORE DATABASE [DatabaseForFileBackups] FILE = N'DatabaseForFileBackups'
FROM DISK = N'C:\SQLBackups\Chapter9\DatabaseForFileBackups_FG1_Full.bak'
WITH REPLACE
GO

RESTORE DATABASE [DatabaseForFileBackups] FILE = N'DatabaseForFileBackups_Data2'
FROM DISK = N'C:\SQLBackups\Chapter9\DatabaseForFileBackups_FG2_Full.bak'
WITH NORECOVERY
GO
```

Listing 9-19: Restoring the full file backups.

```
Processed 184 pages for database 'DatabaseForFileBackups', file 'DatabaseForFileBackups'
on file 1.
Processed 6 pages for database 'DatabaseForFileBackups', file 'DatabaseForFileBackups_log'
on file 1.
The roll forward start point is now at log sequence number (LSN) 23000000026800001.
Additional roll forward past LSN 23000000036700001 is required to complete the restore
sequence.
This RESTORE statement successfully performed some actions, but the database could not be
brought online because one or more RESTORE steps are needed. Previous messages indicate
reasons why recovery cannot occur at this point.

RESTORE DATABASE ... FILE=<name> successfully processed 190 pages in 0.121 seconds (12.251
MB/sec).
Processed 16 pages for database 'DatabaseForFileBackups', file
'DatabaseForFileBackups_Data2' on file 1.
Processed 2 pages for database 'DatabaseForFileBackups', file 'DatabaseForFileBackups_log'
on file 1.
RESTORE DATABASE ... FILE=<name> successfully processed 18 pages in 0.105 seconds (1.274
MB/sec).
```

Figure 9-6: Output message from restoring the full file backups.

Notice that we didn't specify the state to which to return the database after the first
RESTORE command. By default this would attempt to bring the database back online,
with recovery, but in this case SQL Server knows that there are more files to process, so it

keeps the database in a restoring state. The first half of the message output from running this command, shown in Figure 9-6, tells us that the roll forward start point is at a specific LSN number but that an additional roll forward is required and so more files will have to be restored to bring the database back online.

The second part of the message simply reports that the restore of the backup for the secondary data file was successful.

Since we specified that the database should be left in a restoring state after the second restore command, SQL Server doesn't try to recover the database to a usable state (and is unable to do so). If you check your Object Explorer in SSMS, you'll see that `Database-ForFileBackups` is still in a restoring state.

After the full file backups, we took a transaction log backup (`_TLOG`), but since we're rolling forward past the subsequent differential file backups, where any data changes will be captured for each filegroup, we don't need to restore the first transaction log, on this occasion. So, let's go ahead and restore the two differential file backups, as shown in Listing 9-20.

```
USE master
GO

RESTORE DATABASE [DatabaseForFileBackups] FILE = N'DatabaseForFileBackups'
FROM DISK = N'C:\SQLBackups\Chapter9\DatabaseForFileBackups_FG1_Diff.bak'
WITH NORECOVERY
GO

RESTORE DATABASE [DatabaseForFileBackups] FILE = N'DatabaseForFileBackups_Data2'
FROM DISK = N'C:\SQLBackups\Chapter9\DatabaseForFileBackups_FG2_Diff.bak'
WITH NORECOVERY
GO
```

Listing 9-20: Restore the differential file backups.

The next step is to restore the second transaction log backup (_TLOG2), as shown in Listing 9-21. When it comes to restoring the transaction log backup files, we need to specify NORECOVERY on all of them except the last. The last group of log backup files we are restoring (represented by only a single log backup in this example!) may be processing data for all of the data files and, if we do not specify NORECOVERY, we can end up putting the database in a usable state for the user, but unable to apply the last of the log backup files.

```
USE master
GO

RESTORE DATABASE [DatabaseForFileBackups]
FROM DISK = N'C:\SQLBackups\Chapter9\DatabaseForFileBackups_TLOG2.trn'
WITH NORECOVERY
GO
```

Listing 9-21: Restore the second log backup.

Finally, we need to apply the tail log backup, where we know our third data load is captured, and recover the database.

```
RESTORE DATABASE [DatabaseForFileBackups]
FROM DISK = N'C:\SQLBackups\Chapter9\DatabaseForFileBackups_TLOG_TAIL.trn'
WITH RECOVERY
GO
```

Listing 9-22: Restore the tail log backup and recover the database.

A simple query of the restored database will confirm that we've restored the database, with all the rows intact.

```
USE [DatabaseForFileBackups]
GO

SELECT * FROM Table_DF1
SELECT * FROM Table_DF2
```

```
Message
----------------------------------------------------
This is the initial data load for the table
This is the second data load for the table
This is the point-in-time data load for the table
This is the third data load for the table


(4 row(s) affected)

Message
----------------------------------------------------
This is the initial data load for the table
This is the second data load for the table
This is the point-in-time data load for the table
This is the third data load for the table


(4 row(s) affected)
```

Listing 9-23: Verifying the restored data.

Restoring to a point in time (native T-SQL)

Listing 9-24 shows the script to restore our DatabaseForFileBackups to a point in time either just before, or just after, we inserted the two rows in Listing 9-11.

```
USE master
GO


RESTORE DATABASE [DatabaseForFileBackups] FILE = N'DatabaseForFileBackups'
FROM DISK = N'C:\SQLBackups\Chapter9\DatabaseForFileBackups_FG1_Full.bak'
WITH REPLACE
GO


RESTORE DATABASE [DatabaseForFileBackups] FILE = N'DatabaseForFileBackups_Data2'
FROM DISK = N'C:\SQLBackups\Chapter9\DatabaseForFileBackups_FG2_Full.bak'
WITH NORECOVERY
GO
```

```
RESTORE DATABASE [DatabaseForFileBackups] FILE = N'DatabaseForFileBackups'
FROM DISK = N'C:\SQLBackups\Chapter9\DatabaseForFileBackups_FG1_Diff.bak'
WITH NORECOVERY
GO


RESTORE DATABASE [DatabaseForFileBackups] FILE = N'DatabaseForFileBackups_Data2'
FROM DISK = N'C:\SQLBackups\Chapter9\DatabaseForFileBackups_FG2_Diff.bak'
WITH NORECOVERY
GO


RESTORE DATABASE [DatabaseForFileBackups]
FROM DISK = N'C:\SQLBackups\Chapter9\DatabaseForFileBackups_TLOG2.trn'
WITH RECOVERY, STOPAT = '2012-02-07T13:18:00' -- enter your time here
GO
```

Listing 9-24: Filegroup restore to a point in time.

Notice that we include the **REPLACE** keyword in the first restore, since we are trying to replace the database and in this case aren't starting with a tail log backup, and there may be transactions in the log that haven't been backed up yet. We then restore the second full file backup and the two differential file backups, leaving the database in a restoring state each time.

Finally, we restore the second transaction log backup, using the **STOPAT** parameter to indicate the time to which we wish to restore the database. In my example, I set the time for the **STOPAT** parameter to be about 30 seconds before the two **INSERTs** were executed, and Listing 9-25 confirms that only the first two data loads are present in the restored database.

```
USE DatabaseForFileBackups
GO
SELECT  * FROM    dbo.Table_DF1
SELECT  * FROM    dbo.Table_DF2
```

```
Message
--------------------------------------------------
This is the initial data load for the table
This is the second data load for the table

(2 row(s) affected)

Message
--------------------------------------------------
This is the initial data load for the table
This is the second data load for the table

(2 row(s) affected)
```

Listing 9-25: Checking on the point-in-time restore data.

Great! We can see that our data is exactly what we expected. We have restored the data to the point in time exactly where we wanted. In the real world, you would be restoring to a point in time before a disaster struck or when data was somehow removed or corrupted.

Restoring after loss of a secondary data file

One of the major potential benefits of file-based restore, especially for VLDBs, is the ability to restore just a single data file, rather than the whole database, in the event of a disaster.

Let's imagine that we have a VLDB residing on one of our most robust servers. Again, this VLDB comprises three data files in separate filegroups that contain completely different database objects and data, with each file located on one of three separate physical hard drives in our SAN attached drives.

Everything is running smoothly, and we get great performance for this database until our SAN suddenly suffers a catastrophic loss on one of its disk enclosures and we lose the drive holding one of the secondary data files. The database goes offline.

We quickly get a new disk attached to our server, but the secondary data file is lost and we are not going to be able to get it back. As this point, all of the tables and data in that data file will be lost but, luckily, we have been performing regular full file, differential file, and transaction log backups of this database, and if we can capture a final tail-of-the-log backup, we can get this database back online using only the backup files for the lost secondary data file, plus the necessary log files, as shown in Figure 9-7.

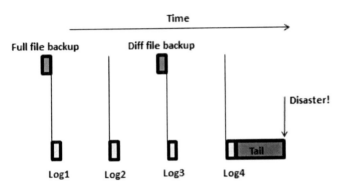

Figure 9-7:   Example backups required to recover a secondary data file.

In order to get the lost data file back online, with all data up to the point of the disk crash, we would:

- perform a tail log backup – this requires a special form of log backup, which does not truncate the transaction log

- restore the full file backup for the lost secondary data file

- restore the differential file backup for the secondary data file, at which point SQL Server would expect to be able to apply log backups 3 and 4 plus the tail log backup

- recover the database.

Once you do this, your database will be back online and recovered up to the point of the failure! This is a huge time saver since restoring all of the files could take quite a long time. Having to restore only the data file that was affected by the crash will cut your recovery time down significantly.

However, there are a few caveats attached to this technique, which we'll discuss as we walk through a demo. Specifically, we're going to use SQL Backup scripts (these can easily be adapted into native T-SQL scripts) to show how we might restore just a single damaged, or otherwise unusable, secondary data file for our `DatabaseForFile-Backups_SB` database, without having to restore the primary data file.

Note that if the primary data file went down, we'd have to restore the whole database, rather than just the primary data file. However, with Enterprise Edition SQL Server, it would be possible to get the database back up and running by restoring only the primary data file, followed subsequently by the other data files. We'll discuss that in more detail in the next section.

This example is going to use our `DatabaseForFileBackups_SB` database to restore from a single disk / single file failure, using SQL Backup T-SQL scripts. A script demonstrating the same process using native T-SQL is available with the code download for this book.

If you recall, for this database we have `Table_DF1`, stored in the primary data file (`DatabaseForFileBackups_SB.mdf`) in the `PRIMARY` filegroup, and `Table_DF2`, stored in the secondary data file (`DatabaseForFileBackups_SB_Data2.ndf`) in the `SECONDARY` filegroup. Our first data load (one row into each table) was captured in full file backups for each filegroup. We then captured a first transaction log backup. Our second data load (an additional row into each table) was captured in differential file backups for each filegroup. Finally, we took a second transaction log backup.

Let's perform a third data load, inserting one new row into `Table_DF2`.

```
USE [DatabaseForFileBackups_SB]
GO
INSERT  INTO Table_DF2
VALUES  ( 'This is the third data load for Table_DF2' )
GO
```

Listing 9-26: Third data load for `DatabaseForFileBackups_SB`.

Now we're going to simulate a problem with our secondary data file which takes it (and our database) offline; in Listing 9-27 we take the database offline. Having done so, navigate to the **C:\SQLData\Chapter9** folder and delete the secondary data file!

```
-- Take DatabaseForFileBackups_SB offline
USE master
GO
ALTER DATABASE [DatabaseForFileBackups_SB] SET OFFLINE;
GO

/*Now delete DatabaseForFileBackups_SB_Data2.ndf!*/
```

Listing 9-27: Take `DatabaseForFileBackups_SB` offline and delete secondary data file!

Scary stuff! Next, let's attempt to bring our database back online.

```
USE master
GO
ALTER DATABASE [DatabaseForFileBackups_SB] SET ONLINE;
GO
```

```
Msg 5120, Level 16, State 5, Line 1
Unable to open the physical file "C:\SQLData\DatabaseForFileBackups_SB_Data2.ndf".
Operating system error 2: "2(failed to retrieve text for this error. Reason: 15105)".
Msg 945, Level 14, State 2, Line 1
Database 'DatabaseForFileBackups_SB' cannot be opened due to inaccessible files or
insufficient memory or disk space.  See the SQL Server errorlog for details.
Msg 5069, Level 16, State 1, Line 1
ALTER DATABASE statement failed.
```

Listing 9-28: Database cannot come online due to missing secondary data file.

As you can see, this is unsuccessful, as SQL Server can't open the secondary data file. Although unsuccessful, this attempt to bring the database online is still necessary, as we need the database to attempt to come online, so the log file can be read.

We urgently need to get the database back online, in the state it was in when our secondary file failed. Fortunately, the data and log files are on separate drives from the secondary, so these are still available.

We know that there is data in the log file that isn't captured in any log backup, so our first task is to back up the log. Unfortunately, a normal log backup operation, such as shown in Listing 9-29 will not succeed.

```
-- a normal tail log backup won't work
USE [master]
GO
EXECUTE master..sqlbackup '-SQL "BACKUP LOG [DatabaseForFileBackups_SB]
TO DISK = ''C:\SQLBackups\Chapter9\DatabaseForFileBackups_SB_TLOG_TAIL.sqb''
WITH NORECOVERY"'
GO
```

Listing 9-29: A standard tail log backup fails.

In my tests, this script just hangs and has to be cancelled, which is unfortunate. The equivalent script in native T-SQL results in an error message to the effect that:

```
"Database 'DatabaseForFileBackups_SB' cannot be opened due to inaccessible files or
insufficient memory or disk space."
```

SQL Server cannot back up the log this way because the log file is not available and part of the log backup process, even a tail log backup, needs to write some log info into the database header. Since it cannot, we need to use a different form of tail backup to get around this problem.

What we need to do instead, is a special form of tail log backup that uses the NO_ TRUNCATE option, so that SQL Server can back up the log without access to the data files. In this case the log will not be truncated upon backup, and all log records will remain in the live transaction log. Essentially, this is a special type of log backup and isn't going to remain useful to us after this process is over. When we do get the database back online and completely usable, we want to be able to take a backup of the log file in its original state and not break the log chain. In other words, once the database is back online, we can take another log backup (TLOG3, say) and the log chain will be TLOG2 followed by TLOG3 (not TLOG2, TLOG_TAIL, TLOG3). I would, however, suggest attempting to take some full file backups immediately after a failure, if not a full database backup, if that is at all possible.

```
USE [master]
GO
EXECUTE master..sqlbackup '-SQL "BACKUP LOG [DatabaseForFileBackups_SB]
TO DISK = ''C:\SQLBackups\Chapter9\DatabaseForFileBackups_SB_TLOG_TAIL.sqb''
WITH NO_TRUNCATE"'
GO
```

Listing 9-30: Performing a tail log backup with NO_TRUNCATE for emergency single file recovery.

Note that if we cannot take a transaction log backup before starting this process, we cannot get our database back online without restoring all of our backup files. This process will only work if we lose a single file from a drive that does not also house the transaction log.

Now that we have our tail log backup done, we can move on to recovering our lost secondary data file. The entire process is shown in Listing 9-31. You will notice that there are no backups in this set of RESTORE commands that reference our primary data file. This data would have been left untouched and doesn't need to be restored. Having to restore only the lost file will save us a great deal of time.

```
USE [master]
GO
-- restore the full file backup for the secondary data file
EXECUTE master..sqlbackup '-SQL "RESTORE DATABASE [DatabaseForFileBackups_SB]
FILE = ''DatabaseForFileBackups_SB_Data2''
FROM DISK = ''C:\SQLBackups\Chapter9\DatabaseForFileBackups_SB_Data2.sqb''
WITH NORECOVERY"'

-- restore the differential file backup for the secondary data file
EXECUTE master..sqlbackup '-SQL "RESTORE DATABASE [DatabaseForFileBackups_SB]
FILE = ''DatabaseForFileBackups_SB_Data2''
FROM DISK = ''C:\SQLBackups\Chapter9\DatabaseForFileBackups_SB_Data2_Diff.sqb''
WITH NORECOVERY"'

-- restore the subsequent transaction log backup
EXECUTE master..sqlbackup '-SQL "RESTORE DATABASE [DatabaseForFileBackups_SB]
FROM DISK = ''C:\SQLBackups\Chapter9\DatabaseForFileBackups_SB_TLOG2.sqb''
WITH NORECOVERY"'

-- restore the tail log backup and recover the database
EXECUTE master..sqlbackup '-SQL "RESTORE DATABASE [DatabaseForFileBackups_SB]
FROM DISK = ''C:\SQLBackups\Chapter9\DatabaseForFileBackups_SB_TLOG_TAIL.sqb''
WITH RECOVERY"'
```

Listing 9-31: Single file disaster SQL Backup restoration script.

What we have done here is restore the full file, the differential file and all of the transaction log file backups that were taken after the differential file backup, including the tail log backup. This has brought our database back online and right up to the point where the tail log backup was taken.

Now you may be afraid that you didn't get to it in time and some data may be lost, but don't worry. Any transactions that would have affected the missing data file would not have succeeded after the disaster, even if the database stayed online, and any that didn't use that missing data file would have been picked up by the tail log backup.

Quick recovery using online piecemeal restore

When using SQL Server Enterprise Edition, we have access to a great feature that can save hours of recovery time in the event of a catastrophic database loss. With this edition, SQL Server allows us to perform an online restore. Using the **Partial** option, we can restore the primary data file of our database and bring it back online without any other data files needing to be restored. In this way, we can bring the database online and in a usable state very quickly, and then apply the rest of the backups at a later time, while still allowing users to access a subset of the data.

The tables and data stored in the secondary data files will not be accessible until they are restored. The database will stay online throughout the secondary data file restores, though. This way, we can restore the most important and most used data first, and the least used, archive data for instance, later, once we have all of the other fires put out.

Let's take a look at an example; again, this requires an Enterprise (or Developer) Edition of SQL Server. Listing 9-32 creates a new database, with two tables, and inserts a row of data into each of the tables. Note, of course, that in anything other than a simple test example, the primary and secondary files would be on separate disks.

```
USE [master]
GO
CREATE DATABASE [DatabaseForPartialRestore] ON PRIMARY
( NAME = N'DatabaseForPartialRestore',
  FILENAME = N'C:\SQLData\DatabaseForPartialRestore.mdf' ,
  SIZE = 5120KB , FILEGROWTH = 5120KB ), FILEGROUP [Secondary]
( NAME = N'DatabaseForPartialRestoreData2',
  FILENAME = N'C:\SQLData\DatabaseForPartialRestoreData2.ndf' ,
  SIZE = 5120KB , FILEGROWTH = 5120KB ) LOG ON
( NAME = N'DatabaseForPartialRestore_log',
  FILENAME = N'C:\SQLData\DatabaseForPartialRestore_log.ldf' ,
  SIZE = 5120KB , FILEGROWTH = 5120KB )
GO
```

```
USE [DatabaseForPartialRestore]
GO
IF NOT EXISTS ( SELECT  name
                FROM    sys.filegroups
                WHERE   is_default = 1
                AND name = N'Secondary' )
    ALTER DATABASE [DatabaseForPartialRestore] MODIFY FILEGROUP [Secondary] DEFAULT
GO

USE [master]
GO
ALTER DATABASE [DatabaseForPartialRestore] SET RECOVERY FULL WITH NO_WAIT
GO

USE [DatabaseForPartialRestore]
GO
CREATE TABLE [dbo].[Message_Primary]
    (
        [Message] [varchar](50) NOT NULL
    )
ON  [Primary]
GO
CREATE TABLE [dbo].[Message_Secondary]
    (
        [Message] [varchar](50) NOT NULL
    )
ON  [Secondary]
GO

INSERT  INTO Message_Primary
VALUES  ( 'This is data for the primary filegroup' )
INSERT  INTO Message_Secondary
VALUES  ( 'This is data for the secondary filegroup' )
GO
```

Listing 9-32: Creating our database and tables for testing.

This script is pretty long, but nothing here should be new to you. Our new database contains both a primary and secondary filegroup, and we establish the secondary filegroup as the DEFAULT, so this is where user objects and data will be stored, unless we specify otherwise. We then switch the database to FULL recovery model just to be sure that we can take log backups of the database; always validate which recovery model is in use, rather than just relying on the default being the right one. Finally, we create one table in each filegroup, and insert a single row into each table.

Listing 9-33 simulates a series of file and log backups on our database; we can imagine that the file backups for each filegroup are taken on successive nights, and that the log backup after each file backup represents the series of log files that would be taken during the working day. Note that, in order to keep focused, we don't start proceedings with a full database backup, as would generally be recommended.

```
USE [master]
GO

BACKUP DATABASE [DatabaseForPartialRestore] FILEGROUP = N'PRIMARY'
TO  DISK = N'C:\SQLBackups\Chapter9\DatabaseForPartialRestore_FG_Primary.bak'
WITH INIT
GO

BACKUP LOG [DatabaseForPartialRestore]
TO DISK = N'C:\SQLBackups\Chapter9\DatabaseForPartialRestore_LOG_1.trn'
WITH NOINIT
GO

BACKUP DATABASE [DatabaseForPartialRestore] FILEGROUP = N'SECONDARY'
TO  DISK = N'C:\SQLBackups\Chapter9\DatabaseForPartialRestore_FG_Secondary.bak'
WITH INIT
GO

BACKUP LOG [DatabaseForPartialRestore]
TO DISK = N'C:\SQLBackups\Chapter9\DatabaseForPartialRestore_LOG_2.trn'
WITH NOINIT
GO
```

Listing 9-33: Taking our filegroup and log backups.

With these backups complete, we have all the tools we need to perform a piecemeal restore! Remember, though, that we don't need to be taking file backups in order to perform a partial/piecemeal restore. If the database is still small enough, we can still take full database backups and then restore just a certain filegroup from that backup file, in the manner demonstrated next.

Listing 9-34 restores just our primary filegroup, plus subsequent log backups, and then beings the database online – without the secondary filegroup!

```
USE [master]
GO


RESTORE DATABASE [DatabaseForPartialRestore] FILEGROUP = 'PRIMARY'
FROM DISK = 'C:\SQLBackups\Chapter9\DatabaseForPartialRestore_FG_Primary.bak'
WITH PARTIAL, NORECOVERY, REPLACE
GO


RESTORE LOG [DatabaseForPartialRestore]
FROM DISK = 'C:\SQLBackups\Chapter9\DatabaseForPartialRestore_LOG_1.trn'
WITH NORECOVERY
GO

RESTORE LOG [DatabaseForPartialRestore]
FROM DISK = 'C:\SQLBackups\Chapter9\DatabaseForPartialRestore_LOG_2.trn'
WITH RECOVERY
GO
```

Listing 9-34: Restoring our primary filegroup via an online piecemeal restore.

Notice the use of the **PARTIAL** keyword to let SQL Server know that we will want to only partially restore the database, *i.e.* restore only the primary filegroup. We could also restore further filegroups here, but the only one necessary is the primary filegroup. Note the use of the **REPLACE** keyword, since we are not taking a tail log backup.

Even though we recover the database upon restoring the final transaction log, we can still, in this case, restore the other data files later. The query in Listing 9-35 attempts to access data in both the primary and secondary filegroups.

```
USE [DatabaseForPartialRestore]
GO

SELECT   Message
FROM     Message_Primary
GO
SELECT   Message
FROM     Message_Secondary
GO
```

Listing 9-35: Querying the restored database.

The first query should return data, but the second one will fail with the following error:

```
Msg 8653, Level 16, State 1, Line 1
The query processor is unable to produce a plan for the table or view 'Message_Secondary'
because the table resides in a filegroup which is not online.
```

This is exactly the behavior we expect, since the secondary filegroup is still offline. In a well-designed database we would, at this point, be able to access all of the most critical data, leaving just the least-used data segmented into the filegroups that will be restored later.

The real bonus is that we can subsequently restore the other filegroups, while the database is up and functioning! Nevertheless, the online restore is going to be an I/O-intensive process and we would want to affect the users as little as possible, while giving as much of the SQL Server horsepower as we could to the restore. That means that it's best to wait till a time when database access is sparse before restoring the subsequent filegroups, as shown in Listing 9-36.

```
USE [master]
GO
RESTORE DATABASE [DatabaseForPartialRestore]
FROM DISK = 'C:\SQLBackups\Chapter9\DatabaseForPartialRestore_FG_SECONDARY.bak'
WITH RECOVERY
GO
```

```
RESTORE LOG [DatabaseForPartialRestore]
FROM DISK = 'C:\SQLBackups\Chapter9\DatabaseForPartialRestore_LOG_2.trn'
WITH RECOVERY
GO
```

Listing 9-36: Restoring the secondary filegroup.

We restore the secondary full file backup, followed by all subsequent log backups, so that SQL Server can bring the other filegroup back online while guaranteeing relational integrity. Notice that in this case each restore is using WITH RECOVERY; in an online piecemeal restore, with the Enterprise edition, each restore leaves the database online and accessible to the end-user. The first set of restores, in Listing 9-34, used NORECOVERY, but that was just to get us to the point where the primary filegroup was online and available. All subsequent restore steps use RECOVERY.

Rerun Listing 9-35, and all of the data should be fully accessible!

Common Issues with File Backup and Restore

What's true for any backup scheme we've covered throughout the book, involving the management of numerous backup files of different types, is doubly true for file backups: the biggest danger to the DBA is generally the loss or corruption of one of those files.

Once again, the best strategy is to minimize the risk via careful planning and documentation of the backup strategy, careful storage and management of the backup files and regular, random backup verification via test restores (as described in Chapter 2). If a full file backup goes missing, or is corrupt, we'll need to start the restore from the previous good full file backup, in which case we had better have a complete chain of transaction log files in order to roll past the missing full file backup (any differentials that rely on the missing full one will be useless).

A similar argument applies to missing differential file backups; we'll have to simply rely on the full file backup and the chain of log files. If a log file is lost, the situation is more serious. Transaction log files are the glue that holds together the other two file backup types, and they should be carefully monitored to make sure they are valid and that they are being stored locally as well as on long-term storage. Losing a transaction log backup can be a disaster if we do not have a set of full file and file differential backups that cover the time frame of the missing log backup. If a log file is unavailable or corrupt, and we really need it to complete a restore operation, we are in bad shape. In this situation, we will not be able to restore past that point in time and will have to find a way to deal with the data loss. This is why managing files carefully, and keeping a tape backup offsite is so important for all of our backup files.

File Backup and Restore SLA

File backup and restore will most likely be a very small part of most recoverability strategies. For most databases, the increased management responsibility of file backups will outweigh the benefits gained by adopting such a backup strategy. As a DBA, you may want to "push back" on a suggestion of this type of backup unless you judge the need to be there. If the database is too large to perform regular (e.g. nightly) full database backups and the acceptable down-time is too short to allow a full database restore, then file backups would be needed, but they should not be the norm for most DBAs.

If file backups are a necessity for a given database, then the implications of this, for backup scheduling and database recovery times, need to be made clear in the SLA. Of course, as we've demonstrated, down time could in some circumstances, such as where online piecemeal restore is possible, be much shorter.

As with all backup and restore SLAs, once agreed, we need to be sure that we can implement a backup and recovery strategy that will comply with the maximum tolerance to data loss and that will bring a database back online within agreed times in the event of a disaster, such as database failure or corruption.

Considerations for the SLA agreement, for any databases requiring file backups include those shown below.

- **Scheduling of full file backups** – I recommend full file backup at least once per week, although I've known cases where we had to push beyond this as it wasn't possible to get a full backup of each of the data files in that period.

- **Scheduling of differential file backups** – I recommend scheduling differential backups on any day where a full file backup is not being performed. As discussed in Chapter 7, this can dramatically decrease the number of log files to be processed for a restore operation.

- **Scheduling of transaction log backups** – These should be taken daily, at an interval chosen by yourself and the project manager whose group uses the database. I would suggest taking log backups of a VLDB using file backups at an interval of no more than 1 hour. Of course, if the business requires a more finely-tuned window of recoverability, you will need to shorten that schedule down to 30 or even 15 minutes, as required. Even if the window of data loss is more than 1 hour, I would still suggest taking log backups hourly.

For any database, it's important to ensure that all backups are completing successfully, and that all the backup files are stored securely and in their proper location, whether on a local disk or on long-term tape storage. However, in my experience, the DBA needs to be exceptionally vigilant in this regard for databases using file backups. There are many more files involved, and a missing log file can prevent you from being able to restore a database to a consistent state. With a missing log file and in the absence of a full file or differential file backup that covers the same time period, we'd have no choice but to restore to a point in time before the missing log file was taken. These log backups are also your "backup of a backup" in case a differential or full file backup goes missing.

I would suggest keeping locally at least the last two full file backups, subsequent differential file backup and all log backups spanning the entire time frame of these file backups, even after they have been written to tape and taken to offsite storage.

It may seem like a lot of files to keep handy, but since this is one of the most file intensive types of restores, it is better to be more safe than sorry. Waiting for a file from tape storage can cost the business money and time that they don't want to lose.

Restore times for any database using file backups can vary greatly, depending on the situation; sometimes we'll need to restore several, large full file backups, plus any differential backups, plus all the necessary log backups. Other times, we will only need to restore a single file or filegroup backup plus the covering transaction log backups. This should be reflected in the SLA, and the business owners and end-users should be prepared for this varying window of recovery time, in the event that a restore is required. If the estimated recovery time is outside acceptable limits for complete restore scenarios, then if the SQL Server database in question is Enterprise Edition, y consider supporting the online piecemeal restore process discussed earlier. If not, then the business owner will need to weigh up the cost of upgrading to Enterprise Edition licenses, against the cost of extended down-time in the event of a disaster.

As always, the people who use the database will drive the decisions made and reflected in the SLA. They will know the fine details of how the database is used and what processes are run against the data. Use their knowledge of these details when agreeing on appropriate data loss and recovery time parameters, and on the strategy to achieve them.

Forcing Failures for Fun

After a number of graceful swan dives throughout this chapter, get ready for a few belly-flops! Listing 9-37 is an innocent-looking script that attempts to take a full file backup of the secondary data file of the DatabaseForFileBackups database. We've performed several such backups successfully before, so try to figure out what the problem is before you execute it.

```
USE [master]
GO


BACKUP DATABASE [DatabaseForFileBackups] FILE = N'SECONDARY'
TO DISK = N'C:\SQLBackups\Chapter9\DatabaseForFileBackups_FG1_Full2.bak'
WITH STATS = 10
GO
```

Listing 9-37: File/filegroup confusion.

The error is quite subtle so, if you can't spot it, go ahead and execute the script and take a look at the error message, shown in Figure 9-8.

```
Messages
Msg 3235, Level 16, State 1, Line 2
The file "SECONDARY" is not part of database "DatabaseForFileBackups". You can only list files that are members of this database.
Msg 3013, Level 16, State 1, Line 2
BACKUP DATABASE is terminating abnormally.
```

Figure 9-8: The file "SECONDARY" is not part of the database...

The most revealing part of the error message here states that *The file "SECONDARY" is not part of database "DatabaseForFileBackups.* However, we know that the SECONDARY filegroup is indeed part of this database. The error we made was with our use of the FILE parameter; SECONDARY is the name of the filegroup, not the secondary data file. We can either change the parameter to FILEGROUP (since we only have one file in this filegroup), or we can use the FILE parameter and reference the name of the secondary data file explicitly (FILE= N'DatabaseForFileBackups_Data2').

Let's now move on to a bit of file restore-based havoc. Consider the script shown in Listing 9-38, the intent of which appears to be to restore our DatabaseForFileBackups database to the state in which it existed when we took the second transaction log backup file.

```
USE [Master]
GO


RESTORE DATABASE [DatabaseForFileBackups] FILE = N'DatabaseForFileBackups'
FROM DISK = N'C:\SQLBackups\Chapter9\DatabaseForFileBackups_FG1_Full.bak'
WITH NORECOVERY, REPLACE
GO

RESTORE DATABASE [DatabaseForFileBackups] FILE = N'DatabaseForFileBackups_Data2'
FROM DISK = N'C:\SQLBackups\Chapter9\DatabaseForFileBackups_FG2_Full.bak'
WITH NORECOVERY
GO

RESTORE DATABASE [DatabaseForFileBackups] FILE = N'DatabaseForFileBackups'
FROM DISK = N'C:\SQLBackups\Chapter9\DatabaseForFileBackups_FG1_Diff.bak'
WITH NORECOVERY
GO

RESTORE DATABASE [DatabaseForFileBackups]
FROM DISK = N'C:\SQLBackups\Chapter9\DatabaseForFileBackups_TLOG2.trn'
WITH RECOVERY
GO
```

Listing 9-38: File restore failure.

The error in the script is less subtle, and I'm hoping you worked out what the problem is before seeing the error message in Figure 9-8.

```
Messages
Processed 168 pages for database 'DatabaseForFileBackups', file 'DatabaseForFileBackups' on file 1.
Processed 3 pages for database 'DatabaseForFileBackups', file 'DatabaseForFileBackups_log' on file 1.
RESTORE DATABASE ... FILE=<name> successfully processed 171 pages in 0.641 seconds (2.074 MB/sec).
Processed 16 pages for database 'DatabaseForFileBackups', file 'DatabaseForFileBackups_Data2' on file 1.
Processed 2 pages for database 'DatabaseForFileBackups', file 'DatabaseForFileBackups_log' on file 1.
RESTORE DATABASE ... FILE=<name> successfully processed 18 pages in 0.551 seconds (0.242 MB/sec).
Processed 56 pages for database 'DatabaseForFileBackups', file 'DatabaseForFileBackups' on file 1.
Processed 1 pages for database 'DatabaseForFileBackups', file 'DatabaseForFileBackups_log' on file 1.
RESTORE DATABASE ... FILE=<name> successfully processed 57 pages in 0.682 seconds (0.642 MB/sec).
Msg 4305, Level 16, State 1, Line 2
The log in this backup set begins at LSN 21000000044500001, which is too recent to apply to the database.
An earlier log backup that includes LSN 21000000044200001 can be restored.
Msg 3013, Level 16, State 1, Line 2
RESTORE DATABASE is terminating abnormally.
```

Listing 9-39: The backup set is too recent...

We can see that the first three RESTORE commands executed successfully but the fourth failed, with a message stating that the LSN contained in the backup was too recent to apply. Whenever you see this sort of message, it means that a file is missing from your restore script. In this case, we forgot to apply the differential file backup for the secondary data file; SQL Server detects the gap in the LSN chain and aborts the RESTORE command, leaving the database in a restoring state.

The course of action depends on the exact situation. If the differential backup file is available and you simply forgot to include it, then restore this differential backup, followed by TLOG2, to recover the database. If the differential file backup really is missing or corrupted, then you'll need to process all transaction log backups taken after the full file backup was created. In our simple example this just means TLOG and TLOG2, but in a real-world scenario this could be quite a lot of log backups.

Again, hopefully this hammers home the point that it is a good idea to have more than one set of files on hand, or available from offsite storage, which could be used to bring your database back online in the event of a disaster. You never want to be in the situation where you have to lose more data than is necessary, or are not be able to restore at all.

Summary

In my experience, the need for file backup and restore has tended to be relatively rare, among the databases that I manage. The flipside to that is that the databases that do need them tend to be VLDBs supporting high visibility projects, and all DBAs need to make sure that they are well-versed in taking, as well as restoring databases from, the variety of file backups.

File backup and restore adds considerable complexity to our disaster recovery strategy, in terms of both the number and the type of backup file that must be managed. To gain full benefit from file backup and restores, the DBA needs to give considerable thought to the file and filegroup architecture for that database, and plan the backup and restore process accordingly. There are an almost infinite number of possible file and filegroup architectures, and each would require a subtly different backup strategy. You'll need to create some test databases, with multiple files and filegroups, work through them, and then document your approach. You can design some test databases to use any number of data files, and then create jobs to take full file, differential file, and transaction log backups that would mimic what you would use in a production environment. Then set yourself the task of responding to the various possible disaster scenarios, and bring your database back online to a certain day, or even a point in time that is represented in one of the transaction log backup files.

Chapter 10: Partial Backup and Restore

Partial backups are similar to file and filegroup backups in that they allow us to back up only a subset of the data files that comprise a database. However, whereas file and filegroup backups allow us to back up specific, individual files and filegroups, partial backups will make a backup copy of the primary filegroup and all read/write filegroups, omitting by default any filegroups designated as **READONLY**. This means that partial backups are only relevant for databases that contain read-only filegroups; otherwise, a partial backup will capture exactly the same data and objects as an equivalent full database backup.

Partial backups are available in SQL Server 2005 and later, and were designed to reduce the backup footprint for large databases that contain a high proportion of read-only data. After all, why would we back up the same data each night when we know that it cannot have been changed, since it was in a read-only state? We wouldn't, or shouldn't, be backing up that segment of the data on a regular schedule.

In this chapter, we will discuss:

- why and where partial backups may be applicable in a backup and restore scheme
- how to perform partial and differential partial backups
- how to restore a database that adopts a partial backup strategy
- potential problems with partial backups and how to avoid them.

Why Partial Backups?

Partial backups allow us to back up, on a regular schedule, only the read-write objects and data in our databases. Any data and objects stored in read-only filegroups will not, by default, be captured in a partial backup. From what we've discussed in Chapter 9, it should be clear that we can achieve the same effect by capturing separate file backups of each of the read-write filegroups. However, suppose we have a database that does not require support for point-in-time restores; transaction log backups are *required* when performing file-based backups, regardless, so this can represent an unnecessarily complex backup and restore process.

With partial backups, we only need to take transaction log backups if they are needed for point-in-time recovery, and so they are ideal for use with SIMPLE recovery model databases, as a means to trim database backups down to a more manageable size, without introducing the added administrative overhead of log backups. Note that partial backups are valid for databases operating in *any* recovery model; it's just that they were specifically designed to simplify back up for very large, SIMPLE recovery model databases that contain a large portion of read-only data.

So, in what situations might we want to adopt partial backups on a database in our infrastructure? Let's say we have a SQL Server-backed application for a community center and its public classes. The database holds student information, class information, grades, payment data and other data about the courses. At the end of each quarter, one set of courses completes, and a new set begins. Once all of the information for a current quarter's courses is entered into the system, the data is only lightly manipulated throughout the course lifetime. The instructor may update grades and attendance a few times per week, but the database is not highly active during the day. Once the current set of courses completes, at quarter's end, the information is archived, and kept for historical and auditing purposes, but will not be subject to any further changes.

This sort of database is a good candidate for partial backups. The "live" course data will be stored in a read-write filegroup. Every three months, this data can be appended to a set of archive tables for future reporting and auditing, stored in a read-only filegroup (this filegroup would be switched temporarily to read-write in order to run the archive process). We can perform this archiving in a traditional data-appending manner by moving all of the data from the live tables to the archive tables, or we could streamline this process via the use of partitioning functions.

Once the archive process is complete and the new course data has been imported, we can take a full backup of the whole database and store it in a safe location. From then on, we can adopt a schedule of, say, weekly partial backups interspersed with daily differential partial backups. This way we are not wasting any space or time backing up the read-only data.

Also, it may well be acceptable to operate this database in **SIMPLE** recovery model, since we know that once the initial course data is loaded, changes to the live course data are infrequent, so an exposure of one day to potential data loss may be tolerable.

In our example, taking a full backup only once every three months may seem a little too infrequent. Instead, we might consider performing a monthly full backup, to provide a little extra insurance, and simplify the restore process.

Performing Partial Database Backups

In most DBAs' workplaces, partial backups will be the least used of all the backup types so, rather than walk through two separate examples, one for native SQL Server backup commands and one for SQL Backup, we'll only work through an example of partial backup and restore using native T-SQL commands, since partial backups are not supported in either SSMS or in the Maintenance Plan wizard. The equivalent SQL Backup commands will be presented, but outside the context of a full worked example.

Preparing for partial backups

Listing 10-1 shows the script to create a `DatabaseForPartialBackups` database with multiple data files. The primary data file will hold our read-write data, and a secondary data file, in a filegroup called `Archive`, will hold our read-only data. Having created the database, we immediately alter it to use the `SIMPLE` recovery model.

```
USE [master]
GO


CREATE DATABASE [DatabaseForPartialBackups] ON PRIMARY
(    NAME = N'DatabaseForPartialBackups'
  , FILENAME = N'C:\SQLData\DatabaseForPartialBackups.mdf'
  , SIZE = 10240KB , FILEGROWTH = 10240KB ), FILEGROUP [Archive]
(    NAME = N'DatabaseForPartialBackups_ReadOnly'
  , FILENAME = N'C:\SQLData\DatabaseForPartialBackups_ReadOnly.ndf'
  , SIZE = 10240KB , FILEGROWTH = 10240KB ) LOG ON
(    NAME = N'DatabaseForPartialBackups_log'
  , FILENAME = N'C:\SQLData\DatabaseForPartialBackups_log.ldf'
  , SIZE = 10240KB , FILEGROWTH = 10240KB )
GO

ALTER DATABASE [DatabaseForPartialBackups] SET RECOVERY SIMPLE
GO
```

Listing 10-1: Creating the `DatabaseForPartialBackups` test database.

The script is fairly straightforward and there is nothing here that we haven't discussed in previous scripts for multiple data file databases. The `Archive` filegroup will eventually be set to read-only, but first we are going to need to create some tables in this filegroup and populate one of them with data, as shown in Listing 10-2.

```
USE [DatabaseForPartialBackups]
GO


CREATE TABLE dbo.MainData
    (
        ID INT NOT NULL
                IDENTITY(1, 1) ,
        Message NVARCHAR(50) NOT NULL
    )
ON   [PRIMARY]
GO

CREATE TABLE dbo.ArchiveData
    (
        ID INT NOT NULL ,
        Message NVARCHAR(50) NOT NULL
    )
ON   [Archive]
GO

INSERT  INTO dbo.MainData
VALUES  ( 'Data for initial database load: Data 1' )
INSERT  INTO dbo.MainData
VALUES  ( 'Data for initial database load: Data 2' )
INSERT  INTO dbo.MainData
VALUES  ( 'Data for initial database load: Data 3' )
GO
```

Listing 10-2: Creating the MainData and ArchiveData tables and populating the MainData table.

The final preparatory step for our example is to simulate an archiving process, copying data from the MainData table into the ArchiveData table, setting the Archive filegroup as read-only, and then deleting the archived data from MainData, and inserting the next set of "live" data.

Before running Listing 10-3, make sure there are no other query windows connected to the DatabaseForPartialBackups database. If there are, the conversion of the secondary file group to READONLY will fail, as we need to have exclusive access on the database before we can change filegroup states.

```
USE [DatabaseForPartialBackups]
GO

INSERT   INTO dbo.ArchiveData
         SELECT  ID ,
                 Message
         FROM    MainData
GO

ALTER DATABASE [DatabaseForPartialBackups] MODIFY FILEGROUP [Archive] READONLY
GO

DELETE   FROM dbo.MainData
GO

INSERT   INTO dbo.MainData
VALUES   ( 'Data for second database load: Data 4' )
INSERT   INTO dbo.MainData
VALUES   ( 'Data for second database load: Data 5' )
INSERT   INTO dbo.MainData
VALUES   ( 'Data for second database load: Data 6' )
GO
```

Listing 10-3: Data archiving and secondary data load.

Finally, before we take our first partial backup, we want to capture one backup copy of the whole database, including the read-only data, as the basis for any subsequent restore operations. We can take a partial database backup before taking a full one, but we do want to make sure we have a solid restore point for the database, before starting our partial backup routines. Therefore, Listing 10-4 takes a full database backup of our DatabaseForPartialBackups database. Having done so, it also inserts some more data into MainData, so that we have fresh data to capture in our subsequent partial backup.

```
USE [master]
GO

BACKUP DATABASE DatabaseForPartialBackups
TO DISK = N'C:\SQLBackups\Chapter10\DatabaseForPartialBackups_FULL.bak'
GO

INSERT  INTO DatabaseForPartialBackups.dbo.MainData
VALUES  ( 'Data for third database load: Data 7' )
INSERT  INTO DatabaseForPartialBackups.dbo.MainData
VALUES  ( 'Data for third database load: Data 8' )
INSERT  INTO DatabaseForPartialBackups.dbo.MainData
VALUES  ( 'Data for third database load: Data 9' )
GO
```

Listing 10-4: Full database backup of `DatabaseForPartialBackups`, plus third data load.

The output from the full database backup is shown in Figure 10-1. Notice that, as expected, it processes both of our data files, plus the log file.

```
Processed 176 pages for database 'DatabaseForPartialBackups', file
'DatabaseForPartialBackups' on file 1.
Processed 16 pages for database 'DatabaseForPartialBackups', file
'DatabaseForPartialBackups_ReadOnly' on file 1.
Processed 2 pages for database 'DatabaseForPartialBackups', file
'DatabaseForPartialBackups_log' on file 1.
BACKUP DATABASE successfully processed 194 pages in 0.043 seconds (35.110 MB/sec).
```

Figure 10-1: Output from the full database backup.

Partial database backup using T-SQL

We are now ready to perform our first partial database backup, which will capture the data inserted in our third data load, as shown in Listing 10-5.

```
BACKUP DATABASE DatabaseForPartialBackups READ_WRITE_FILEGROUPS
TO DISK = N'C:\SQLBackups\Chapter10\DatabaseForPartialBackups_PARTIAL_Full.bak'
GO
```

Listing 10-5: A partial backup of `DatabaseForPartialBackups`.

The only difference between this backup command and the full database backup command shown in Listing 10-4 is the addition of the **READ_WRITE_FILEGROUPS** option. This option lets SQL Server know that the command is a partial backup and to only process the read-write filegroups contained in the database.

The output should be similar to that shown in Figure 10-2. Notice that this time only the primary data file and the log file are processed. This is exactly what we expected to see: since we are not processing any of the read-only data, we shouldn't see that data file being accessed in the second backup command.

```
Processed 176 pages for database 'DatabaseForPartialBackups', file
'DatabaseForPartialBackups' on file 1.
Processed 2 pages for database 'DatabaseForPartialBackups', file
'DatabaseForPartialBackups_log' on file 1.
BACKUP DATABASE...FILE=<name> successfully processed 178 pages in 0.039 seconds (35.481
MB/sec).
```

Figure 10-2: Partial backup results.

Differential partial backup using T-SQL

Just as we can have differential database backups, which refer to a base full database backup, so we can take differential partial database backups that refer to a base partial database backup, and will capture only the data that changed in the read-write data files, since the base partial backup was taken.

Before we run a differential partial backup, we need some fresh data to process.

```
USE [DatabaseForPartialBackups]
GO

INSERT   INTO MainData
VALUES   ( 'Data for fourth database load: Data 10' )
INSERT   INTO MainData
VALUES   ( 'Data for fourth database load: Data 11' )
INSERT   INTO MainData
VALUES   ( 'Data for fourth database load: Data 12' )
GO
```

Listing 10-6: Fourth data load, in preparation for partial differential backup.

Listing 10-7 shows the script to run our partial differential backup. The one significant difference is the inclusion of the WITH DIFFERENTIAL option, which converts the command from a full partial to a differential partial backup.

```
USE [master]
GO

BACKUP DATABASE [DatabaseForPartialBackups] READ_WRITE_FILEGROUPS
TO DISK = N'C:\SQLBackups\Chapter10\DatabaseForPartialBackups_PARTIAL_Diff.bak'
WITH DIFFERENTIAL
GO
```

Listing 10-7: Performing the partial differential backup.

Once this command is complete, go ahead and check the output of the command in the messages tab to make sure only the proper data files were processed. We are done taking partial backups for now and can move on to our restore examples.

Performing Partial Database Restores

We will be performing two restore examples: one restoring the DatabaseForPartial-Backups database to the state in which it existed after the third data load, using the full database and full partial backup files, and one restoring the database to its state after the fourth data load, using the full database, full partial, and differential partial backup files.

Restoring a full partial backup

Listing 10-8 show the two simple steps in our restore process. The first step restores our full database backup file, which will restore the data and objects in both our read-write and read-only filegroups. In this step, we include the NORECOVERY option, so that SQL Server leaves the database in a state where we can apply more files. This is important so that we don't wind up with a database that is online and usable before we apply the partial backup.

The second step restores our full partial backup file. This will overwrite the read-write files in the existing database with the data from the backup file, which will contain all the data we inserted into the primary data file, up to and including the third data load. We specify that this restore operation be completed with RECOVERY.

```
USE [master]
GO


RESTORE DATABASE [DatabaseForPartialBackups]
FROM DISK = N'C:\SQLBackups\Chapter10\DatabaseForPartialBackups_FULL.bak'
WITH NORECOVERY
GO

RESTORE DATABASE [DatabaseForPartialBackups]
FROM DISK = N'C:\SQLBackups\Chapter10\DatabaseForPartialBackups_PARTIAL_Full.bak'
WITH RECOVERY
GO
```

Listing 10-8: Restoring the partial full database backup.

The output from running this script is shown in Figure 10-3. We should see all files being processed in the first command, and only the read-write and transaction log file being modified in the second command.

```
Processed 176 pages for database 'DatabaseForPartialBackups', file
'DatabaseForPartialBackups' on file 1.
Processed 16 pages for database 'DatabaseForPartialBackups', file
'DatabaseForPartialBackups_ReadOnly' on file 1.
Processed 2 pages for database 'DatabaseForPartialBackups', file
'DatabaseForPartialBackups_log' on file 1.
RESTORE DATABASE successfully processed 194 pages in 0.760 seconds (1.986 MB/sec).

Processed 176 pages for database 'DatabaseForPartialBackups', file
'DatabaseForPartialBackups' on file 1.
Processed 2 pages for database 'DatabaseForPartialBackups', file
'DatabaseForPartialBackups_log' on file 1.
RESTORE DATABASE ... FILE=<name> successfully processed 178 pages in 0.124 seconds (11.159
MB/sec).
```

Figure 10-3: Partial database backup restore output.

Everything looks good, and exactly as expected, but let's put on our Paranoid DBA hat once more and check that the restored database contains the right data.

```
USE [DatabaseForPartialBackups]
GO

SELECT  ID ,
        Message
FROM    dbo.MainData
SELECT  ID ,
        Message
FROM    dbo.ArchiveData
```

Listing 10-9: Checking out our newly restored data.

Hopefully, we'll see three rows of data in the **ArchiveData** table and six rows of data in the read-write table, **MainData**, as confirmed in Figure 10-4.

Results | Messages

	ID	Message
1	4	Data for second database load: Data 4
2	5	Data for second database load: Data 5
3	6	Data for second database load: Data 6
4	7	Data for second database load: Data 7
5	8	Data for second database load: Data 8
6	9	Data for second database load: Data 9

	ID	Message
1	1	Data for initial database load: Data 1
2	2	Data for initial database load: Data 2
3	3	Data for initial database load: Data 3

Figure 10-4: Results of the data check on our newly restored database.

Restoring a differential partial backup

Our restore operation this time is very similar, except that we'll need to process all three of our backup files, to get the database back to its state after the final data load. You may be wondering why it's necessary to process the full partial backup in this case, rather than just the full backup followed by the differential partial backup. In fact, the full database backup cannot serve as the base for the differential partial backup; only a full partial backup can serve as the base for a differential partial backup, just as only a full database backup can serve as a base for a differential database backup. Each differential partial backup holds all the changes since the base partial backup so, if we had a series of differential partial backups, we would only need to restore the latest one in the series.

Listing 10-10 shows the script; we restore the full database and full partial backups, leaving the database in a restoring state, then apply the differential partial backup and recover the database.

```
USE [master]
GO


RESTORE DATABASE [DatabaseForPartialBackups]
FROM DISK = N'C:\SQLBackups\Chapter10\DatabaseForPartialBackups_FULL.bak'
WITH NORECOVERY
GO

RESTORE DATABASE [DatabaseForPartialBackups]
FROM DISK = N'C:\SQLBackups\Chapter10\DatabaseForPartialBackups_PARTIAL_Full.bak'
WITH NORECOVERY
GO

RESTORE DATABASE [DatabaseForPartialBackups]
FROM DISK = N'C:\SQLBackups\Chapter10\DatabaseForPartialBackups_PARTIAL_Diff.bak'
WITH RECOVERY
GO
```

Listing 10-10: Restoring the partial differential backup file.

Once again, check the output from the script to make sure everything looks as it should, and then rerun Listing 10-9 to verify that there are now three more rows in the MainData table, for a total of nine rows, and still only three rows in the ArchiveData table.

Special case partial backup restore

Here, we'll take a quick look at a special type of restore operation that we might term a "partial online piecemeal restore," which will bring the database online by restoring only the read-only filegroup in the database (requires Enterprise edition), as shown in Listing 10-11. This type of restore can be done with both full partial backups as well as full file backups, provided the full file backup contains the primary filegroup, with the database system information. This is useful if we need to recover a specific table that exists in the read-write filegroups, or we want to view the contents of the backup without restoring the entire database.

```
-- restore the read-write filegroups
RESTORE DATABASE [DatabaseForPartialBackups]
FROM DISK = N'C:\SQLBackups\Chapter10\DatabaseForPartialBackups_PARTIAL_Full.bak'
WITH RECOVERY, PARTIAL
GO
```

Listing 10-11: Performing a partial online restore.

Now, we should have a database that is online and ready to use, but with only the read-write filegroup accessible, which we can verify with a few simple queries, shown in Listing 10-12.

```
USE [DatabaseForPartialBackups]
GO

SELECT  ID ,
        Message
FROM    MainData
GO
SELECT  ID ,
        Message
FROM    ArchiveData
GO
```

Listing 10-12: Selecting data from our partially restored database.

The script attempts to query both tables and the output is shown in Figure 10-5.

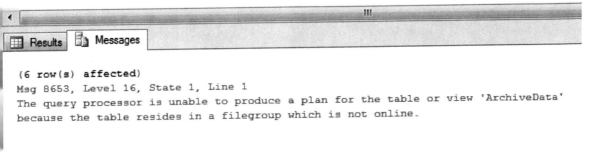

```
Results    Messages

(6 row(s) affected)
Msg 8653, Level 16, State 1, Line 1
The query processor is unable to produce a plan for the table or view 'ArchiveData'
because the table resides in a filegroup which is not online.
```

Figure 10-5: Unable to pull information from the archive table.

We can see that we did pull six rows from the MainData table, but when we attempted to pull data from the ArchiveData table, we received an error, because that filegroup was not part of the file we used in our restore operation. We can see the table exists and even see its structure, if so inclined, since all of that information is stored in the system data, which was restored with the primary filegroup.

SQL Backup Partial Backup and Restore

In this section, without restarting the whole example from scratch, we will take a look at the equivalent full partial and differential partial backup commands in SQL Backup, as shown in Listing 10-13.

```
USE master
GO
-- full partial backup with SQL Backup
EXECUTE master..sqlbackup '-SQL "BACKUP DATABASE [DatabaseForPartialBackups]
READ_WRITE_FILEGROUPS
TO DISK = ''C:\SQLBackups\Chapter10\DatabaseForPartialBackups_Partial_Full.sqb''
WITH DISKRETRYINTERVAL = 30, DISKRETRYCOUNT = 10, COMPRESSION = 3, THREADCOUNT =
2"'
```

```
-- differential partial backup with SQL Backup
EXECUTE master..sqlbackup '-SQL "BACKUP DATABASE [DatabaseForPartialBackups]
READ_WRITE_FILEGROUPS
TO DISK = ''C:\SQLBackups\Chapter10\DatabaseForPartialBackups_Partial_Diff.sqb''
WITH DIFFERENTIAL, DISKRETRYINTERVAL = 30, DISKRETRYCOUNT = 10, COMPRESSION = 3,
THREADCOUNT = 2"'
```

Listing 10-13: A SQL Backup script for full partial and differential partial backups.

The commands are very similar to the native commands, and nearly identical to the SQL Backup commands we have used in previous chapters. The only addition is the same new option we saw in the native commands earlier in this chapter, namely `READ_WRITE_FILEGROUPS`.

Listing 10-14 shows the equivalent restore commands for partial backups; again, they are very similar to what we have seen before in other restore scripts. We restore the last full database backup leaving the database ready to process more files. This will restore all of the read-only data, and leave the database in a restoring state, ready to apply the partial backup data. We then apply the full partial and differential partial backups, and recover the database.

```
-- full database backup restore
EXECUTE master..sqlbackup '-SQL "RESTORE DATABASE [DatabaseForPartialBackups]
FROM DISK = ''C:\SQLBackups\Chapter10\DatabaseForPartialBackups_FULL.sqb''
WITH NORECOVERY"'

-- full partial backup restore
EXECUTE master..sqlbackup '-SQL "RESTORE DATABASE [DatabaseForPartialBackups]
FROM DISK =
''C:\SQLBackups\Chapter10\DatabaseForPartialBackups_Partial_Full.sqb''
WITH NORECOVERY"'

-- differential partial backup restore
EXECUTE master..sqlbackup '-SQL "RESTORE DATABASE [DatabaseForPartialBackups]
FROM DISK = ''C:\SQLBackups\Chapter10\DatabaseForPartialBackups_Partial_Diff.sqb''
WITH RECOVERY"'
```

Listing 10-14: A SQL Backup script for full and differential partial restores.

Possible Issues with Partial Backup and Restore

The biggest issue when restoring a database using partial backups is the storage and management of the read-only data. This data is captured in a full database backup, directly after the data import, and then not backed up again. As such, it is easy for its existence to slip from a DBA's mind. However, the fact that this portion of the database is backed up less frequently, does not mean it is less important; it is still an integral piece of the recovery strategy, so manage each file in your backup strategy carefully and make sure the full database backup doesn't get lost in the archival jungle.

When performing one of the full database backups on a database where the backup strategy includes subsequent partial backups, it's a good idea to perform a checksum on that full database backup (see Chapter 2 for details). This can, and most likely will, slow down the backup speed but if you can take the speed hit, it's nice to have the reassurance that this full backup is valid, since they will be captured infrequently. Of course, performing a test restore with the newly created full backup file is even better!

If you do find that your full database backup has not been stored properly or that the file is somehow corrupted, what can you do? Well, not a whole lot. Hopefully you have multiple copies stored in different locations for just this type of situation. Keeping a copy on long-term storage, as well as locally on a robust disk, are other good ideas when dealing with data that is not backed up on a regular basis. Be diligent when you are managing your backup files. Remember that your data is your job!

Partial Backups and Restores in the SLA

Like file backup and restore, partial backup and restore will most likely form a very small part of your overall recoverability strategy; partial backups are a very useful and time saving tool in certain instances, but they will not likely be the "go-to" backup type in most situations, largely because most databases simply don't contain a large proportion of read-only data.

However, if a strategy involving partial backups seems a good fit for a database then, in the SLA for that database, you'll need to consider such issues as:

- frequency of refreshing the full database backup

- frequency of full partial and differential partial backups

- are transaction log backups still required?

As noted earlier, partial backups are designed with SIMPLE recovery model databases in mind. When applied in this way, it means that we can only restore to the last backup that was taken, most likely a full partial or a differential partial backup, and so we do stand to lose some data modifications in the case of, say, a midday failure. That is something you have to weigh against your database restore needs to decide if this type of backup will work for you. Like every other type of backup, weigh up the pros and cons to see which type, or combination of types, is right for your database.

Just because this type of backup was designed mainly for SIMPLE recovery model databases, it doesn't mean that we can only use it in such cases. For a FULL recovery model database that has a much smaller window of data loss acceptability, such as an hour, but does contain a large section of read-only data, this backup type can still work to our advantage. We would, however, need to take transaction log backups in addition to the partial full and partial differentials. This will add a little more complexity to the backup and restore processes in the event of emergency, but will enable point-in-time restore.

Forcing Failures for Fun

Much as I hate to end the chapter, and the book, on a note of failure, that is sometimes the lot of the DBA; deal with failures as and when they occur, learn what to look out for, and enforce measures to ensure the problem does not happen again. With that in mind, let's walk through a doomed partial backup scheme. Take a look at the script in Listing 10-15 and, one last time, try to work out what the problem is before running it.

```
USE [master]
GO

RESTORE DATABASE [DatabaseForPartialBackups]
FROM DISK = N'C:\SQLBackups\Chapter10\DatabaseForPartialBackups_FULL.bak'
WITH NORECOVERY
GO

RESTORE DATABASE [DatabaseForPartialBackups]
FROM DISK = N'C:\SQLBackups\Chapter10\DatabaseForPartialBackups_PARTIAL_Diff.bak'
WITH RECOVERY
GO
```

Listing 10-15: Forcing a restore error with partial database backup restore.

Do you spot the mistake? Figure 10-6 shows the resulting SQL Server error messages.

```
Messages
Processed 160 pages for database 'DatabaseForPartialBackups', file 'DatabaseForPartialBackups' on file 1.
Processed 16 pages for database 'DatabaseForPartialBackups', file 'DatabaseForPartialBackups_ReadOnly' on file 1.
Processed 2 pages for database 'DatabaseForPartialBackups', file 'DatabaseForPartialBackups_log' on file 1.
RESTORE DATABASE successfully processed 178 pages in 0.511 seconds (2.709 MB/sec).
Msg 3178, Level 16, State 1, Line 2
File DatabaseForPartialBackups is not in the correct state to have this differential backup applied to it.
Msg 3119, Level 16, State 1, Line 2
Problems were identified while planning for the RESTORE statement. Previous messages provide details.
Msg 3013, Level 16, State 1, Line 2
RESTORE DATABASE is terminating abnormally.
```

Figure 10-6: Forced failure query results

The first error we get in the execution of our script is the error *"File DatabaseForPartial-Backups is not in the correct state to have this differential backup applied to it."* This is telling us that the database is not prepared to process our second restore command, using the differential partial backup file.

The reason is that we have forgotten to process our partial full backup file. Since the partial full file, not the full database file, acts as the base for the partial differential, we can't process the partial differential without it. This is why our database is not in the correct state to process that differential backup file.

Summary

You should now be familiar with how to perform both partial full and partial differential backups and be comfortable restoring this type of backup file. With this, I invite you to sit back for a moment and reflect on the fact that you now know how to perform all of the major, necessary types of SQL Server backup and restore operation. *Congratulations!*

The book is over, but the journey is not complete. Backing up databases and performing restores should be something all DBAs do on a very regular basis. This skill is paramount to the DBA and we should keep working on it until the subject matter becomes second nature.

Nevertheless, when and if disaster strikes a database, in whatever form, I hope this book, and the carefully documented and tested restore strategy that it helps you generate, will allow you to get that database back online with an acceptable level of data loss, and minimal down-time.

Good luck!

Shawn McGehee

Appendix A: SQL Backup Installation and Configuration

This appendix serves as a Quick Reference on how to download, install and configure the SQL Backup tool from Red Gate Software, so that you can work through any examples in the book that use this tool. You can download a fully-functional trial version of the software from Red Gate's website, at WWW.RED-GATE.COM/PRODUCTS/DBA/SQL-BACKUP/.

By navigating to the **Support** pages for this tool, you can find further and fuller information on how to install, configure and use this tool, including step-by-step tutorials and troubleshooting guides. See, for example, HTTP://WWW.RED-GATE.COM/SUPPORTCENTER/CONTENT/SQL_BACKUP/HELP/6.5/SBU_GETTINGSTARTED, and the links therein.

With the software package downloaded, there are basically two steps to the installation process, first installing the SQL Backup GUI, and then the SQL Backup services.

SQL Backup GUI Installation

This section will demonstrate how to install the SQL backup GUI tool, which will enable you to register servers for use, and then execute and manage backups across your servers (having first installed the SQL Backup services on each of these SQL Server machines). The GUI tool will normally be installed on the client workstation, but can also be installed on a SQL Server.

Open the SQL Backup zip file, downloaded from the Red Gate website, and navigate to the folder called **SQLDBABundle**. Several files are available for execution, as shown in Figure A-1. The one you want here, in order to install the SQL Backup GUI is

SQLDBABundle.exe, so double-click the file, or copy the file to an uncompressed folder, in order to begin the installation.

Name	Type	Compressed size
HyperBac_Installer_x64.exe	Application	4,619 KB
HyperBac_Installer_x86.exe	Application	4,468 KB
README.TXT	Text Document	1 KB
SQL Storage Compress_6.0.exe	Application	7,790 KB
SQLDBABundle.exe	Application	19,475 KB
SQLMonitor2.3.exe	Application	8,623 KB

Figure A-1: Finding the installation file.

There is the option to install several DBA tools from Red Gate, but here you just want to install SQL Backup (current version at time of writing was SQL Backup 6.5), so select that tool, as shown in Figure A-2, and click the **Next** button to continue.

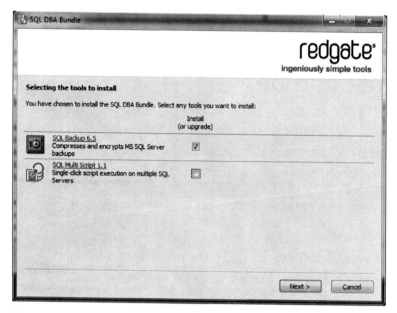

Figure A-2: Installing SQL Backup 6.5.

On the next page, you must accept the license agreement. This is a standard EULA and you can proceed with the normal routine of just selecting the "I accept..." check box and clicking **Next** to continue. If you wish to read through the legalese more thoroughly, print a copy for some bedtime reading.

On the next screen, select the folder where the SQL Backup GUI and service installers will be stored. Accept the default, or configure a different location, if required, and then click **Install**. The installation process should only take a few seconds and, once completed, you should see a success message and you can close the installer program.

That's all there is to it, and you are now ready to install the SQL Backup services on your SQL Server machine.

SQL Backup Services Installation

You can now use the SQL Backup GUI tool to connect to a SQL Server and install the SQL Backup services on that machine. Open the SQL Backup GUI and, once past the flash page offering some import/registration tools and demo screens (feel free to peruse these at a later time), you'll arrive at the main SQL Backup screen.

Underneath the top menu items (currently grayed out), is a tab that contains a server group named after the current time zone on the machine on which the GUI installed. In the bottom third of the screen are several tables where, ultimately, will be displayed the backup history for a selected server, current processes, log copy queues and job information.

Right-click on the server group and select **Add SQL Server**, as shown in Figure A-3.

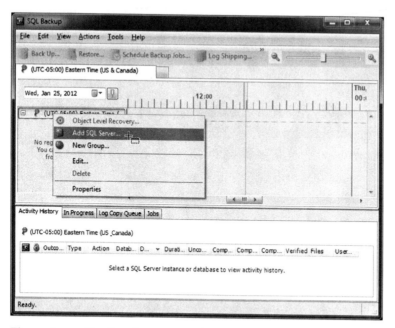

Figure A-3: Starting the server registration process.

Once the **Add SQL Server** screen opens, you can register a new server. Several pieces of information will be required, as shown below.

- **SQL Server**: This is the name of the SQL Server to register.

- **Authentication type**: Choose to use your Windows account to register or a SQL Server login.

- **User name**: SQL Login user name, if using SQL Server authentication.

- **Password**: SQL Login password, if using SQL Server authentication.

- **Remember password**: Check this option to save the password for a SQL Server login.

- **Native Backup and restore history**: Time period over which to import details of native SQL Server backup and restore activity into your local cache.

- **Install or upgrade server components**: Leaving this option checked will automatically start the installation or upgrade of a server's SQL Backup services.

Having have filled in the **General** tab information, you should see a window similar to that shown in Figure A-4.

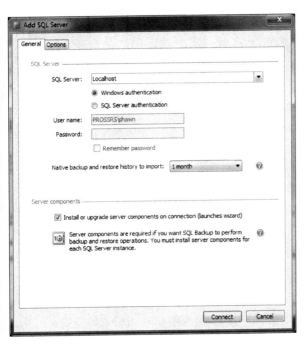

Figure A-4:   SQL Server registration information.

There is a second tab, **Options**, which allows you to modify the defaults for the options below.

- **Location**: You can choose a different location so the server will be placed in the tab for that location.

- **Group**: Select the server group in which to place the server being registered.

- **Alias**: An alias to use for display purposes, instead of the server name.

379

- **Network protocol**: Select the SQL Server communication protocol to use with this server.

- **Network packet size**: Change the default packet size for SQL Server communications in SQL Backup GUI.

- **Connection time-out**: Change the length of time that the GUI will attempt communication with the server before failing.

- **Execution time-out**: Change the length of time that SQL Backup will wait for a command to start before stopping it.

Accept all the defaults for the **Options** page, and go ahead and click **Connect**. Once the GUI connects to the server, you will need to fill out two more pages of information about the service that is being installed. On the first page, select the account under which the SQL Backup service will run; it will need to be one that has the proper permissions to perform SQL Server backups, and execute the extended stored procedures that it will install in the `master` database, and it will need to have the `sysadmin` server role, for the GUI interface use.

You can use a built-in system account or a service account from an Active Directory pool of users (recommended, for management across a domain). For this example, use the `Local System` account. Remember, too, that in SQL Server 2008 and later, the `BUILTIN\Administrators` group is no longer, by default, a `sysadmin` on the server, so you will need to add whichever account you are using to the SQL Server to make sure you have the correct permissions set up.

Figure A-5 shows an example of the security setup for a typical domain account for the SQL Backup service on a SQL Server.

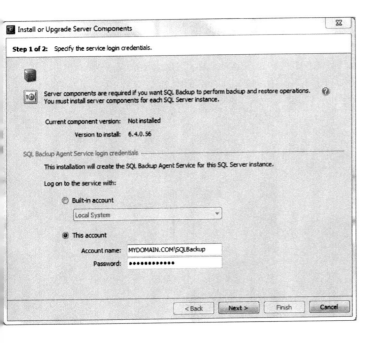

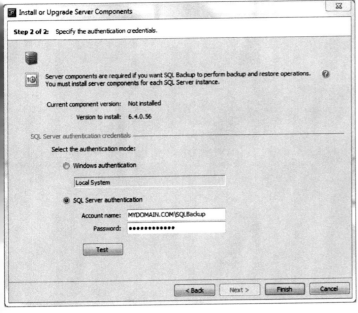

Figure A-5: Security setup for new server installation.

On the next page, you will see the SQL Server authentication credentials. You can use a different account from the service account, but it is not necessary if the permissions are set up correctly. Stick with the default user it has selected and click **Finish** to start the installation. Once that begins, the installation files will be copied over and you should, hopefully, see a series of successful installation messages, as shown in Figure A-6.

Figure A-6: Successful SQL backup service installation.

You have now successfully installed the SQL Backup service on a SQL Server. In the next section, you'll need to configure that service.

SQL Backup Configuration

Your newly-registered server should be visible in the default group (the icon to the right of the server name indicates that this is a trial version of the software). Right-click the server name to bring up a list of options, as shown in Figure A-7, some of which we will be using throughout this book.

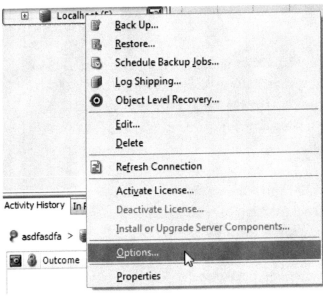

Figure A-7: Getting to the SQL Backup options configuration.

Go ahead and select **Options...** to bring up the **Server Options** window.

File management

The **File Management** tab allows you to configure backup file names automatically, preserve historical data and clean up MSDB history on a schedule.

The first option, **Backup folder**, sets the default location for all backup files generated through the GUI. This should point to the normal backup repository for this server so that any backups that are taken, especially if one is taken off the regular backup schedule, will end up in the right location.

The next option, **File name format**, sets the format of the auto-generated name option that is available with SQL Backup, using either the GUI or T-SQL code. Of course, it is up to you how to configure this setting, but my recommendation is this:

```
<DATABASE>_<DATETIME yyyymmdd_hhnnss>_<TYPE>
```

Using this format, any DBA can very quickly identify the database, what time the backup was taken, and what type of backup it was, and it allows the files to be sorted in alphabetical and chronological order. If you store in a shared folder multiple backups from multiple instances that exist on the same server, which I would not recommend, you can also add the `<INSTANCE>` tag for differentiation.

The next option, **Log file folder**, tells SQL Backup where on the server to store the log files from SQL Backup operations. Also in this section of the screen, you can configure log backup management options, specifying for how long backups should be retained in the local folder. I would recommend keeping at least 90 days' worth of files, but you could keep them indefinitely if you require a much longer historical view.

The final section of the screen is **Server backup history**, which will clean up the backup history stored in the `msdb` database; you may be surprised by how much historical data will accumulate over time. The default is to remove this history every 90 days, which I think is a little low. I would keep at least 180 days of history, but that is a choice you will have to make based on your needs and regulations.

If the SQL Backup server components are installed on an older machine which has never had its `msdb` database cleaned out, then the first time SQL Backup runs the `msdb` "spring clean," it can take quite a long time and cause some blocking on the server. There are no indexes on the backup and restore history tables in `msdb`, so it's a good idea to add some.

Once you are done configuring these options, the window should look similar, but probably slightly different, to that shown in Figure A-8.

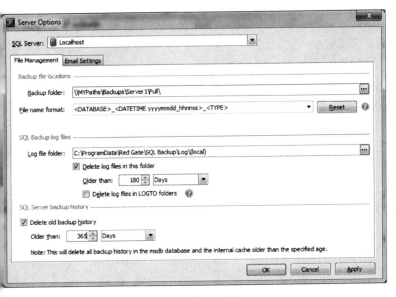

Figure A-8: File management configuration.

Email settings

The **Email Settings** tab will allow you to configure the settings for the emails that SQL Backup can send to you, or to a team of people, when a failure occurs in, or warning is raised for, one of your backup or restore operations. It's a very important setting to get configured correctly, and tested.

There are just five fields that you need to fill out.

- **SMTP Host**: This is the SMTP server that will receive any mail SQL Backup needs to send out.

- **Port:** The standard port is 25; do not change this unless instructed to by your email administration team.

- **Username:** Email account user name. This is not needed if your SQL Server is authorized by Exchange, or some other Email Server, to relay email from an address. Talk to your email admins about getting this set up for your SQL Servers.

- **Password:** Email account password.

- **Send from:** This is the actual name of the email account from which the email will be sent. You can use one email account for all of your SQL Servers (e.g. SQLBackups@MyCompany.com), or use an identifiable account for each server (e.g. MyServer123@MyCompany.com). If your SQL Servers are authorized to relay email without authentication you can just use the second example without having to actually set up the mail account. That is also something to discuss with your email administrators.

Once this screen is configured, it should look similar to that shown in Figure A-9. Always use the **Send Test Email...** button to send a test email and make sure everything was set up correctly.

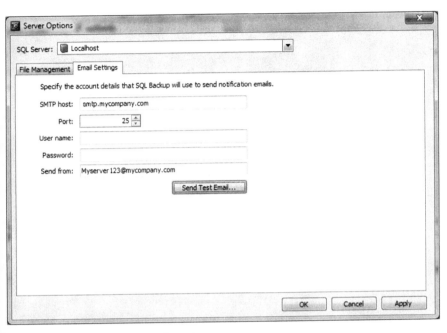

Figure A-9: Setting up email settings.

You are now installed and ready to start with the SQL Backup sections of the book! As noted at the start, if you have any trouble getting SQL Backup installed and running properly, visit the support section of the Red Gate site. There are many FAQs on common issues and a full message board with Red Gate support staff monitoring all of your questions and concerns.

Index

Symbols

SQL Server
and .NET Tools
from Red Gate Software

redgate®

ingeniously simple tools

SQL Backup Pro $795

Compress, encrypt, and strengthen SQL Server backups

↗ Compress SQL Server database backups by up to 95% for faster, smaller backups

↗ Protect your data with up to 256-bit AES encryption

↗ Strengthen your backups with network resilience to enable a fault-tolerant transfer of backups across flaky networks

↗ Control your backup activities through an intuitive interface, with powerful job management and an interactive timeline

"SQL Backup is an amazing tool that lets us manage and monitor our backups in real time. Red Gate's SQL tools have saved us so much time and work that I am afraid my director will decide that we don't need a DBA anymore!"

Mike Poole Database Administrator, Human Kinetics

SQL Virtual Restore $495

Rapidly mount live, fully functional databases direct from backups

↗ Virtually restoring a backup requires significantly less time and space than a regular physical restore

↗ Databases mounted with SQL Virtual Restore are fully functional and support both read/write operations

↗ SQL Virtual Restore is ACID compliant and gives you access to full, transactionally consistent data, with all objects visible and available

↗ Use SQL Virtual Restore to recover objects, verify your backups with DBCC CHECKDB, create a storage-efficient copy of your production database, and more.

"We find occasions where someone has deleted data accidentally or dropped an index, etc., and with SQL Virtual Restore we can mount last night's backup quickly and easily to get access to the data or the original schema. It even works with all our backups being encrypted. This takes any extra load off our production server. SQL Virtual Restore is a great product."
Brent McCraken Senior Database Administrator/Architect, Kiwibank Limited

SQL Storage Compress

Silent data compression to optimize SQL Server storage

↗ Reduce the storage footprint of live SQL Server databases by up to 90% to save on space and hardware costs

↗ Databases compressed with SQL Storage Compress are fully functional

↗ Prevent unauthorized access to your live databases with 256-bit AES encryption

↗ Integrates seamlessly with SQL Server and does not require any configuration changes

Visit **www.red-gate.com** for a 14-day, free trial

SQL Monitor

from $795

SQL Server performance monitoring and alerting

- ↗ Intuitive overviews at global, cluster, machine, SQL Server, and database levels for up-to-the-minute performance data

- ↗ Use SQL Monitor's web UI to keep an eye on server performance in real time on desktop machines and mobile devices

- ↗ Intelligent SQL Server alerts via email and an alert inbox in the UI, so you know about problems first

- ↗ Comprehensive historical data, so you can go back in time to identify the source of a problem

- ↗ Generate reports via the UI or with Red Gate's free SSRS Reporting Pack

- ↗ View the top 10 expensive queries for an instance or database based on CPU usage, duration, and reads and writes

- ↗ PagerDuty integration for phone and SMS alerting

- ↗ Fast, simple installation and administration

> **"Being web based, SQL Monitor is readily available to you, wherever you may be on your network. You can check on your servers from almost any location, via most mobile devices that support a web browser."**
>
> **Jonathan Allen** Senior DBA, Careers South West Ltd

SQL Compare® Pro

$595

Compare and synchronize SQL Server database schemas

↗ Eliminate mistakes migrating database changes from dev, to test, to production

↗ Speed up the deployment of new databse schema updates

↗ Find and fix errors caused by differences between databases

↗ Compare and synchronize within SSMS

> **"Just purchased SQL Compare. With the productivity I'll get out of this tool, it's like buying time."**
> **Robert Sondles** Blueberry Island Media Ltd

SQL Data Compare Pro

$595

Compares and synchronizes SQL Server database contents

↗ Save time by automatically comparing and synchronizing your data

↗ Copy lookup data from development databases to staging or production

↗ Quickly fix problems by restoring damaged or missing data to a single row

↗ Compare and synchronize data within SSMS

> **"We use SQL Data Compare daily and it has become an indispensable part of delivering our service to our customers. It has also streamlined our daily update process and cut back literally a good solid hour per day."**
> **George Pantela** GPAnalysis.com

Visit **www.red-gate.com** for a 14-day, free trial

SQL Prompt Pro

$295

Write, edit, and explore SQL effortlessly

- ↗ Write SQL smoothly, with code-completion and SQL snippets
- ↗ Reformat SQL to a preferred style
- ↗ Keep databases tidy by finding invalid objects automatically
- ↗ Save time and effort with script summaries, smart object renaming and more

> **"SQL Prompt is hands-down one of the coolest applications I've used. Makes querying/developing so much easier and faster."**
>
> **Jorge Segarra** University Community Hospital

SQL Source Control

$295

Connect your existing source control system to SQL Server

- ↗ Bring all the benefits of source control to your database
- ↗ Source control schemas and data within SSMS, not with offline scripts
- ↗ Connect your databases to TFS, SVN, SourceGear Vault, Vault Pro, Mercurial, Perforce, Git, Bazaar, and any source control system with a capable command line
- ↗ Work with shared development databases, or individual copies
- ↗ Track changes to follow who changed what, when, and why
- ↗ Keep teams in sync with easy access to the latest database version
- ↗ View database development history for easy retrieval of specific versions

> **"After using SQL Source Control for several months, I wondered how I got by before. Highly recommended, it has paid for itself several times over."**
>
> **Ben Ashley** Fast Floor

Visit **www.red-gate.com** for a 28-day, free trial

SQL Toolbelt

$1,995

The essential SQL Server tools for database professionals

You can buy our acclaimed SQL Server tools individually or bundled. Our most popular deal is the SQL Toolbelt: fourteen of our SQL Server tools in a single installer, with **a combined value of $5,930 but an actual price of $1,995**, a saving of 66%.

Fully compatible with SQL Server 2000, 2005, and 2008.

SQL Toolbelt contains:

↗ **SQL Compare Pro**

↗ **SQL Data Compare Pro**

↗ **SQL Source Control**

↗ **SQL Backup Pro**

↗ **SQL Monitor**

↗ **SQL Prompt Pro**

↗ **SQL Data Generator**

↗ **SQL Doc**

↗ **SQL Dependency Tracker**

↗ **SQL Packager**

↗ **SQL Multi Script Unlimited**

↗ **SQL Search**

↗ **SQL Comparison SDK**

↗ **SQL Object Level Recovery Native**

"**The SQL Toolbelt provides tools that database developers, as well as DBAs, should not live without.**"
William Van Orden Senior Database Developer, Lockheed Martin

Visit **www.red-gate.com** for a 14-day, free trial

Performance Tuning with SQL Server Dynamic Management Views

Louis Davidson and Tim Ford

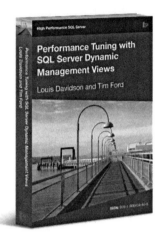

This is the book that will de-mystify the process of using Dynamic Management Views to collect the information you need to troubleshoot SQL Server problems. It will highlight the core techniques and "patterns" that you need to master, and will provide a core set of scripts that you can use and adapt for your own requirements.

ISBN: 978-1-906434-47-2
Published: October 2010

Defensive Database Programming

Alex Kuznetsov

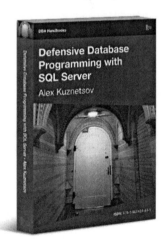

Inside this book, you will find dozens of practical, defensive programming techniques that will improve the quality of your T-SQL code and increase its resilience and robustness.

ISBN: 978-1-906434-49-6
Published: June 2010

Brad's Sure Guide to
SQL Server Maintenance Plans
Brad McGehee

Brad's Sure Guide to SQL Server Maintenance Plans shows
you how to use the Maintenance Plan Wizard and Designer
to configure and schedule eleven core database maintenance
tasks, ranging from integrity checks, to database backups, to
index reorganizations
and rebuilds.

ISBN: 978-1-906434-34-2
Published: December 2009

The Red Gate Guide to SQL Server
Team-based Development
Phil Factor, Grant Fritchey, Alex Kuznetsov,
and Mladen Prajdić

This book shows how to use a mixture of home-grown scripts,
native SQL Server tools, and tools from the Red Gate SQL
Toolbelt, to successfully develop database applications in
a team environment, and make database development as
similar as possible to "normal" development.

ISBN: 978-1-906434-59-5
Published: November 2010

CPSIA information can be obtained at www.ICGtesting.com
Printed in the USA
BVOW040638210912

300956BV00003B/9/P